1495

Hell on Horses and Women

Alice Marriott

Hell on Horses and Women

with drawings by Margaret Lefranc

Foreword by Margot Liberty

UNIVERSITY OF OKLAHOMA PRESS
NORMAN AND LONDON

By ALICE MARRIOTT

Published by the University of Oklahoma Press;
Hell on Horses and Women (1953)
The Valley Below (1949)
María: The Potter of San Ildefonso (1948)
The Ten Grandmothers (1945)

Indians of the Four Corners (New York, 1952)
These Are the People (Santa Fé, 1951)
Indians on Horseback (New York, 1948)
Winter-telling Stories (New York, 1947)

Library of Congress Card Catalog Number 53-5479
ISBN: 0-8061-2482-2

*Manufactured in the U.S.A.
First paperback printing, 1993.*

3   4   5   6   7   8   9   10   11

This book is dedicated to
the other members of the Semi-sewing Circle:
    Lenore
    Alberta
    Ellen Clare
    Mrs. Mibbles
to mark the silver anniversary
of a friendship

Contents

Foreword

by MARGOT LIBERTY

IN the summer of 1985 Manville Kendrick made the remark, "They don't make women any more!" Several of us were visiting the OW Ranch on Hanging Woman Creek in Montana, the old Kendrick Cattle Company headquarters, where Manville and his sister had received their first school lessons at their mother's knee. His meaning was that most ranch wives no longer like to live that far out on bad roads in all seasons of the year, doing what his mother had done before she went off as a political wife to Cheyenne and then to Washington, D.C.

Alice Marriott's book, here reprinted, proves that a lot of ranch wives were made of tough and enduring stuff. In a section entitled "My Own Voice," and in twenty subsequent chapters, she chooses from interviews of fifty-two individuals, gathered in 1951 and 1952 in travels ranging six thousand miles across twelve western states. The chapters extend in time from 1895 to the 1950s, most of them concentrated in the latter years.

Marriott's selection of women for her interviews is biased, she tells us: she did not include the obvious failures. And unlike Teresa Jordan's *Cowgirls*, Marriott's *Hell on Horses and Women* focuses on ranchwomen in traditional feminine roles. The people she talked to were living rewarding and satisfying lives.

My mother, Helena Huntington Smith, who wrote *A Bride Goes West* with Mrs. Nannie Tiffany Alderson (known informally as Domo), was amused by the picture of Western women's agonized isolation presented by such male writers as O. E. Rolvaag, who insisted that "the moaning of the wind drove women crazy." "Nonsense," she said. "Domo had a wonderful time surrounded by all those cowboys. She used to ride and run horse races with them, and they took wonderful care of her. It was only after she had children and had to stay home to care for them that her life became difficult."

Perhaps all women's life stories should be divided into two periods, BC and AC—before and after children. Marriott's ranchwomen responded to the needs of their children, and their lives often were dominated by them. As anthropologists have long pointed out, pastoral societies that depend on the herding of large animals are almost always male dominated and patrilineal. (Matrilineal cultures most often subsisted on gardening and/or the care of small animals, activities close to home and therefore compatible with the care of young children.) In emphasizing the popular masculine imagery of ranching, Marriott also draws parallels to the age of knights and chivalry, when women existed in a world of horseback men (who were lifted above others by their equestrian status), where the masculine image reigned supreme. Perhaps our association of men and the word "cowboy" makes "cowgirl" seem such a jarring expression, one that ranchwomen themselves, no matter how skilled in working with livestock, virtually never use.

Hell on Horses and Women, published in 1953, was the first collection of accounts by or about ranch women.[1] The ranch people whose stories are recorded here wanted them written. According to Marriott, the book is for them and also for the twenty-first-century historian, "a skeleton of the life of one industry in four years of the middle twentieth century." She says that in spite of many changes, "a portion of it is timeless, representing thought and word patterns that will persist among the men and women of the cattle country, whatever their share of it may be."

I believe she was right. As fresh today as they were thirty years ago, the stories herein take the reader into the heart of ranching life. Now that family ranches, along with family farms, are becoming an endangered species, these stories will grow in value—as a record of a special way of life—as time goes by.

NOTE

1. The only comparable book is Teresa Jordan's *Cowgirls: Women of the American West*, published in 1982. Important early works include Agnes Morley Cleaveland, *No Life for a Lady* (1941) and Nannie Tiffany Alderson and Helena Huntington Smith, *A Bride Goes West* (1942). See also Haydie Yates, *Seventy Miles from a Lemon* (1946); Mary Kidder Rak, *A Cowman's Wife* (1934); Clarice Richards, *A Tenderfoot Bride* (1920); Eulalia Bourne, *Woman in Levi's* (1967); Jo Jeffers, *Ranch Wife* (1964); Sherry Thomas, *We Didn't Have Much But We Sure Had Plenty: Stories of Rural Women* (1981); Melva Cummins, *Mom and Me* (1971); Helena Thomas Rubottom, *Red Walls and Homesteads* (1987); and Jean Jardon and Dollie Iberlin, *The White Root: A Story About German-Russian Immigrants in the Clear Creek Valley in Wyoming* (1988). Contemporary ranchwoman authors of nonfiction include Cynthia Vannoy-Rhodes, *Seasons on a Ranch* (1986) and Linda Hasselstrom, *Going Over East: Reflections of a Woman Rancher* and *Windbreak: A Woman Rancher on the Northern Plains* (both 1987).

In contrast to the scarcity of studies about women in the field of Western women's history, now in an expanding raised-consciousness phase linked to the New Western History—see *The Women's West*, edited by Susan Armitage and Elizabeth Jameson (1987), and Larry McMurtry's "How the West Was Won or Lost: The Revisionists' Failure of Imagination," *The New Republic*, October 22, 1990—anthropological studies of women have been going on for years, exemplified by the work of Margaret Mead in the thirties and continuing ever since. For one overview of these studies and the titles of ninety-one relevant works, see Naomi Quinn's "Anthropological Studies on Women's Status" in the 1977 *Annual Review of Anthropology*, edited by Bernard J. Siegal et al. A number of outstanding studies by or about American Indian women have long existed. A useful guide to these is *American*

Hell on Horses and Women

Indian Women: Telling Their Lives, by Gretchen M. Bataille and Kathleen Mullen Sands (University of Nebraska Press, Lincoln, 1984).

"The cow business is a damn fine business for men and mules, but it's hell on horses and women."—Unidentified cowman

Hell on Horses and Women

1. *In My Own Voice*

FOR the past several months I have been trying to find the geographic common denominator of the cattle country. Just when I think I have found it, and am ready to express it in terms of rivers or mountains or rolling plains, I remember another landscape and my mathematical factor is gone. I am left at this moment of writing with the bald-faced statement that the cattle country extends wherever grass will grow on the continent of North America, and that is a right fair stretch of country. And it is right fair country, when you look at it.

The cattle business is an old, old business. In Ur of the Chaldees, the city of Abraham the Patriarch, archaeologists of the British Museum found mosaics and sculptures which showed that even in those uncountably early days men had and cared for large herds of cattle. Moreover, the cattle looked—if they resembled their contemporary portraits—very much like modern cattle. They looked even more like the cattle that were landed on the east coast of Mexico by the Spanish *conquistadores*.

For in the beginning the cattle business belonged to the Old World, not to the New. What quirk it was, what Neolithic genius or plain lazy soul first perceived that it was easier to tame and feed cattle and keep a meat supply at home than to run them down in their wild state, we shall never know. We do know that cattle were domesticated and that beef raising and

3

dairy keeping were established industries before man discovered the malleability and many uses of iron. And we also know that the cattle business, like most other dominant elements of our lives, originated in Asia Minor.

From its starting-point the industry spread all around the Mediterranean and thence northward to the British Isles and the wild coasts of Normandy. Cattle that had been sleek and smooth-coated, with spreading horns, became rough and shaggy and developed shorter horns and more compact bodies as their generations faced the northern fogs and cold. In the south, including the Iberian Peninsula, the stock remained tall and rangy and big-boned. The first Spanish settlers took animals of this latter sort to Cuba, and from there ferried them across the narrow waters to the continental coasts of North America.

Sometimes I wonder whether certain chapters of American history will ever be written. Why do we know so little about the breeding of those first cattle? We know a great deal about the history of horses in North America, for the history of horses is the history of conquest. But the history of cattle is the history of settlement, of consolidation, and of peace. The plod of the feet of grazing cattle in thick grass is not as stirring to our ears as the remembered drumbeat of galloping hooves. Our historians are thwarted cavaliers, and for that reason our history has been written as it has. Perhaps someday we shall know more about the early cattle and the men who handled them.

Since the first cattle in North America were those brought to Florida by De Soto and since the stock was meant as a walking commissary for an army, the first American cowboys were certainly soldiers. The cattle these men cared for were tough beasts. They had to be, to have survived the voyage by open boat across the Caribbean. Probably all were steers, and certainly, after plugging through the swamplands between the West Coast of Florida and the Mississippi, they must have made tough eating. We know that those cattle did not last long, but they survived long enough to convince the later Spanish conquerors, when they sailed for Mexico, that a walking commissary was a practical idea.

4

Perhaps it was its early association with an army that put the American cattle industry on horseback. There had been mounted herdsmen in the Old World, true enough, but there were never very many of them and the cattle they tended usually belonged to royal herds. Cattle range was more restricted in countries where lands were smaller and populations were dense. Cattle could be herded by men and boys afoot quite as easily as by horsemen.

The American cattle industry has been enormously influenced by the very fact that the first cowboys on the continent were soldiers. Take the matter of horses, for instance. Most of the Spaniards rode rather small, tough, wiry horses, of basically Barb stock. The tradition of our own West still speaks of *cow ponies* rather than *cow horses*. Able to travel far and fast on little feed and less water if they had to; maneuverable, able to "turn on a dime and hand you a nickle's change," they were beautiful horses. Many of them were light buckskin in color with light or very dark points—the kind of markings that we still call by the Spanish names: *palomino* and *bayo coyote*. Western horsemen still hold such horses as ideals, still breed for the same qualities that marked the mounts of the earliest Spanish *vaqueros*.

Then take the question of equipment. The cow hand of today rides a saddle that a sixteenth-century Spaniard would recognize and feel at home in. If you were to go to the Metropolitan Museum tomorrow and examine the tilting saddles and the military saddles of the late Renaissance, you would find them, with their high horns and their high-rolled cantles, perfectly functional stock-roping saddles. The use of the rope itself follows an old Spanish custom, too. Back in the days of the Roman legions, the ropers and slingers of Iberia were renowned throughout the Mediterranean world for their skilled use of these novel weapons. From roping enemies to roping steers isn't such a long jump.

Of course stirrups and bits and bridles and girths, and all the other things that go with a stock saddle, had their Spanish counterparts. The cowman's ten-gallon Stetson hat today is modeled on the slouched felt headgear popular among courtiers in sixteenth-century Spain. Chaps (or *chaparejos*)—folds of leather used to protect a man's legs in riding through brush—are actually leggings and a lot older garments than trousers. Even the blue denim of the cow hand's jeans started out as the coarse linen fabric used to make laborers' clothes a long way away and a long time ago.

A lot of mental and emotional attitudes connected with the cattle business are just as old and just as time-honored as the cowman's clothes and equipment, much as these intangibles have been colored by recent events. The cattle business of the New World has always been a business of frontiers, largely for economic reasons. Cattle live on grass, and the best grass and the most of it for a long time were found just beyond the rim of settlement. But stock raising doesn't have to be a frontier business. You can raise beautiful cattle on fenced pastures within easy walking distance of a city if you have to. The cattle business in the New World had started with frontier troops, and it remained in the hands of men who lived on the margin of settlement until the frontiers were gone. Even then some of the men tried to carry on the tradition of border warfare against the farmers who were surrounding them with settlements and fences.

Men are conservative critters, anyway. Men are the people who hold class reunions just to reune. It's not that they want to see each other, especially; it's more that they think they *ought* to want to see each other. I think the same reasoning was behind a lot of the later manifestations of the frontier spirit. It seems to me there were an awful lot of unnecessary shootings in the history of the West. But tradition called for an occasional scrap, and the cow hands shot it out in exactly the same spirit as that in which a lot of their descendants go on Saturday afternoons to watch Dear Old Alma Mater wallop the tar out of Dear Old Traditional Enemy. They get cold and tired and build up the makings of a hangover there in those concrete stands, but they go and do it because it's the thing to do on a Saturday afternoon in the autumn.

Also, it seems to me, the western man's attitude towards

women, from then right along until now, has had just as much tradition and just as little real reasoning behind it. That, in fact, is my point in repeating all this history. It helps you to understand what is behind the life of a woman on a ranch and why her men treat her as they do, from southern Texas to northern Montana and back again to Florida by way of California.

Because even today a ranch woman gets a stiff dose of chivalry most of the time. And a ranch woman is about the only person left in the world who has reason to remember the origin of the word. *Chivalry* has a side that is all roses and moonlight and sweetness and music. It has another side that is just plain hard work. *Chivalry*, according to the dictionary, means a mounted society, a world of horseback men. All the jessamine and guitars and sweet talk in the world can't change that basic definition.

Mark Twain blamed the tradition of southern chivalry on Sir Walter Scott and his imitators, but Mark Twain was thinking only of the moonlight and honeysuckle aspect of the tradition when he spoke. He could have gone right on back to the Courts of Love and the troubadours of the Middle Ages and come up with the point I want to make.

After all, chivalry never did protect women from the hardest, dirtiest, most dangerous, and most painful work the world knows—childbearing. In fact, a great deal of the Protect the Women movement grew up as a side issue to Protect the Descendants. Once Father had fulfilled his biological function, he could get on his trusty horse and depart on a Crusade or a Punitive Expedition or just go off projecting for a year or so. Mother was left holding the diaper bag and running the place until he got home.

I hope I am not hurting anybody's feelings when I mention this. A lot of men and women who have been mighty good to me are going to be annoyed, I'm afraid. But I don't see how I can write about women and the cattle business, and especially about the parts of the cattle business that can be hell on horses and women, without giving a little of the background and a few pertinent facts concerning the matter.

Let's go back a few paragraphs and add things up. The cattle business as we know it today started with soldiers stationed on the frontiers of conquered lands. It was a most masculine business, because women have always been scarce around armies and on frontiers. Moreover, some of the early stockmen of the Spanish colonies were soldiers who had left the army informally and taken the stock with them so the cows wouldn't get lonesome. Such men were better off as independent—altogether independent—operators.

A matter of two or three centuries and half-a-dozen wars went by, and meanwhile our frontiers extended themselves westward and northward. The Tidewater and Piedmont plantations of the southern Atlantic states began to overflow into the western lands. A one-crop economy, plus slavery, led to the exhaustion of the soil. Before that the same economic factors had combined to make large-scale cattle raising an unsound investment in the South. Long before even his mother had thought of Horace Greeley, young men were going west into Texas and Arkansas and Missouri and starting in as cattle operators on the new grasslands they opened up and took over.

Some of these young men were Indians, by the way. It is the boast of the Chickasaw Nation today that it moved itself lock, stock, and saddle from Mississippi into the Indian Territory, paying its own expenses and supporting its people as it went. The Chickasaws are ethnologically uninteresting today because the story of their removal is a success story. They picked out the best grasslands west of the Mississippi, drove the best beef cattle east of the river on to the new pastures, settled down, and went into business. That's the story of the Chickasaws. No trail of tears for them.

Getting back to the other Southerners who came west and started raising cattle: naturally, they brought with them the tongues in their heads and the speech on those tongues. They spoke with a flatter *a* and a slower drawl than their English ancestors, but they spoke an upper-class English that preserved many now obsolescent grace-notes of words. And their speech has lingered in the South and West, to soften and make gracious

8

the speech of their descendants. So even today you may hear an elderly Texan speak of the days when "I was a bare-bottomed boy at my Granny's," and even Shakespeare could not phrase it better—nor would he have phrased it differently.

The southern men brought the chivalry business to the West with them. They traded their flat, low-horned saddles, patterned after English hunting saddles, for the more practical Spanish type. They bred their Thoroughbred mares to the little, tough, wiry western stallions, to get mounts that were resistant to disease and hardship. They changed the cut of their pantaloons and wore neckerchiefs instead of cravats; they made all manner of alterations in their outward style, but they were men and therefore conservatives, and their habits of thought did not change. Especially when the intellectual climate was congenial to the flourishing of well-rooted and firmly established thought patterns, they saw no reason to experiment with new rootstock.

The world of the West was from the beginning a man's world. Women were nice to have around, and they came in handy at cooking and washing and taking care of the place when a man was away from home, but women were a secondary interest to the men of the western frontier. And I don't think it was at all because the life was too rough for women to live. After all, if women hadn't been able to survive living in caves and medieval cities, none of us would be here now. I think it was because the men had a chance to get things their own way and to keep things their own way that women played such a minor part in the scheme of things western. Perhaps there's something in this "Momism" business of Philip Wylie's. Perhaps the men of the Old West were fugitives from Momism and wanted to establish a world where women would be kept in their place—a properly subordinate one.

They could call it chivalry if they wanted to. It operated exactly like chivalry in the Old World. The women who insisted on going with their men to the frontier got the small end of the deal. They had little water and less soap; if they were lucky, they got to a town for church and shopping once a year; often they were literates married to men who could neither read nor write anything but cattle brands; often they were city women, used to buildings and parks and trees, caught and imprisoned like flies in amber in the blazing emptiness of sun and plains.

And they loved it. Never once in the months and miles that went into research for this book did I hear a *woman* acknowledge the truth of the statement that "The cow business is a damn fine business for men and mules, but it's hell on horses and women." Never once did I hear a woman take credit for having first spoken those words, though I met women to whom the first speaking of them was credited by men-folks. Ask the women of the cattle country if their life is hell, and they all deny it. "Maybe it was, way back yonder," they say to a woman, "but it never has been in my lifetime." And I pursued across eighteen states, and finally ran down and hog-tied, the pioneer women who are left in possession of their faculties, only to hear the same story. "Maybe it was, 'way back yonder," sighed one who has lived on frontiers for the past seventy years, "but never in my lifetime."

After a lot of talking and more listening and a fair amount of thinking, I have come to the conclusion that that oft-quoted statement originated with a man. Maybe—let's be Freudian about this—the men had deep convictions of guilt about the lives they let their women lead. So, self-accusing, they compared the lives of women in the cattle country with the lives of women in the eastern cities, and coined an epigram. And, manlike, they said the words and attributed them to women, without asking the women how they really felt.

This book is not going to reflect a battle of the sexes; not my own—I haven't any battling feelings on the subject—nor anybody else's. I hope it is going to reflect a society where the man's work is sharply distinguished from the woman's; where lines are drawn and behavior compartmentalized to a degree that is unknown in the rest of twentieth-century white America. So I am emphasizing the differences right at the beginning, as a means of getting them into the record.

For the cattle country is anywhere that grass grows and water can be found, and the frontier is now. There was a land opening, for homesteading, in Colorado, in the winter of 1950. There is still land in the West that may someday be opened to settlement. Lands in Louisiana and Florida that have since the beginning of time been uninhabitable are being reclaimed by stockmen who are bold enough to reverse the usual procedures of soil care and stock management, and who are benefiting from their daring.

True, barbed wire is everywhere, and cattle guards across the roads mark the limits of men's lands. True, the long-horned descendants of the Spanish cattle have vanished except from zoos and have been largely replaced by flat-backed, square-rumped, low-slung beasts whose breeds originated in the cold and fogs of the British Isles. True enough, as much herding is done by jeep or even on foot as is done by horsemen today. And yet, and yet—as long as the Big Horns soar white-crested against the turquoise of a Wyoming August, as long as the sixty measured miles of the Big Bend south of Marfa shimmer with the blaze of ocotillo in May, and as long as the Missouri runs muddy and yellow all the year through, just so long certain thought patterns and words will persist among the men and women of the cattle country, wherever their share of it may be.

This is their book. They wanted it written; they wanted to show the world how they lived and thought. I have put into this one chapter all that I intend to put in the book of my own comments and ways of thought. From now on, I shall try to be a telephone. And I want to say, before I go any further, that I have not put into the introduction any ideas I haven't talked over with my friends on ranches. Some of them laughed, some of them argued, and a few of them applauded. But all of them listened to me, because in the cattle country you still have the right to your own ideas and the expression thereof, whether your hearers agree with you or not.

Each chapter in the book is about real people in a real place and about real things that happened to them. I have changed the names of people, because the universality of persons and events is more interesting and more important to readers not directly connected with either than a Who's Who of the Cow

Country. Some of the things in this book I saw happen, some were told to me, and some I learned of through letters. They are all true, and each one is worth telling as a story in itself. I have not changed place names, because in each story the place is an important element in what happened to people who lived there.

Many times since this book began, I have been asked about the tragedies of the cow country, about the failures. What of the women who surrendered, who, defeated, returned to a more familiar world? What of losses by drought and grasshoppers, plagues, and deaths from accidents? Have all the stories of the cattleman's world happy endings?

Of course not. I would not give the impression that they do. But I should like to remind my readers that the stories in this book are success stories because, in one way or another, most people do succeed. That's why we notice failures when they do occur—and perhaps attach undue importance to them. Also, please remember that these stories were largely told to me by their participants. People like to remember—and to tell about—the pleasant things that have happened in their lives. Most of all, remember that I talked to women who *lived* on ranches; I did not search out former ranch women who had moved to small towns or to cities.

So this is, largely, a book of successes and of good times, and I hope that fact in itself will not convey a wrong impression of ranch life. It can be hard and tough and truly hell for the women who live it, but it can also come about as close to Heaven as any life a woman can live today. Is it unrealistic to say that there are flashes of Heaven in every human life? Just as there are occasional sparks from hell?

The original plan of this book called for two stories about each cattle-raising state: one concerned with its pioneer period, the other with the life of a ranch woman of today. This plan had to be abandoned early in the undertaking, for several reasons.

In the first place, the words "pioneer" and "modern" are comparative and to some degree meaningless. The pioneer cattle days of New Mexico and California were in the eighteenth century. It is obviously impossible to interview the pioneer cattle women of those states now. The pioneer period in Oklahoma began with the run of 1889 and ended with Statehood, in 1907. First-hand recollections of those days are abundant, but, thanks to the Oklahoma Historical Society, so well recorded that little can or need be added to our knowledge of them. The pioneers of cattle raising in Louisiana went to work yesterday—1947, to be exact—and their stories are not yet ready to tell.

In the second place, no part of our national life is so thoroughly documented as the early story of the cattle industry in the Western states. The great period of the open-range industry lasted at most twenty years, from the late eighteen sixties to the late eighteen eighties. That is the period usually referred to as "pioneer," and it was a time of great economic development throughout the whole United States, when the great trend of freedom and free enterprise was towards the West. But again the story has been told, well and ably, by specialized historians who have devoted their lives to the telling and by local writers who have delved industriously into their county-sized microcosms of the period. This is the span of years we have all come to know well, through the novels of such men as Owen Wister and Eugene Manlove Rhodes, the paintings of Frederic Remington and Charley Russell, the truly epic motion pictures that have come from Hollywood—and through the Hopalong Cassidy vogue of our children.

It has seemed to me that rather than write another book about the pioneers of the cattle business, it is important to show the cattle people of today, their lives and interests. In some cases the roots of the stories have been in the past, and I have included them. In others the past has been repetitiously familiar, and I have tried to tell a new story—the story of the now.

There are stories still untold throughout the cattle country. There are stories that may never reach paper, and there are others that will. But my aim has been to show one part of America how another part exists; not to hold a mirror that will reflect familiar features to familiar eyes. Our country has become too large and its pattern of life too complex for any one of us to comprehend more than a fragment of the whole. This book is intended to add one more scrap of substance to the total; to leave for the historian of the twenty-first century, digging in the dead leaves of the past for his own roots, a skeleton of the life of one industry in four years of the middle twentieth century.

All of the cattle-raising states could not be included, to my regret. Time failed, strength faltered before the whole round could be made. That is more my loss than anybody else's. And I fear I may be accused of favoritism even among the places I did visit. One ranch recurs in story after story, but nothing happens there that does not also happen elsewhere. Let the JL on Powder River stand to the reader, as it does to me, as the archetype of small-to-medium ranches, where humor, courage, and determination, more than money to hire hands, make the wheels go round.

I have said that this is the book of many people. All had so large a share in its making that it would be presumption on my part to thank them. You will find their names listed by states at the end of the book. You will also find a partial list of books about the cattle country, if this one has given you a taste for further reading. There is no glossary; I hope that none is necessary. Ranchers and their wives nowadays usually talk just like other people.

PART ONE

Where Do They Come From, and What Kind of Women Are They?

RANCH WOMEN *come from everywhere. Some of them were born on ranches, and some traveled long distances to reach the places that became their homes. And some women who were born on ranches have turned their backs on their native sod, for one reason or another, and gone elsewhere.*

If the women who came to the ranches from other lives have a quality in common, it is their adaptability. If they share another personality trait, it is that mixture of courage and humor at their own expense that Americans frequently designate as "guts."

Here is the story of a woman who was not born on a ranch, who came to ranch life as an adult. What happened to her—how she felt and thought—is typical of the woman who makes the transition from city life to ranch life now or fifty years ago.

2. A Well-stocked Pantry Is the Housewife's Pride

NEW YORK–NEVADA, 1940

ALL the way out of the city, Ada was silent. Down the speedway, through the tunnel, and across the Jersey marshes, up and over those malodorous flats and down again to the smooth level of four-lane concrete highway, she looked for something to say—and found nothing. Now, when at last the radiator cap was pointed nowhere but west, she found the words she had searched for.

"Well," she announced, "that's over."

Harry looked at her sidewise and turned back to the wheel and the road. "You sound as if you were glad of it," he remarked.

Ada hesitated, and considered that aspect of the situation.

"I don't know whether I'm glad or sorry," she said at last. "I only know it's going to be different from now on. A Harvard graduate working on a newspaper in New York is one person. A Nevada rancher is somebody else. I feel as if I were committing bigamy."

Harry chuckled. "All the conveniences and none of the legal problems," he observed.

The road was smooth and the car was carefully loaded and well balanced. Their furniture and winter clothes and all the books and the other heavy things had gone by freight. The car contained only the answers to their immediate necessities and their spring-weight clothing. The coming of spring had precipitated the move. One week ago today Harry had walked into the apartment in the East Sixties and announced that he had resigned—"as of now."

Ada asked him what he was going to do. It was a natural question. No one quits an editorial job with the prospect of a five-figure salary a few years ahead, without something to look forward to. Harry told her that he had, indeed, a new job in mind. "I'm going back to the ranch and get busy," he informed her. "I've wasted too much time as it is."

She knew about the ranch; had known about it ever since they were first married. His father's homestead exemption—whatever that was—increased by claims for other members of the family and by shrewd purchases of land relinquishments—again, whatever those were—and leases of government land. It all represented real estate, Harry said once in an explanatory mood. Ada visualized a suburban development with neat, small, white houses set at regular intervals in geometric progression. It couldn't be like that, but she had no other idea what it could be like.

Through their ten years of marriage, the ranch and the stock had run like an undercurrent. There was a "tenant" on the place, and once, in the first year that she was an absentee landlady, Ada asked what rent the tenant paid.

"Thirty-three and one-third per cent of the crop," Harry replied.

"How much is that—in money?" she inquired.

"Well ————," Harry hesitated before answering; then he plunged. "This year we had a drought, so I owe him about two hundred dollars he spent for feed for my calves."

Ada was completely bewildered by the statement and the idea it embodied. She was half-owner of a ranch she had never seen, on which the landlord paid rent to the tenant. The theory was confusing enough; she began to hope she would never face the actuality. And then Harry announced that they were going to the theoretical ranch to live.

He surged through the apartment like a high wind, leaving

18

in his wake stacks of books and heaps of crumpled papers. "Got to get packed," he insisted. "Got to get packed and get going."

Patiently, Ada tried to extract from him the cause of this up-heaval. As nearly as she could tell, there was no one cause. He had come to the end of his rope, that was all. He hated the city, and he'd be—a string of profanity, stained and scented with saddle-leather, followed—if he'd live there a moment longer than he had to. No, nothing had happened. That was, nothing much. Not what a New Yorker would call anything. He'd gone for a walk, that was all, on his way home, and he'd crossed the bridle path in Central Park, and he'd smelled manure. Manure! Ada tried to imagine, in complete bewilderment, a state of mind in which the smell of manure could produce insane homesickness.

There was no arguing, no coping with him. Ada saw that at once. Without trying to explain that leaving the city would mean to her what leaving the ranch had meant to him, she got busy with the endless detailed work involved in deserting a New York apartment in the spring. She argued with the landlord about the lease; she induced a friend to sublease. She got pack-ers in and watched them carefully, to be sure that the things to go in the car were sorted from the things to go in the van. Now, at last, she was thankful for the car. It eased a lot of problems. Anything she was uncertain about could go in the back seat. For years she had protested against what seemed to her an ex-travagance, when subways and buses and taxis were within reach at all hours. Harry always gave her the same answer, "A man afoot is no man at all," and went on paying exorbitant rental for a garage to shelter the car which they conscientiously ex-ercised once a week and which she had never learned to drive.

Now they were out and away from the city, turned a-loose, as Harry said, and headed west. She should have found herself frightened and panicky at the prospect of a kind of life she was still unable to visualize. Instead, she was tired. She turned her face against the back of the seat and slept.

She slept for three days, while Harry drove. He waked her sometimes for a meal, or to leave the car and stagger groggily into a tourist court and sleep again. When she did rouse enough to perceive dimly the country through which they were passing, she was not alarmed or even interested. It all looked rather like Westchester, she thought. And Westchester, while "country," was familiar country. That was where they usually took the car for what Harry called its Sunday stroll.

When they were beyond Chicago, she suddenly woke up, woke all over, to feel herself tingling and energetic. "We're climbing," Harry announced, and he drove all that day with his face split by the smile of a Cheshire cat. That night the tourist court was unexpectedly lavish in its equipment, more like a fine hotel than those farther east. She noticed that at least half the men in the restaurant wore high-heeled boots.

When they stopped for lunch at noon the next day, Harry announced that he was going to leave her for half an hour and do some shopping. He disappeared into a dry goods store, as it called itself, that filled almost a block on one side of the main street of the little town. When her husband returned, he, too, minced in high-heeled boots. Above the boots were tight-fitting fawn-colored trousers and jacket and a small-checked shirt. Spreading its glory over the rest of the costume was a wide-brimmed, pale gray felt hat, like the hats Ada had seen in Madison Square Garden on rodeo riders.

"Does a man good to get into some decent clothes," Harry declared. "These are bench-made boots and they're stiff, but what can you expect for thirty-five dollars? I'll put in an order from the ranch and have Rudi make me some real ones."

"All right," Ada said faintly. As long as she had known him, her husband had objected passionately to paying as much as ten dollars for a pair of shoes. She rallied a little. "What do you call those trousers?" she inquired. "Do you think you can sit down and drive a car in them?"

"I can sit a horse in them," said Harry. "These are ready-made and they don't fit as well as I'd like them to; there's more room in them than there ought to be in a pair of frontier pants. I'll feel better in them if they shrink when they're cleaned."

Frontier pants. Ada filed the name away in her mind. They went into the hotel for lunch.

Now, for the first time, she was conscious of a change in the wording of the menu. Suddenly a great many things seemed to be fried: meats and vegetables and even bread, apparently, for she saw men at the counter eating corn cakes with their dinners. "What," she asked her husband, "is a chicken-fried steak?"

"Say!" exclaimed Harry. "Have they got chicken-fried steak here? Best meat you ever ate, honey. Sinews of America. Battles have been fought and great works done and great songs written on chicken-fried steak." Without further discussion, he ordered two portions.

"I can see how battles would be fought on this," said Ada thoughtfully, sampling hers, "but singing—no, I don't think I'd want to sing about it. What *is* it? A mistreated veal cutlet?"

"It's chicken-fried steak," Harry asserted, as if that reply were sufficient, and from then on he ate it every day and three times a day. Ada gave it up after her first attempt. Instead she tried fried chicken—batter-coated like the steak, stringy and pink under the batter, and totally unappetizing to one accustomed to being served broiled chicken. She experimented with fried ham, and decided it would do very well to patch a tire. After she burned her mouth with the sauce that dripped from a Bar-B-Q hamburger, she gave up the search for edible meat in public eating places and confined herself to familiar fried eggs.

It was dark and late when they came to Winnemucca, and the hotel that received them was dim and old and comfortable. Ada stumbled a little going up the stairs to their room, while Harry urged her forward in the intervals of a lecture on the history of the West. A large part of it, she gathered, had been written in this vicinity.

Morning brought a deluge of sunshine and a feeling of cheer that was intensified by her first glimpse of the menu in the hotel dining room. Evidently someone west of the Mississippi realized that Easterners might travel, for here was listed food that was familiar and welcome to her. She ate with pleasure: fresh orange juice, not prunes; coddled, not fried, eggs; buttered toast that was neither stiffly cold nor grease-soaked. The coffee was coffee;

no one had slipped paint-remover into the pot by mistake. She relaxed; she felt restored and ready for anything.

"Got to go out for an hour or so," Harry said as he finished his last hot cakes and fried ham and fried eggs. "I want to see about ordering those boots, and I've got to check at the courthouse and see where we stand on taxes and some other things. What do you want to do? Go to the grocery and order some stuff? I don't think you'll need to get much. We'll probably be back in town next week. Just pick up enough to carry us through."

For a moment Ada hesitated. She loved to cook; it had always been fun in the apartment, with the kitchenette that was so small she had only to turn around to reach everything she needed. She hadn't had to move a step from the stove to prepare a meal. Often, to be sure, she prepared the meal without cooking anything, unless making tea or coffee counted as cooking. There was a wonderful delicatessen on the corner, and with the Viennese bakery in the next block. . . . It would be fun to go shopping for groceries again, but would she know how to buy for a week at a time? She had never tried to keep food on hand from one day to the next in the city apartment.

"Well," she said, considering, "suppose you meet me at the grocery. I'll pick out the things I'm sure of, and you get whatever else you think we'll need."

When they left town late in the afternoon, she knew her decision had been a wise one. Harry's order had engulfed hers. When he included a whole ham and a ten-pound beef roast, she knew she would have to leave the shopping to him for some time to come. She didn't know what kind of household she would have or how to plan for it.

Again it was late and dark when they arrived at a destination. Ada could see the shape of a long, one-story house and the spidery frame of a porch before it. Harry fumbled with the latch and the door swung inward. A smell of recent disuse, strong with dust and stale coffee, musty with an underlying scent of mice, drifted out to the porch. The house, she saw when her husband lighted the first kerosene lamp, was reasonably clean—

at least in this quarter-light it seemed to be so. The place was also fairly orderly, although it looked alarmingly bare. The kitchen was the only room that was really furnished. It held a huge round table and an assortment of chairs of various patterns with straight backs in differing stages of paint-scale, two glass-fronted wall cupboards, and an enormous range. Ada had seen objects like that stove in the movies—never anywhere else.

"We'll get along," said Harry, viewing the scene. "I had them leave a couple of beds and the dresser's in the bedroom. Oh, there's Grandma's old rocker in the corner. Nice of them to leave that. I'll get the bedding from the car."

It was only because of his foresight that they had sheets and blankets with them, Ada realized. The room was chilly with neglect and with the thin night air that washed through the open door. She decided to light the oven, and investigated the stove to that end.

There were no handles. She could not turn on the gas. She searched in vain for the connection to the outlet so she could release the valve. Harry returned with his arms full of blankets and pillows and found her on her knees behind the stove.

"What in the world are you doing?" he demanded.

"I'm trying to turn it on," Ada replied and was amazed and offended when he broke into howls of laughter. It was a matter of minutes before he quieted down enough to explain to her that this was a wood-and-coal combination stove. It had no handles to turn because it didn't burn gas or electricity. Ada withdrew to the bedroom—a little startled to find that it opened off the kitchen—and made up the bed while he built a fire and lighted it, and set the kettle on to boil. He made her a cup of hot chocolate with canned milk, and, warm and mollified, she dropped off to sleep.

There was no interval between her surrender to slumber and a shattering awakening when the alarm clock screamed its summons. Harry was out of bed and across the room before she could get a hand out from beneath the covers. "What time is it?" she inquired. She was hardly able to comprehend his answer. She *thought* he said four o'clock, and asked him to repeat. He did. It was four o'clock in the morning and time to get up, on this or any other ranch.

"You stay where you are till I get the fire going," he added kindly. "You're pretty tired. Don't try to get up till I get the chill off the kitchen."

Outraged at the hour and relieved that she did not have to battle with the stove, Ada drew the covers up to her ears, enclosing the tip of her nose, which always got chilly at night. Dimly she listened to the crash of stove lids, the duller thud of fuel, the tickling scratch of a match against the metal of the firebox. She heard, ever more faintly, Harry's "Damn!" when the first match went out, and the scratching of the second. Then there was a series of tiny, warming pops as the kindling lighted, and then deep, warm silence as she slept again.

The room was full of daylight when she reawakened. At first she thought that it was also full of silence, but after a moment she heard the stove sounds again and was glad to hear them. That meant she had not slept too long; she had not disgraced herself on her first morning as a ranch wife. How she knew that it was a disgrace to oversleep, she could not have told. Harry had never, as far as she could remember, told her anything of the sort. In fact, she decided as she struggled into a chilly cotton housedress, he had never told her anything *real* about the ranch at all. He had said it was there, and that it was a nice place, and that he had been born in the house and had gone away to school from it, but that was all. What the ranch was actually like, this place she had reached in physical darkness and spiritual blind faith, she had no idea.

Now she was awake, and her mind suddenly seemed to have waked with her body. She had been numbed by city noise, perhaps; certainly she had been unexpectedly stupid about something important to her husband all her married life. This ranch meant so much to Harry that he, a man who had made his living from his use of words, had brought her here without description—without verbal preparation of any sort. And she, because she sensed that this country and this life meant more to him than anything else ever could, had come thus far with him. Why, or into what, she had come, she had not stopped before to analyze.

So she looked at the mustard-yellow paint on the door between the bedroom and the kitchen with the eyes of quick perception, as she felt the slight roughness of the knob's cast-iron surface against the palm of her hand, and turned it. She stepped into the kitchen and closed the door behind her. She looked across the room at the stove and at the strange man who was stoking it with firewood.

The man raised his bristly chin as he turned in her direction. His face, even to his pale-blue eyes, was blank, and his voice was expressionless when he spoke.

"Howdy," he said. "You're Harry's good lady?"

"I—well, yes—I am."

"Pleased to meet you. I live neighbors to you. Name's Dunham—down the creek."

Ada hesitated. It seemed a little abrupt to demand of Mr. Dunham-Down-the-Creek what he was doing in her kitchen, stoking her stove at—she blinked incredulously at the clock—ten-thirty in the morning. He seemed to be at home and a great deal more accustomed to her surroundings than she was. As he probably was, at that.

"I rode over to say howdy to Harry," Mr. Dunham announced, "and he said he thought you was real fagged and maybe was going to stay in bed all day. So I left him down in the south pasture, mending fence, and rode on up to see maybe could I fix us all a bite to eat."

"That was very kind of you," Ada hazarded. From the rich, well-ripened odor of horse and accoutrements that filled the part of the kitchen near the stove, she decided Mr. Dunham had ridden hard and for a long time. "I think I can manage, though."

"Now you don't have to bother about a thing," said Mr. Dunham, reassuringly. "I'm an old hand at this—I've batched and liked it ever since my wife quit me for a section hand twenty years ago. She always was a flighty kind of gal," he added reminiscently. "Said she liked to live near town, where she could look out the window and see lights at night. I never could figure her out," he continued, peering into the grocery boxes Harry had left on the floor, "stars was good enough night lights for my grandpappy—he was one of ole Jim Bridger's boys back in the forties—and they're plenty good enough for me. Now I've got a nice, strong pot of coffee brewed up, ma'am, and you just set down there in the rocker—Harry's gran'mammy had it brung out by ox-team; she was a great one for her comfort, she was— and drink a cup, and by that time I'll have the dinner started so's by the time Harry and the others rides in, it'll be all ready. You don't have to worry about it a bit. Where's your sourdough crock, ma'am?"

"I-I-I-don't know . . . ," Ada stammered. She poured a cup of coffee and subsided into the rocker, which creaked comfortingly as it enfolded her.

"Well, now, I don't 'spect you've had time to get you a mess started, at that," Mr. Dunham consoled her. "I'll bring you over a starter this evening. This the bacon-powder? If you ain't got sourdough, you can always get by with bacon-powder, I reckon, though most folks thinks it don't make as good biscuits. I got you a kittle of beans started, but laws, why'd you let Harry get them little squinchy navy ones? Takes a week to get 'em cooked proper, and by that time they're all gone. You won't be able to eat none of these till tomorrow, even if I did put plenty of salt in 'em to make 'em mush up. You tell Harry you want pintos the next time. He told me he done the shopping, but I guess he's been out of practice so long the next time you better do it yourself."

Mr. Dunham continued to prowl his way through the preparations for what looked to Ada like a colossal meal. One thing at a time, as he needed the various articles, her neighbor unpacked the grocery boxes, and each article that he unpacked he put tidily away on the shelves of the kitchen cupboard. While he worked, Mr. Dunham-Down-the-Creek continued to talk, endlessly, in the same rather high voice, without intonation or inflection, on every subject under the ranchman's Heaven. Ada, stunned by the outpouring of words, could only sit and rock and clutch her coffee cup.

26

Weeks later, when she found sanity in herself and in her surroundings, she realized the magnitude of her debt to Mr. Dunham. It was through his endless, amiable, innocent flow of words that she learned most of the really significant things about her husband and the life he had chosen for both of them, for the first time. Into her unconscious, from the flood of words Mr. Dunham poured over her, had seeped the facts that the tenants had neglected the ranch shamelessly and that what should have been a gold mine under proper management had become a hole in the ground into which she and Harry must pour all their capital. She learned for the first time that her husband had once made a good hand, but that he was now so out of practice that he couldn't hardly string a fence wire straight *with* somebody to help him. And she realized, from watching Mr. Dunham's movements around the kitchen, that she was not only going to have to keep house without the delicatessen on the corner and the Viennese bakery in the next block, without a gas stove or electric lights or refrigerator, but without even running water.

Her mind reeled, and the rocking chair galloped under her. Then she recovered part of her self-possession. There were two things she could do, two courses plainly open to her. She could go into the bedroom and change back into the neat navy blue suit in which she had traveled west, take up her unpacked bags, and demand that Harry, Mr. Dunham, or somebody else—anybody else—take her into town to the railroad station and the first train east. Or she could make up her mind to stay where she was, to get up at four in the morning and to cook enormous meals involving some substance known as "sourdough," and see the whole thing through to some conclusion. From what Mr. Dunham said, she gathered that Harry, unless he worked like a day laborer, would lose the ranch. The most difficult thing for her to accept and adjust to was the thought that her husband would rather be broke on a ranch in Nevada than solvent on a newspaper in New York. But so it was. They had an investment here. Maybe, with time and with much back-breaking, muscle-stretching hard work, they could realize something on it.

All this and a great deal more churned and riled in her mind while the rocker cantered and Mr. Dunham talked. Mr. Dunham was an old-timer in the neighborhood and had taken up his homestead exemption at the same time Harry's father had taken up his. He sure did love Nevada, hadn't never lived nowhere else and didn't aim to. Yes, ma'am, he'd been out of the state some; he'd been as far east as Denver and north to Calgary for the Stampede, and even out to the West Coast one time to take delivery of some stock on a ranch in Oregon, and you couldn't tell him nothing about other parts of the country. There just wasn't any country anywhere any nicer than what you'd got right here.

In the intervals of his autobiography and philosophical reflections thereon, Mr. Dunham compounded what he called bacon-powder biscuits. He discovered the butter and beamed at it—hadn't tasted butter in more'n a month, he confided. He produced enamel plates and battered steel knives and forks from what he designated as the cab'net, and he set the objects on the bare oilcloth of the table top. He also discovered, in the bottom of a grocery box, that ten-pound roast of beef.

The beef was still wrapped. Mr. Dunham stripped off the paper and held the chunk of meat out in front of him on his palm. "Now, ain't that pretty?" he marveled. "That's the nicest piece of meat I've seen in I don't know when. How was you aiming to cook it, ma'am?"

"Why, I thought I'd roast it," Ada began, when Mr. Dunham interrupted her.

"I knew it!" he exclaimed. "That's what ladies always wants to do with a nice piece of meat like that. Why, ma'am, it's a shame to roast this. You know what you want to do with this? You just let me cut some nice steaks off of it, and we'll fix them for dinner. You've got to cook it or it won't keep, and there sure ain't time to roast this here between now and noon. You just let me fix some steaks and we'll have them ready for dinner in no time flat."

For the first time in her life, Ada experienced what her Irish grandmother had been wont to call A Warning. Clutching the arms of the rocker, she rose to her feet. "Mr. Dunham," she demanded, "*how* are you going to cook those steaks?"

"Why, ma'am, the only way a steak's fit to eat. Naturally, when you're out on roundup and cooking over a campfire, you've just about got to broil your meat, but I don't relish it that way. Never gets done in the center. You can cook it till its outside's a coal, and it's still pink in the middle. Any cowman will tell you that's no way to eat a steak. Now you just set back and relax, and I'll cook these steaks right. Just give 'em even heat and plenty of grease, and they'll come out the same color all the way through. Yes, ma'am, I'll chicken-fry these steaks like nothing you'd ever get to eat in the East."

For a moment Ada felt her temper rising, but only for a moment. Never, never, in her house should anyone eat chicken-fried steak! Then she remembered Harry's delight when he found the unspeakable substance listed on the menu, the eagerness with which he ordered and ate it, his paean in its praise. How the meat was cooked was a little thing in itself. The important thing, the thing that really mattered, was that they had meat. Thanks to Mr. Dunham and his bacon-powder biscuits, they had bread as well.

"Aren't you going to cook any vegetables, Mr. Dunham?" Ada asked when there was again a lull in his speech.

Mr. Dunham, turning from the oven, his back still bent, pondered. "Well, I tell you, ma'am," he said after what was for him a considerable pause. "I know ladies always likes vegetables. My wife, she used to get to plumb craving for them. I got so I always planted a garden for her, ever' spring. Even got so I could eat some of the things myself. Next time I come, when I bring you the sourdough starter, I'll bring you some green things. But for now, I don't know. We got steak and biscuits and if some of these beans softens up a little we can eat them. I tell you what—," he announced suddenly, turning to face her with his eyes wrinkling in the first smile she had seen him produce, "Harry got you some canned tomaytoes. I can fix them up. That'll give you a vegetable and the men won't mind eatin' them."

The men—what men? Himself and Harry, Ada supposed. She would be glad of the tomaytoes and relieved that the men wouldn't mind them. But her heart sank when she saw how her neighbor "fixed" the vegetables, with salt and sugar and broken slices of store bread from the package in the supply box. That was no way to treat a perfectly good vegetable, according to Ada's training, but she steeled herself against argument and watched him set the saucepan that contained the mess on the back of the stove to simmer out whatever vitamins it might still contain.

The door opened and Harry came in. "Dinner ready?" he asked. He saw his wife sitting there in the rocking chair and beamed. "My," he said, "it looks good to see somebody in that chair again. I can remember my grandmother and my mother sitting in it as far back as I can remember anything. They'd get dinner all ready to put on the table and then sit down there to rest and wait for the men to get in from work. I want you to meet the wife, boys. Come on in."

Eight men crowded the doorway behind him, eight men who looked enormous and thoroughly hungry.

"These are our neighbors," Harry said, and he introduced them one at a time. "They all wanted to meet you, and I bet they wanted to see what kind of a meal you could put out. I told them it might be different from what they're used to—city people eat different from people on ranches—but they said they'd take a chance. Looks like she's done all right, too, boys," he announced proudly. "Of course it's her first day here, and she's kind of tired from the trip and not used to things, but I guess we won't any of us go hungry."

Ada, shaking hands, repeating names, motioning towards the table, wanted to protest against the undeserved honor and to shriek with laughter. Then, as she opened her mouth to refuse the unearned credit, she caught sight of Mr. Dunham. He stood behind Harry, facing her. As she watched him, he made sure he had caught her eye. Then one of his own pale ones closed, momentarily but deliberately, in a ponderous wink.

PART TWO

Is Their Life Hell?

I HAVE SAID BEFORE *that ranch women do not think their life is hell. I want to repeat the statement. No matter how difficult existence is on a ranch, no matter how nearly tragedy approaches a ranch woman, she would rather be where she is, doing what she is doing, than trade lives with any other woman who breathes.*

Each of the women who told me her story in the section that follows told it as something that had happened to her: something funny, something exciting, something from which she learned another fact or perceived another facet of ranch life. The incidents were never related as things which the protagonists found themselves unable to endure.

Tragedy need not be melodrama, although we often confuse the two. Tragedy is a cow with a broken leg more often than a husband suddenly struck dead. Remember, always, that these are the stories of participants. Women who have lived through things have usually gone beyond them.

From which observation can be drawn the conclusion that hell is where you make it; it can be a runner in a stocking or a misplaced jar of cold cream as easily—perhaps more easily—than physical danger and physical hardship.

3. *Give Us This Day*

COLORADO, 1936

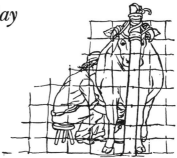

LSIE LITTLE was born in a sod-roofed, semi-dugout claim shack at a time when such dwellings were the homes of landed gentry and at a spot on the earth's surface where the corners of four states coincided. Since none of the four states required registration at the time of Elsie's appearance and since the family home and the state boundaries were equally flexible in location for some years after the event, Elsie occasionally said that she had her choice of states to be born in.

She was named, as were many girl children at the time, for her mother's girlhood heroine, Elsie Dinsmore. Mrs. Little, a gentle Philadelphian, had modeled her own behavior and character on that of the insipidly aggravating creature as nearly as she might, and it was her fondest hope that her daughter would grow up to do likewise. Probably if Mrs. Little had remained in Philadelphia and married the young Mennonite minister who courted her in her youth, Elsie would have complied. But Mrs. Little had chosen to flout.convention by going out west to teach school, and later to throw her cap clear over Philadelphia's windmills by marrying a cowboy. Elsie, an amiable creature, tried all her life to conform to her mother's standards of behavior. It was certainly never her fault that circumstances forced her, from time to time, into activities which would probably have caused

33

her namesake to faint from shock had they been described to her.

The Littles were not rich and they were not poor. Mr. Little had homesteaded his land, taking up a claim each for himself and for his wife. When opportunity offered, he added further small pieces of land to the original tract, until he controlled ten sections. That was enough to graze the hundred head of stock that would support a family without other income in that area, but it didn't satisfy Mr. Little. Cattle were tricky, as he well knew, since his life had been devoted to them. So he ran a few sheep—to keep the wolves out in the woods where they belonged and away from the door, to use his own words. He put in hay meadows, he planted wheat and oats and turnips, and he had silage stored up and ready to carry his cattle through the worst of any winter. This was in direct contradiction to the economic theories of his neighbors, who one and all contended that it was simpler and more satisfactory to let the cattle do their own harvesting and a waste of time to gather in feed for them. Mr. Little replied that he was raising ten hands of his own and they all liked to eat. Let them work for the cattle, and he would work along with them. In time the stock would pay them all off.

There were enough children in the Little family to justify a district school. The county and state support was paid to a teacher who lived with the family. Additional funds were paid to Mr. Little to provide for the building of a schoolhouse on his land. He added some money—and much of his own labor and his sons'—and built the schoolhouse away from the family home and near the county road so other children could attend as they were born or moved into the neighborhood. Selfishness was no part of the Little pattern. They housed and boarded the teacher free.

Elsie was the oldest daughter and the second child. She grew up with a full knowledge of responsibility and a sense of the pleasure of life. The two were never separated in her mind or experience. She took over much housework and the care of the younger children from her mother. Mrs. Little had her hands fuller than full and needed all the assistance she could get. When

34

Elsie, aged twenty-one years and three weeks, married Albert Jones, most of the neighbors distributed over the surrounding 120 miles wondered audibly if Albert knew exactly how well he had done for himself.

Albert didn't seem greatly to care whether he had done well or ill. He loved his Elsie completely and almost wordlessly, and he would probably have been just as content to marry her if she had never washed a dish or a baby in her life. It was bonus luck that she was almost as well able to run the place as he was.

Albert had a place of his own when they married. He had bought his land from an old homesteader who had gone broke ten years before. Like most western men, Albert had waited a while to marry. He had planted a few wild oats in the form of poker-playing Saturday nights. When the crop of headaches and I.O.U.'s began to sprout, he decided it wasn't worth raising and plowed it under. From that day on, when Albert went out on a Saturday night, he went to a square dance, that most effective form of social insurance. The man doesn't live who can drink and dance in a square, or drink and call for the fiddler, and you can't play poker when your hands and feet are both busy do-si-do-ing. So Albert spent his poker money on fences, and when he married Elsie a month after he first met her at a square dance, he had something worthwhile to offer her.

It was a good thing Albert's place was free and clear to begin with. The drought came along two years later, just a year after the first baby. From the day when the earth first rose in its moving might and assaulted the heavens, Colorado ranchers confronted despair. Some of them, defeated, left the doors swinging behind them when they went to see if somewhere the grass still grew green. Others, like the Joneses, stayed where they were, too busy scratching for food to think about leaving.

No rain in the autumn, no snow in the winter, dust in the spring, and grasshoppers in August. It was a poor year for everybody in the Plains country; it was a worse than poor year for Albert and Elsie. Now they learned why the original owner of their land had lost his shirt. Most of the place was high, and there was rock near the surface. The meadows were covered

35

with tall grass, but the growth was shallow-rooted. With the strong spring winds the poor, dry earth sifted out through the arches of the grass roots and went away somewhere else. The young couple, staying right at home, were in the strictest sense displaced persons. They no longer had their own land.

They struggled through the first year. There was a hay meadow with a spring-fed creek running through it near the house. Albert had started raising milking shorthorns. He brought his best cows into the meadow and kept them there. When they dropped their calves, he kept the cows on grass and milked the half-wild creatures as well as he could. The milk not only kept the family alive; there was enough of it for Elsie to make a little butter once in a while. She sold the butter to her neighbors, and the income from it was the only cash money in the house from midwinter until the next autumn. Then Albert sold the short calf crop for whatever he could get, to save the grass in the meadow for the cows.

Milking those cows was more than a chore; it was a full-time job. The creatures regarded their calves as the only satisfactory milkers on the market and looked on Albert's best efforts as amateurish. They were likely to try to persuade him to quit by kicking over the milking bucket in an effort to bash in the side of his head. They resisted his blandishments at milking time, and in order to get them into the lot where he had set a pair of stanchions, Albert had to take Ole Paint out with a stock saddle and a rope and chouse the cows up to the corral as if he were going to brand them. When he had four cows in the lot, he milked them; when he had eight, he milked four and turned the others loose. Four were all he could hope to deal with in the time he could allow himself for milking.

Elsie had done her share of milking at home when she was growing up, and she knew more than the theory of the business. But she never went near the shorthorns, and Albert encouraged her not to. God only knew, he sometimes said, what the cows would do if they saw a skirt come fluttering into the barn lot. They had never seen human beings wear anything but pants, and they'd probably think a skirt meant a new kind of animal and charge it. And, he once added shyly, he always liked the way Elsie stuck to skirts, with divided skirts for riding. It was kind of pretty and ladylike to see her that way all the time.

At the beginning of the second bad drought year, Mr. Little offered his daughter a Jersey milch cow, but Elsie refused it. The Jerseys were used to better pasture than she and Albert could offer them. They were also used to supplemental feeding of fancy chopped silage. While she knew she could easily milk a Jersey, she doubted her ability to feed it properly. So she shook her head at her father's offer and continued to use the variable amounts of milk Albert coaxed from the shorthorns. He once remarked with a certain bitterness that it was a good thing those cows were named "milking shorthorns." Otherwise you sure wouldn't have been able to tell them from beef cattle.

The second year was worse than the first. The dust started to rise in mid-March and the grasshoppers arrived the end of June. Albert took one look at the devastation the insects wrought on the first night of their march across country. Without a word he went in the house and packed his duffle and suggans. He rounded up one shorthorn cow—by good luck the only fresh one left—and tied her in the barn lot with her calf in the small corral alongside. He next came in the house and kissed his wife and child good-bye. "So long, honey," he said. "I'm going out to look for a job, and if I find it you won't see me for a while. Turn the calf in with the cow when you get through milking." He then climbed aboard Ole Paint and departed.

Elsie was not in the least dismayed by this performance. In fact, she thought her husband was acting very sensibly. Not only he, but she and little Mavis, had to eat. It was up to him to get out and find something that would pay the grocery bill. It was up to her to keep things running, smoothly if possible, but running, here at home. So she got out her wash tubs on a Wednesday morning, hauled buckets of water two at a time from the creek, and did some laundry to calm herself. No use wasting her energy. If she were going to get all worked up about being left alone for a while, she might as well work off her unhappiness in a way that would do her some good.

The washing was as soothing as she expected it to be. After lunch Elsie decided to go ahead and iron. She had to dry the clothes in the kitchen because if she left them outside the dust fogged them up and the grasshoppers left green spots all over them. The best way of making room to cook supper in was to iron the clothes and put them away. She tied Mavis to the table leg with a length of old hair rope and got busy.

The ironing was almost finished and she was down to the sheets and pillow cases, when she realized that Mavis was getting restless. That was a sure sign the baby was also getting ready for supper and bed. Elsie looked at the clock. Almost five; time she was starting the evening meal. Then she remembered something, with a jolt. It was also time for Albert to go out to the lot and start milking. The noise, so familiar that she hardly heard it, that floated in on the evening wind was the bawling of the old cow out in the lot, ready and past ready for milking.

Elsie made sure that Mavis was still securely fastened; she did not want the unnecessary complication of a baby underfoot in the barn lot. Mavis had learned a lot about doors and how they opened recently. Satisfied on that point, Elsie picked up the scalded milk pail and the folding stool and started out.

Not until she reached the barn lot did she remember Albert's remarks about skirts and cows. Oh, well, she reflected, probably he was exaggerating, manlike. They loved to feel important; any man who could set himself up even over a pair of jeans would most likely do it. She opened the lot gate and stepped inside the enclosure.

Elsie escaped the cow's charge by jumping the fence. Afterwards she thought she probably had climbed it like a ladder, but at the time she was sure only that she was on one side of the fence and the cow, milk pail, and stool were on the other. The cow was jabbing her horns into the fence. Elsie decided that if the old girl went on that way for long, she'd get them in and be unable to get them out. And serve her right.

A more practical revenge on the cow immediately occurred to her. Milk the beast. Wait till she hung herself up on the fence and then go in the lot and milk her. Since it was highly improbable that the cow would be so obliging as to impale the fence with her horns and so fix herself permanently in a milking position, Elsie left her to demolish the bucket if she could and returned to the house.

Albert's old jeans and denim jacket hung on the back porch, so stiff with time and cow-lot dirt that a hook was hardly needed to support them. Those jeans could walk out to the lot and milk the cow by themselves, Elsie thought as she looked at them. A corollary thought promptly followed. Her nose wrinkled, but she had to do it. Standing on the porch, she took off her apron and housedress and put on the jeans. She grasped another bucket from the bench by the back door and dusted it out with the cheese cloth that covered it. As an afterthought she picked up Albert's old lariat, which he had hung on the hook under the jeans. So equipped, Elsie headed back for the cow lot.

Her first loop missed the cow's horns, but she caught them on the second try. Triumphantly she snubbed the cow to a fence post and let herself into the corral. She retrieved the milking stool and advanced on the cow. The cow turned her head and eyed Elsie with haughty and menacing suspicion, then subsided briefly, soothed by the sight and smell of the familiar jeans. A moment later, stirred by an unfamiliar touch on her udder, the cow rigidly refused to give down her milk. Furious with resentment, she kicked forward, barely missing Elsie's head and lamming in the side of the milk bucket. It pinged like an accordion and collapsed on itself accordion-wise.

Elsie was completely angry for one of the few times in her gentle life. In righteous wrath she picked up the milking stool and returned to the porch for a third bucket. When she regained the lot she was in no mood for foolishness from any cow. The light was almost gone, Mavis was getting hungry, she herself was tired. Deliberately, she drew back her left foot and cold-bloodedly she planted it in the cow's side.

The kick worked like a charm. The cow subsided into stormy muttering if not amiability, and Elsie milked her, getting down about half her milk. When she had finished, she put the bucket and milking stool outside the corral and opened the gate to the

39

calf's pen. The calf rushed to its mother and began its supper. Elsie carried her share of the milk back to the house, where she strained it and set it aside to cool under a thick covering of cheesecloth. She fed Mavis. Then she returned to the cow lot to secure the calf in its pen again, against the cow's raucous protests. Last of all, Elsie climbed on the fence and loosened the rope from the cow's horns. Her final return to the house and her lonely supper were not cheered by the reflection that she had it all to do over again the next morning.

She managed it. She managed three days of it. Then she was awakened by bellowings and contralto screams from the meadow. She went out clad in the old jeans, to see by the dawn's earliest light what was going on down there.

Something had panicked the cows in the maternity ward. Most of them had gone completely off their heads and were galloping from one end of the meadow to the other. Elsie yelled at them at the top of her voice and a gray shadow faded under the fence and out and away towards the buttes to the west. It was—it couldn't be—it was!—a lobo wolf. They were all supposed to have been killed off long ago. But its shape and color were wrong for a coyote and its size was far too large. As Elsie recovered from her astonishment, she saw one of the cows lying on the ground and struggling to get up.

Elsie investigated. Somehow, with the awkwardness peculiar to cows, the creature had managed to trip and fall as she fled from the intruder. In falling she had landed on the one surface rock for a mile in any direction and she had broken her hind leg.

The proper thing to do with any animal under such circumstances, Elsie well knew, was to shoot it and butcher out its meat. She had herself done the unpleasant job before. But this cow was far along with her calf and shooting her would mean the loss of two head of stock instead of one. Maybe, just possibly, Elsie could save the cow until the calf was born. The first thing to do, even before she called the State Game Department, collect, to report the wolf, was to get the cow up to the barn lot and away from further harm. Luckily the distance was only a quarter-mile.

Elsie tried to get the cow to stand and walk on three legs, but the animal either could not or would not do it. For the first time since Albert had left Elsie felt inadequate. She had been born on a ranch, she had grown up and gone to school on a ranch, she had been convinced all her previous life that she knew all she needed to know about ranching. And she *did* know what she needed to know, even about this situation. The difficulty was that she lacked the physical strength to put her knowledge to use.

Well, she decided, if woman-power couldn't get the job done, perhaps horse-power could. She removed her bra and tied it to the cow's horns. A fluttering piece of cloth would keep away any animal except an antelope, and an antelope couldn't hurt a cow. The classic thing to use was a handkerchief, but she hadn't a handkerchief with her, and the bra was the easiest of her garments to remove. She left the pasture and went back to the horse lot, a quarter of a mile beyond the house on the other side, for her horse. On the way she looked through the bedroom window. Mavis was sleeping soundly and the sides of the crib were up and locked in place, but Elsie tied a length of light cord from the baby's leg to the table, just in case. It never paid to take unnecessary chances with anything.

When Elsie got back to the pasture, the cow still lay where she had fallen. The bra drooped rakishly from one horn and across her eye. Elsie dismounted and retrieved her garment. She substituted a rope as a horn ornament, fastening it around the boss so it looped both horns. She backed her horse off and made him haul. The cow's resistance was passive, but it was effective. Elsie feared the horns might be pulled out by the roots before the cow budged.

She finally solved the problem by tying the rope around the cow's body forward of the hind legs and towing the stubborn brute slowly up to the barn lot. She had to cut wire and retie it to get the cow out of the pasture. Stopping to rest the horse, the cow, and herself, sometimes getting down to move obstructions so that the cow would not be bruised, Elsie toiled on. Foot by foot, almost inch by inch, they traveled that nightmare quarter-mile. By the time the cow was safely lodged in the barn, with the bars up to keep the milch cow from getting in and killing her, Elsie was soaked with sweat and the horse was lathered and gasping. Elsie left the shorthorn unmilked for the time being. Everything else could wait till she and the saddle horse were rested and fed.

The State Game Department sent a man out later in the day. He set traps around the pasture and tied rags to the fence wires between them. He also found and mended two wire breaks, but he said nothing about that until he saw Albert in town, months later. The game warden had brought two weeks' accumulation of mail out from the post office with him. In the assortment of bills, letters from the family, and fliers advertising sales of farm equipment, Elsie found a letter from Albert. She read it while Mavis trotted busily around the kitchen, pretending to be Mother in Daddy's clothes going out to milk.

"Dear Elsie," the letter began. "I thought you would like to know I got me a job. I am now Assistant State Brand Inspector at the north station on the state line. You can write to me here. The salary is two hundred a month, board, room, and horse feed. It isn't a lot, but it's better than nothing. I will be home in the fall after the stock stops moving. I would like you and Mavis to come and see me when you can, but I have only one room and no running water here, so don't feel you have to stay and cook for me unless you want to. It is pretty uncomfortable for a woman and a baby. I enclose a check for part of the first two weeks' pay. I had to keep out some for tobacco and laundry. Your loving husband, Albert." The check was for ninety dollars.

Off and on, for the rest of the day, Elsie considered the matter. Albert would like to have them come, no matter how uncomfortable his quarters were, she could tell that. She could probably get a job cooking for the outfit and earn as much as her husband. They needed extra money—how badly only God knew besides themselves. It would be possible to get one of her brothers to stay on the place and hold things together until fall. Her father had sold off all his breeding stock when the second drought year threatened and there really wasn't enough to do at home to keep all the boys busy. They would work this place on shares, willingly.

The injured cow decided her. When Elsie went out to milk, she found the milch cow in a high state of nerves, trumpeting her annoyance with the intruder sky high and jabbing her horns between the slats of the barn gate. She couldn't quite get at the stranger, but she was doing her dead level best to commit murder. The other cow, lying on the barn floor, bloated from being so long in one position, was uttering feeble little moaning toots of protest and submission. Elsie, anxious to relieve the cow, caught hold of her tail and the uninjured hind leg, and heaved. The cow, with an enormous blast of wind and a sigh of relief, twisted over on her other side. Elsie gave her water and part of the corn chops she had been hoarding for horse feed. She felt reckless. She had the check in the silver drawer in the sideboard, and she could blow the whole works on cow feed if she took a notion to. While she milked, she was busy planning how she could reorganize her day to get out to the barn and turn the cow twice, morning and afternoon.

That evening, with Mavis in bed and the June bugs that come in August butting their heads against the screen in an effort to reach her light, Elsie wrote to her husband.

"Dear Albert," she started her letter. "It sure is good news that you got such a nice job. Mavis and I will be coming over to see you one of these days, as soon as I can get one of the boys to stay on the place over Sunday. I think we will just pay you a visit, though, because I am pretty busy around here. Since you went away a wolf got into the pasture . . . ."

4. *Blizzard Winter*

"... and there is at no time cause for alarm. The process is entirely natural ...."

MARY BELLE EHRENBERG shut the baby book decisively. There was no sense in sitting there reading the same chapter over and over. If she didn't know by now—intellectually—what the onset of labor pains was like, reading the chapter in the Pocket Book for the hundredth time wouldn't make it any clearer.

Joe was the person who ought to read that chapter anyway. He was the one who would have to take care of her, most likely. That was, if he were anywhere around the house to do it. The chances were that he'd be out taking care of some cow's labor pains about the time his wife's started.

Once again Mary Belle recalled a story Joe's mother told about him when he was eight years old. He came in from the corral and asked her to come out and help him for a minute. Mother Ehrenberg naturally thought he wanted help in some normal eight-year-old project and kept putting him off while she washed the dishes and set a baking of bread. Finally he confronted her with tears in his eyes.

"Durn it, Maw," he yelled, "that ole muley cow's out in the lot having her calf this minute. If somebody don't come and

44

hold her while I pull it, she'll be dead 'fore Dad and the men gets home."

And his mother, a ranch wife first, last, and all the time, held the old muley cow's head while her son performed his first delivery with the handles of a pair of fence pliers as forceps.

That had been thirty years ago. Undoubtedly Joe was now as accomplished an obstetrician to cows as there was in the state. Whether that qualified him to deliver a human baby or not his wife was uncertain. She wasn't ranch-raised herself, and in the small Iowa town where she grew up ladies didn't discuss such matters in mixed company. Some remnants of her girlhood tabus still persisted after six years of marriage to prevent her asking too many too intimate questions of her husband.

Of course Mary Belle wanted this baby. She had got married in the first place with the firm intention of having at least six, and the delay in the arrival of the first had been heartbreaking. Childbirth had had many pleasant connotations for her before now. It had meant her friends in their white hospital beds, suddenly slim again, flat under the covers. It had meant flowers—vases of them on dressers and pillow corsages pinned beside carefully made-up faces and freshly done hair. It had meant coaxings to eat specially prepared foods. Never, in her farthest stretches of imagination, had Mary Belle visualized anything like a snowbound ranch house, cut off from everything that could not be reached by means of a fence-line telephone, even the radio possibly immobilized, and a wall of barren mountains enclosing the flat where house and outbuildings stood. Mary Belle had never contemplated having a baby at home, alone except for her husband.

In the first years of her marriage she had tried to keep her mouth shut and never to complain. It was dreadful for a man to be married to a nagging wife, her mother always said. The system of silent suffering was too much for Joe. "For God's sake, TALK!" he exploded at her one day when they had been married about six months. "If you don't like it here, *say so*. Don't go around drooping like an old mare with a bellyache." She rounded on him in a furious temper, and their first quarrel was

45

a knock-down drag-out scrap, verbally. When it was over and she had sobbed herself calm on Joe's shoulder, Mary Belle was astonished to learn that she felt much better. She was fresh and rested and thoroughly relaxed. "There," Joe said. "You see. It's a good thing to let go once in a while. The only women who go crazy on ranches are the ones who keep their mouths shut." Mary Belle adopted the principle of getting things off her chest and put it into effect, forthwith.

Acting upon this principle, she addressed her husband when he came in at five o'clock. She had not seen him since he finished breakfast and went out "to see to some cows" twelve hours earlier.

"I'm worried," she said.

Joe surveyed her briefly and obliquely. "You don't have to be—yet," he commented.

"How do you know what I'm worried about?"

"There's only one thing a woman worries about when she's in—" he grinned delicately—"the shape you are. And you don't have to worry yet. You've got a good two and a half months and six inches to go."

"How can YOU tell?"

"You're still oblong, honey. You don't have to worry till you're square. Wait till you're as wide as you are high, and then it'll be time to think about getting out the car. That's the way we tell with cows."

"I knew you'd lump me in with the livestock!"

"Why not? That's where I learned everything I know. Cows are the best schoolteachers I ever had." He pulled his chair up to the table. "How are the groceries holding out? It's going to snow again, and it looks like it might go on for a while."

"We've got plenty of food in the storeroom. If you want to bring in some fresh meat from the freeze-room, I can use it by the time it thaws."

"I'll do that." He began to eat as the phone rang. Mary Belle went to answer it.

She had trouble hearing over the line and more trouble making herself heard. The phone batteries must be getting low.

46

She'd have to get Joe to take them out to the pump house and hitch them up to the Wincharger for reloading. She finally managed to recognize George Allen's voice, from three houses down the valley. He was nearest the highway of anybody on the line, only twenty-two miles from the turn-off.

"Wait a minute, George," Mary Belle screamed, when she began to grasp the urgency of what he was trying to say. Phones must be off all along the fence; that was what made his voice so faint. "I'll get Joe."

She went to put her husband's plate in the oven while he took the phone. When she turned from the stove—it really was hard for her to bend over to the oven, whatever Joe said—he was still listening intently. "Yeah," he said. "Sure. I see. Well, all right, we'll be looking out for it. Our radio tubes are kind of weak, and we aren't using them unless we have to. Ten to ten-fifteen every morning. We can do that. Sure. Well, if you can get tubes in to us——" He stopped, and shook the receiver briskly. Then he tapped on the mouthpiece and listened with close attention. "All right, George. We'll make out the best we can. This end's dead. I hope he could hear me," he added calmly, as he hung up.

"What's happened?" Mary Belle demanded.

"Storm warning," Joe said. "The worst winter in a hundred years, they say, and the snow's headed right for us. It's been bad in the East for a couple of weeks, and now it's on its way out here."

"How much snow?"

"Now, honey, how can anybody tell about that now? Ask me in a couple of months."

"A couple of months!"

"Don't worry, darling. I was just kidding."

He might have been or he might not have been; Mary Belle had never been entirely certain when he was or wasn't. Men who lived as much alone as most North Dakota ranchers developed their own highly individual senses of humor. Joe was no exception. She remembered what her brother, a fraternity brother of Joe's at Ames, had said about him. "He came here

47

to school, not because it's the best Ag school in the country, but because talking to the other Norskies was like talking to himself and he wanted to know what people were like."

It wasn't quite that bad, naturally. But there was no doubt about the fact that the local humor was peculiar unto itself. Mary Belle went to the back door to look at the sky before she went to bed. The sky was nowhere to be seen; it had hidden itself behind the straight-falling cataract of snow that poured down, separated from her by the width of the porch. A sound at her feet made Mary Belle look downward. The old barn cat was crouched on the floor before her, whining rather than mewing, looking up beseechingly. "Come on in, kitty," Mary Belle invited, holding the door open. She shivered, and turned back inside. "Joe," she asked, "do you think I could be getting a chill? It can't be as cold as I think it is and go on snowing."

Joe stood with his back to the circulating oil heater, warming, and he shook his head. "If you've got a chill, I've got one, too," he observed. "I never felt anything like that draft in my life. You want that old cat in here? She belongs in the barn."

"It's too cold out there for her; she told me so. And she's going to have kittens, too."

"You girls got to stick together, huh? All right. I'll go get her a box of dirt right now. The house won't be fit to live in by morning, otherwise."

Was it morning, or was it still night, Mary Belle wondered when she opened her eyes. The room was filled with a white darkness, and some invisible substance seemed to bind it with silence. Then, as she struggled with her nightmare waking, she realized that the silence was outside the house and that the white bandage beyond the windows held in closer wrappings all the sounds that normally belonged within. The kettle was boiling in the kitchen—she could hear it plainly, even though it was two rooms away. The cat stretched herself under the bed, and Mary Belle could make out the tiny grating of claws against the boards beneath the rag rug. A stick broke and fell in the cookstove, and she could hear its crack as plainly as she did the snap of a board in the house wall somewhere near the window. There was snow outside and the morning was bitterly cold.

Joe was gone, and when she entered the kitchen, Mary Belle found plain evidence that he had prepared his own breakfast and put up a lunch for himself before he started out. She let the cat out and then had to let her in again. She sliced herself some bacon and dropped it in the pan. She hesitated over eggs. There were plenty of dried ones in the storeroom down cellar, but only a dozen fresh ones left in the refrigerator. She decided to let the eggs go. Joe would enjoy the fresh ones as long as they lasted—he had used six for his breakfast and lunch and left the shells in plain view on the kitchen table—and they could always scramble the dried ones with water or canned milk later. She dropped an extra strip of bacon in the pan for the cat and buttered a slice of toast for herself. She lifted the butter dish and found a note on the table beneath it. "Listen to the radio from ten to ten-fifteen," it instructed her. "Get the weather forecast and the news broadcast if you can. I'm going to try to move the stock down from the upper pasture before it gets too cold. Expect me when you see me." The note had apparently been meant to end there, for Joe's afterthought was hastily scrawled and its slant was different from that of the other writing. "Take care, honey," he had added. "I love you." She blinked twice and poured extra canned milk into the cat's dish before she looked at the clock. It was nine-fifteen! She had wasted a good third of her day sleeping, and she had as much housework to do as usual. A snowstorm outside did not mean less to do indoors—quite the contrary.

Mary Belle was so busy with her housecleaning that she almost missed the news broadcast. In fact, it was ten-two before she turned the radio on, and cut into the middle of a sentence, ". . . the worst storm the country has experienced in the last one hundred years. Cattlemen and feed-lot operators are warned to get all livestock under cover or into sheltered areas, if grave losses are to be avoided. Trains were stalled at Fargo, North Dakota, for five hours last night, but heavy snow-moving equipment, rushed from Miles City, Montana, cleared the tracks, and traffic was proceeding slowly by rail, although more highways were reported closed hourly in the prairie and mountain states. Highway patrols warned drivers to keep off the roads except in cases of extreme emergency. Elsewhere in the nation, the weather picture was sunnier. Miami Beach, Florida, reported eighty-seven degrees . . . ."

Mary Belle turned the radio off with a snap. The local weather forecast was the only news she and Joe were interested in. As she went about her housework during the rest of the morning, she found herself haunted by a phrase. Eighteen-hundred-and-froze-to-death. Where in the world had she heard those words and why in the world should they come to pester her now? The word "pester" called up a picture of her New England grandmother, with her crisp white apron, crisp white curls, and bright blue eyes, rocking by a window at home and telling stories. There was one Grandmother had learned from *her* grandmother—that was how Mary Belle came to know the expression. Eighteen-hundred-and-froze-to-death. Hadn't that been 1848? Just exactly one hundred years ago? Then this might be nineteen-hundred-and-froze-to-death.

All day long she kept herself busy, and all day long she waited for Joe. Snow fell and fell and fell. It had been as deep as the window sills when she awakened, and it continued falling until it had reached the top of the lower sash. The tide-level stood there when darkness came, and she was unable to watch the snow's progress against the upper pane. She was matter-of-fact and calm, hopeful, and despairing, by turns. Real daylight might have been encouraging—or it might not. This white dusk was oppressive, but the worst was not being able to see far enough to know the worst. She could not penetrate the mist of snow between her and the barn sufficiently to know whether Joe had gone on horseback or had taken out the tractor.

At the worst moments she panicked, her hand on the phone or the radio, wondering how long she and the cat would be left alone together, perhaps to bear their kittens in one another's company, midwifing each other. At one point, in order to soothe what she realized were unnecessary fears, Mary Belle read aloud from the baby book for almost an hour. The cat listened, her ears moving slightly, graciously back and forth on the dome of her head, as she lay with her paws tucked under her chest before the oil burner. The tiger-striped fur along her spine crawled a little at the sound of fright in Mary Belle's voice. Otherwise the cat was immobile, and her tranquility soothed Mary Belle. After that the day was better. She kept coffee on the stove all day long, waiting to be heated while Joe got out of his boots. She baked a chocolate cake and mixed a bowl of batter for corn bread, ready to bake for supper while he drank the coffee.

At half-past five Mary Belle heard her husband stamping on the porch, and she rushed to open the door. Joe came in sheathed in ice like armour, and at first he could not speak, only stretch out a hand to hold her off. "Let me thaw slowly, honey," he finally croaked. "If I get warm too fast, I'll be sick."

She worked his gloves off and drew a chair to the door so that he could sit down, his bearskin coat still a rigid shell around him. Then she knelt before him, clumsily, and loosened the clasps on his fleece-lined overshoes. She lifted his old fur cap— like the coat, it had belonged to his father—from his head and left him to work his feet free of the overshoes while she went to move the coffeepot to the hottest part of the stove. The ice began to melt from his clothes, and she brought old towels to spread on the floor around the chair and soak up the moisture.

She brought Joe his first cup of coffee before he took off his overcoat. The liquid was too hot; he could not drink it right away, but the warmth loosened his throat. "That Brownie is a mighty good horse," he remarked hoarsely. While she went to put more wood in the stove, he took off his overcoat and loosened the snaps of the leather jacket beneath it.

It took half an hour to get him undressed down to his jeans and his blue shirt, and by then he was shivering. He worked his way nearer the fire, moving his fingers and toes first experimentally, then confidently. "Nothing frozen, not even my ears," he reported at last. "I was feared they might be."

"Did you save the stock?" she asked, and he threw back his head and roared with laughter.

51

"Now you're talking like a ranch woman!" he said. "I'll bet you're glad we're a small spread because the big ones will have tremendous losses. Sure, honey. You bet I saved the stock—or Brownie did. We found them drifted along the fence, right about where I thought we would. There was an opening between drifts down to the creek, and they went that way without any driving. After that it was a business of giving them their heads and following them till we got them down into the feed-lot corrals. When they had any doubt how to go, I didn't try to tell them. I let Brownie figure it out and pass the word along. If it hadn't been for him, we'd never have made it. The way it is, he's safe in the barn with all the corn he's got room for; the cows are in the corral with hay to chew on, and I'm safe indoors, about to dig into a pan of corn bread and follow up with a chocolate cake. What did you and Puss hear on the radio today?"

"The worst storm in a hundred years and no relief in sight," she said. "Joe, does getting the stock in this way mean you're through till it's over? You won't have to go out again?"

"Only to feed. I won't have to go farther than the barn and the corral."

Mary Belle stood looking at the cake knife in her hand.

"Joe, probably I'm silly. But I've been thinking all day about the stories my grandmother used to tell us. She talked a lot about the winter of eighteen-hundred-and-froze-to-death. That was just a hundred years ago. One story she used to tell was about a man who got lost in the snowstorm and froze to death halfway between his house and the barn, within sight of both of them. And she said her grandfather didn't get frozen because when he went out in the storm the first time, he tied a rope to the back door and carried the end of it with him. That way he could find his way back to the house if he got lost. Afterwards he left the rope tied and he could feel his way along it whenever he had to go out. Joe, will you do that, please? For me?"

Her husband looked at her, astonished. "Why, sure, honey, if it will make you feel any better. Anything to please the little woman. Let's eat. I'm starved."

For over a week there was no break in the snowfall. Then they waked to a morning that Mary Belle knew must be different because of the way the air felt. The snow was piled above the windows all around the house, and Joe told her it was above the eaves on the north side. He had kept a tunnel open from the house to the barn and from the barn to the feed lot. The cattle were huddled under the shed there, as the horses were bunched together in the barn. He reported two calves born during the excitement. Not until months later did he tell Mary Belle that both the little creatures died of cold before they were an hour old.

Two exciting things happened on the morning the snow stopped. The old cat had her kittens behind the kitchen stove— and they heard the airplane. The cat attended to business as if it were a routine matter for her, which it probably was. Mary Belle did not realize that anything was going on until she heard the first kitten squeak. By then it was too late for her to be of any help to the cat. She did get a box from the storeroom and transfer the cat and kitten to an old towel she wadded in the bottom. Momentarily she rebuked herself for not being prepared; then she remembered that the cat was the barn cat and had never lived in the house. There had been no calendar to determine how near her time might be.

The fourth kitten had just been born and was being cleaned up by its mother when the plane went over. The mother cat raised her head and spat at the strange sound angrily. Then she lowered herself protectively above the kittens. Mary Belle hoped as she went towards the back door that the little things would survive the blast of cold air that would follow her opening it.

The plane was invisible behind the snow wall, although she could hear it more distinctly when she was outdoors. The noise seemed to hang directly overhead. It sounded like an extremely busy and rather busy-bodyish bee. She listened for a while and then went back indoors. After all it was ten o'clock and time to turn the radio on.

The tubes were lasting better than Joe had feared they would. If she kept the volume low she could make out every word the announcer said. She sat crouched over the instrument, her ear glued to the loud-speaker panel.

"The U. S. Army Air Force today moved into the disaster area," the voice from the air informed her. "Operation Haylift began in three of the eight stricken states. It will be extended over the entire area by late afternoon. First deliveries from helicopters were made over the Navaho Indian Reservation in Arizona." That's a long way south for this snow to go, Mary Belle thought. "There was unfortunately one casualty, when an Indian woman was hit on the head and killed by a falling sack of groceries. Families in disaster areas are asked to signal their need of help by spreading something black on the snow where airmen can see it. Bulldozers and full-track tanks will be despatched on rescue operations to areas where there are no other means of communication . . . ." Mary Belle realized that the cold draft between her shoulders came from the door Joe had opened behind her. She moved around to face the radio and watch him standing on the back porch with the door ajar and his head bent, listening. "It is planned to patrol the storm area by helicopter at least once every forty-eight hours, more often if possible, unless further snow should begin to fall. According to U. S. Weather Bureau forecasts, further snowfall can be expected within the next thirty-six hours, beginning in northern Arizona and spreading northward as the storm returns. Reports have just reached this studio that Operation Haylift is to be regarded as an Emergency Relief measure *only*. Cattle in some storm-stricken states have been reported as starving to death when bales of hay exploded on drifts ten feet from their pens. To avoid further waste of man power and time, ranchers are urged . . . ."

Joe tiptoed into the room, and closed the door behind him. The cat mewed demandingly. He crossed the kitchen and peered behind the stove, then grinned delightedly and bent to thrust one gloved finger into the box. Mary Belle could see a tigerish paw wave a little and then bat confidingly at the finger. Joe straightened again and crossed the kitchen to the bedroom door. He returned presently, in time for the end of the broadcast, with his dress trousers over his arm.

54

"Joe!" Mary Belle exclaimed as she shut off the radio. "Where are you going with the pants to your tux?"

"I'm going to take them out and lay them on the snow," he answered. "That 'copter went on north. They'll likely come back over before they report in to the field."

"What do you want to signal them for? We've got enough fuel oil and plenty to eat!"

"I want them to get a full-track in here for you, honey. We may be in for a long spell of bad weather yet. I'd like you to get into town to the hospital and the doctor while there's a chance of somebody getting through."

Mary Belle sat still, considering. "The cows aren't afraid of you and the old cat isn't afraid of you. I don't know why I should be. If this baby's born before we can get the car through, you'll just have to take a pair of pliers and pull him like a calf. But he'll make a hand when he gets here. He'll wait till it's handy for me to have him."

Seventy-four days later the telephone rang, and Mary Belle rolled across the kitchen floor, dodging kittens as she went, to answer it.

"Hello, George!" she screamed. "Yes, we're fine, thanks. How are all of you? Oh, sure, we've still got plenty to eat. Joe says have them get something in for me when they can; I ought to get to the hospital in about a week, he says. And, he says, when the full-track makes it through, have them bring him a couple of cartons of tailor-mades. He's down to his last two sacks of Durham today."

5. *The Ordeal*

TEXAS, 1952

JIM SOMERTON and Dolores Gadsden met when they were students at S.M.U. and attended the same fraternity dance. Dolores was somebody else's date, but that made little difference to Jim. He wangled an introduction, and immediately afterwards Dolores forgot who her original date for the evening was. That young gentleman went off and got drunk, and a week later he enrolled in Seminary courses with the firm intention of ending his days as a reformed rake and Methodist minister.

By that time Jim had given Dolores his pin and she had put hers away in the little blue velveteen box it came in. She stowed the jewelers' box in her stocking case, and there it remained. A year later, when they graduated, she traded Jim back his pin for a plain gold band. She decided that life was blindingly beautiful.

Their honeymoon, spent in Monterrey, convinced her that marriage was an uninterrupted sequence of dates and best clothes and twanging guitars accompanied by sighing accordions, all against a backdrop of mountains and moon. It was unbelievably beautiful—it was much too good to last.

Dolores did not fall out of love with Jim when they left Monterrey. Fundamentally she was a highly practical person. Also fundamentally, she was—as are most women—thoroughly

56

realistic. When she discovered, as most women do, that the man she had married was a different person on and off his home grounds, she set about in a businesslike way to fall in love with the stranger she found herself living with.

The odd thing about this state of affairs, as Dolores saw it, was that Jim seemed to feel that he was married to a stranger, too. He seemed to be doing almost as much adjusting as she was. About once a month during their first year of married life one of a series of climaxes occurred. They would bounce together for an hour to a mountain-top of emotionalism, then find that there stretched before them a tranquil plateau of understanding. It was the unpredictability of the bounces that startled Dolores.

The whole background of the ranch and its life was strange to her. She remembered her father's saying once that Texas had the right to divide itself into five states if it wanted to, but that it never would because of the problem of who should have the Alamo. Her life at home in Dallas, where elegant new residences lounged on carefully manicured lawns alongside deliberately coursing Turtle Creek, could not have been further from the life she lived in the Chisos Mountains, had she contrived to exist in one lifetime on two separate planets.

Here there was nothing, and the nothing was everything. She and Jim came home from their honeymoon early in June, just after the spring rains and before the midsummer drought. San Antonio was wonderful; they ate a delicious meal and then they paddled along a little river that flowed through the down-town section of the city, under arched bridges and between parked banks. It reminded Dolores of the old geography books and their pictures of Venice.

The next day they started west. The country immediately grew barer and drier. Uvalde was a pretty little town, surprising because it was green in the midst of tawny country. Del Río, where they stopped for lunch, was larger and it had a charm and character of its own even at midday. Oleanders were planted as fences there. They grew as big as trees, their tan and white and rosy blossoms puffing out a strange, dry scent with a hint of dust in it that was like nothing Dolores had ever smelled before.

57

There was no relationship between these giant bushes and the pot plants standing beside her mother's front door.

Then the road was entirely barren under the afternoon sun. They swung around a hairpin curve, across an incredibly high and slender bridge, with one higher still—and slenderer—a mile beyond it, around another steeply twisting S before the asphalt flattened and leveled out, it seemed, forevermore. There were lizards in the dust beside the road, and tarantulas angled deliberately across it, their thick fur daring the might of the car. Dolores suspected rattlesnakes under each clump of sagebrush. Jim raised the needle of the speedometer to eighty and held it there.

They stopped for gas and cokes in Sanderson much later that afternoon, and Dolores was tempted by the sight of a white-stuccoed, air-conditioned tourist court, but Jim shook his head when she gestured towards it. "Time we were getting home," he said. "If you're tired, we'll spend the night in Marfa." Again he set his foot on the accelerator, and they listened to the song of the big convertible along the road.

It was long after dark when they reached Marfa, and Dolores had never known that she could be so tired or so hungry, or so numb just from sitting. Jim parked before a café. They went in and were served steaks without ordering, tremendous steaks. With them came mounds of french-fried potatoes. Tired chips of unripe tomato drooped against wilting hunks of lettuce, hardly able to support their burden of store-bought salad dressing.

The food revived Dolores; she laughed a little as the waitress brought her second cup of coffee. "I don't know what we want to eat steaks here for," she said. "I suppose we'll have all we want of them on the ranch."

Jim stared at her. "I suppose *not*," he exclaimed. "What do you think we are—butchers? Oh, the Mexican hands kill a beef once in a while for a barbecue, but it's too tough for a white man to eat. We ship our beef out for fattening and slaughter, sweetheart," he said more calmly. "Mighty few ranchers in this part of Texas know what their own beef tastes like unless they meet it by accident on somebody else's table." He switched the subject. "Let's sleep the night here in town," he suggested. "I'd kind of like to drive you through the ranch by daylight the first time, so you can get a good look at it."

That, although Dolores did not realize the fact until some months later, was the first episode in their mutual adjustment. The second came the next morning. Jim was up and moving around the room with the first blush of daylight, and they ate breakfast as soon afterwards as the hotel dining room opened— at six o'clock. Dolores could remember her father and brothers getting up at six for a fishing trip, but she had never dreamed that she herself would eat breakfast at that hour. And not only eat it, but hear a husband say, "It sure is late to get started. Breakfast's an hour earlier at the ranch this time of year."

A chill ran through Dolores, and her shocked surprise must have shown on her face. Jim grinned at her reassuringly. "It's all right, Doll. You don't have to get up in the middle of the night if you don't want to. I can go over to the bunkhouse and eat with the hands or have breakfast with Dad at the big house. Mom's always up."

Dolores lifted her head to look him square in the eye.

"Don't you start babying me, Jim Somerton. I'm young and healthy, and I can get up as well as you can. Do you know this is the first time, right this minute, that you've said anything to me about where we're going to live? All this time I thought there was just one house at the ranch and we'd live there with your parents."

"Didn't Mom tell you about the little house?"

"I hardly even got to talk to her. She was just in Dallas the one day—the day of the wedding—remember? And then she flew back to El Paso that night, to meet your Dad when he came in to ship the cattle. And there were so many people around, we just said hello. We didn't get acquainted, or . . ." she was surprised to hear herself sniffling, ". . . or anything."

"Poor Dolly! All alone among strangers! They won't be strangers for long, sweet. They're the most wonderful people in the world."

"Of course they are. They're your people."

Jim looked at her closely for a moment, as if to see whether to suspect sarcasm, and then smiled as if he were reassured. She truly meant what she said. She loved these unknowns already and was determined that they should love her. She went blithely out to the car and slid into her place beside Jim.

They drove through the town at a thoroughly illegal pace. Marfa was beginning to stir and stretch and throw off sleep. They slid between the last fringe of filling stations and tourist camps, and out to a highway that stretched at right angles to the road they had come in on the night before. A cluster of low stone buildings, surrounded by dense trees, lay on the right of the pavement, and the notes of a bugle soared across the walls and followed them with sweetness. "Fort D. A. Russell," Jim said in answer to his wife's unspoken question. "If anything ever happens to me, sweet, get me to the doctors there. They're bound to take care of an ex-GI, even if there's no law that says they have to, and they've got better equipment than the city hospital. It's an old cavalry post, and they keep up a lot of old customs like the bugle there," he added. "Robert E. Lee founded the fort as a frontier post against the Indians."

"Before the War Between the States?"

"Way before."

They drove across a saucer-shaped valley and up to its farther rim. For a moment they clung to the crest, and Dolores looked out and down, ahead of her. As far as she could see, the ground fell away in an easy slope, and the whole earth-plane blazed beneath the early sun. The crimson moved and shimmered in an utterly living, utterly ghostly flame as strange as the blue mountains that soared, free of the desert encompassing their feet, on the right. Could any solid mountains hang so in midair, without touching the substantial earth? Dolores gasped at the blueness and the redness and the beauty, and Jim understood; he turned his eyes away from the flaming land before them to meet hers.

"It's the ocotillo," he said, his own voice hushed by the glory. "It's a real thorny desert plant, but it's not a cactus. All the rest of the year it looks as if somebody had stuck a bunch of dried-up clothes poles in the ground. Then it blossoms and comes alive all over, about this time of year."

"The blossoms are right at the ends of the sticks. Just one clump to a plant."

"Just one, but there's sixty miles of plains there straight ahead of us and not another plant on it that grows as tall as the ocotillo."

"What are the mountains, honey?"

"The Chisos. No, I'm not swearing. It's a Spanish word, and it means Ghosts."

That first sight of her new world flung before her eyes like a map was only a beginning of strangeness. The next big crisis came four months later. It was almost fall, and time for the late roundup. Jim and his father and the four Mexican cowboys and the cook—who frequently declared in the hearing of the others that he was not a wet-*back* but a Latino Americano—departed with horses and the chuck wagon. They were gone for ten endless days. Mrs. Somerton invited Dolores to stay at the big house for a visit. It was always an experience of some formality to leave her own small adobe house for dinner at her mother-in-law's. Mrs. Somerton believed firmly in separate homes and separate lives for young married couples. The hundred yards that divided the two houses might have been the width of the city of Dallas, for all that they saw of each other.

Dolores packed for her visit as if she were really going away from home; she packed so much and so carefully that she had to put her suitcases in the car and drive them over to the big house. When she arrived, Mrs. Somerton, who had observed the loading from her own bedroom window, sent the house boy out to bring the bags indoors.

The big house lived up to its name. It was more than a hundred years old—nobody was quite sure how much more. It had certainly been built in the days when the menace of Indian raids hung over every household that had the temerity to locate in the Big Bend, for its walls were three feet thick—every inch of them hard-packed, sun-baked adobe. Within those walls the temperature stood almost constant. Jim had once remarked that it was almost always twenty degrees cooler inside, as it was in the air-conditioned theaters in town. He added that when the thermometer reached zero, the interior temperature was damned cold.

The furniture in the house was old and solid and fine. Only the best was worth the wagon freight that had to be paid to bring goods overland from San Antonio in the days when the house was furnished. The square rosewood piano in the living room had come out west before the War—The War Between the States, naturally—and annually a piano tuner was imported to keep it in condition. The four-posters in the bedrooms—four of them—had been brought from Tidewater Virginia by Mr. Somerton's great-grandfather. Those massive beds had been his younger son's share of the family plantation and estate. Just why those highly impractical and unsuitable objects should have accompanied him inland, across the Mississippi, to his first plantation on the Neches and his first ranch on the Brazos, and on to the third place when he bought it from a Mexican *hacendero*, nobody now living knew. The explanation was lost in the genealogical mists. The whole twenty rooms of the big house were filled with such puzzles.

Nobody knew, for instance, where the apothecary's scales in the pantry or the copper measuring cans in the kitchen had come from; only that they were of foreign manufacture and very old. But there they were, quite at home with cast aluminum on the one hand and misshapen Mexican pottery *casuelas* on the other. Because they were all a part of Jim's old home, Dolores loved them all equally.

The ten days' visit dragged although she kept busy. She and Mrs. Somerton polished silver and mended sheets. Mrs. Somerton supervised the Mexican maid who washed and stretched and ironed the drawing-room curtains. "It sounds a little pretentious to call it a drawing room, I know," Mrs. Somerton said with her nearest approach to apology, "but then, it *is* a little

pretentious. After all, a room sixty by thirty, with two fireplaces
. . . ." And later the older woman said, "I always save certain jobs
to do while the men are on roundup. It makes the time pass
more quickly."

It seemed like a good idea to Dolores. She considered it, and
also pondered the state of her own house. At last she remarked
to her mother-in-law, "It's fall, but I believe I'll do my spring
housecleaning while Jim's away."

"That's a fine thing, dear," Mrs. Somerton said, amused.
"Why don't you come over and have your meals with me while
you do it? The men should be back in a day or two now."

That afternoon Dolores packed her bags, and the house boy
carried them downstairs and put them in the car. She drove the
hundred yards to her own house, opened the door, and un-
loaded the bags.

She plunged headlong into her housecleaning. She washed
windows and mirrors, cleaned out dresser drawers, put the fresh
shelf-paper she had been saving for spring on the kitchen
shelves. They'd certainly go into town for Christmas shopping
and she could replace it then. She jotted "Shelf paper" down on
her permanent revolving list and dropped into bed that night
well satisfied.

She started on the floors the next morning. The little house
had once been the *mayor domo's* quarters, and it had been built
with a floor of earth mixed with deer's blood and straw. That
floor had withstood as much usage as the rest of the building,
and showed it far less. The little house was supposed to be even
older than the big house. Jim talked of having a hardwood floor
put down when they could afford it, but his mother told him
that as long as the floor wax held out, the floor he had was better
than any he could buy at a lumber yard. Now, in preparation for
waxing the surface, Dolores swept and dry-mopped it with
careful thoroughness.

She heard the noise outside as she reached under the bed.
She ran to the door, still clutching the mop. A wave of cows
rolled slowly towards the low adobe wall that protected the yard
of the little house. At either side of it men rode, drooping a little

in their saddles. Jim was in the lead on the left, and Dolores greeted him joyously, waving the mop in the air in welcome.

Jim's hands rose slowly and he gestured to her with a calm fury. Dolores supposed his movements were those of greeting, and she waved the mop with increased enthusiasm in return. Her husband's mouth opened, and she knew he was addressing her, but the noise of the herd was too great for her to distinguish what he said. At the same time his gestures became definitely those of one who puts a lid on something. By no stretch of imagination could they be interpreted as gestures of welcome, or even of greeting.

Offended, Dolores withdrew into the house. She was still tempestuously cleaning an hour later, when the door slammed open and Jim appeared. Her anger did not outlast his squeeze; she was too thoroughly happy to have him back to stay mad. When he released her the fourth time, she headed for the kitchen and the coffeepot before he could grab her again. Not until much later did she remember to ask him what he meant when he waved his arms that way.

Jim frowned, puzzled. Then his face cleared. "I meant for you to get the hell in the house with that mop, sweet," he said. "You could have spooked the whole herd, waving it that way, and somebody could've got hurt bad. We might have lost some cattle, too."

The next great crisis occurred two months later, and marked the end of Dolores' initiation into ranch life. It also served as a dividing line between her thinking of herself as a bride and as a wife.

The cattle had been sold and shipped. Christmas was coming. It didn't feel exactly like Christmas to Dolores—she was attuned to seasons set by department-store advertisements and street decorations—but the calendar said that the date was only three weeks away, so she knew it was true.

Jim, to whom ranch Christmases were normal Christmases, withdrew to the shop. This institution had begun as the ranch blacksmith's shop and was still equipped with forge and bellows for the repair of wagon tires and the making of horseshoes.

With the passage of years and generations the functions of the shop had increased and expanded. It was now equipped for fine carpentry and radio repair, as well as for routine automobile and tractor mechanics.

Jim loved the shop. Like many ranchmen he was a born putterer. He spent a great deal of his spare time in the construction of fascinatingly useless gadgets. Christmas speeded up his production and put a lock on the shop door—one of the prime requisites of a Christmas gift, in his eyes, was that it should be a complete surprise to the recipient.

Dolores visited her mother-in-law on the evenings Jim spent in seclusion. She was learning to sew and she was ambitious, like all beginners. Her personally constructed Christmas gift for Jim was a set of matching pajamas and dressing gown, in spite of all Mrs. Somerton could say to warn her of the difficulties of tailoring. That lady, presiding over the cutting table and sewing machine, had behind her the authority of many years' experience. She observed Dolores' struggles with only the most necessary comments.

There came an evening three weeks before Christmas, when the door of the sewing room was hurled open. The Latino-Americano cook stood on the threshold, stuttering and choking in his efforts to separate two languages and produce a coherent statement in either.

"Meez Soomerton," he finally enunciated, and then, "Meester Jeem. You come—queek."

Jim was behind the cook, and even as the women caught sight of him, they saw him stagger. His hands were clutched before him and a red trail coursed down the front of his jeans and along the hall behind him. His face was laundry-starch white.

Mrs. Somerton seized her yardstick and cracked it in two against the edge of the cutting table. She caught up a heavy piece of material and twisted a tourniquet around her son's arm, above the injured hand. Dolores could not force herself to look at him—the red stream seemed to flow before her eyes and cover everything. Then her cheek stung and the red faded out. She

opened her eyes—she had not realized that they were closed—
and saw her mother-in-law confronting her, one hand still upraised.

"Get Mr. Somerton and the car, Dolores. Hurry. You can
faint later."

The cook had gone before her, and the sedan was warming
up in short, angry bursts before the house. Dolores, the cook
trailing her now, turned and ran back along the hall. Her mother-in-law supported Jim where he stood, and between them,
with some awkward help from the cook, they led him down the
hall and out to the car. Mr. Somerton left the driving seat long
enough to help them load Jim into the back. Then they were all
inside and doors were slammed. The car rocketed across the
banging cattle guard and out on the ranch road.

Dolores thought Jim was unconscious. His eyes were closed
and his face was a moonlike blur of whiteness in her lap. His
mother leaned over the front seat of the car to hold his arm upward and at an angle before her. From time to time she loosened
the tourniquet and blood spurted across the car and stained the
upholstery and the skirt of Dolores' housedress. Then the twist
was drawn tight again and the flow was temporarily stopped.

Dolores forced herself to speak only once, and then she did
not ask the question that engulfed her consciousness. She spoke
from the memory level just below the agony of keeping Jim
alive. "Fort D. A. Russell," she said to her father-in-law's back.
"He told me, if anything happened, to be sure and take him
there."

She saw the older man nod his head and she thought she saw
Jim's eyelids stir and twitch, although she could not be quite
sure that they moved. Gravel spurted against the undersides
of the fenders and the car lurched sidewise, sickeningly. Dolores
tightened her grip on Jim's shoulders, clutching him against her
on the car seat. They stopped; a car on the road ahead of them
barred their way.

"Somerton?" said the voice behind the flashlight. "Your
mayor domo phoned patrol headquarters for an escort. We got
out here as fast as we could. You want one of us to drive?"

"I'll drive," Mr. Somerton said. "You keep ahead of me, if you can."

"Post or City Hospital?"

"Post."

The ride became an accelerating horror, and the scream of the patrol car, always ahead of them to clear the way, cut through Dolores' ears and brain like a stabbing flame. She wondered how Jim could bear it, was glad he was unconscious and did not have to, and held him tight so he would not be jarred. The screaming stopped. There were lights and a thud of brakes. Men and a stretcher were beside the car. Jim was lifted from her arms and rushed away from her.

"Mother," she sobbed, and felt arms around her.

"Hush, dear," Mrs. Somerton said soothingly. "It's all right now. He'll be all right now."

The trooper came over and stood awkwardly beside them. Now that the wild ride was over, they were all bewildered by their sudden idleness, stunned by the emptiness of loss of occupation and cessation of movement.

"You want to go to the hotel, Mrs. Somerton?" the officer asked.

"I think we'll wait here," Jim's mother answered. "It won't be very long before we know."

"Probably need a transfusion," Mr. Somerton added. His voice was slowly becoming matter-of-fact and normal again.

"You leaned over the back of that seat and took care of that tourniquet the whole time, didn't you?" the trooper said in an awed voice to Mrs. Somerton. "Gosh! Not many men who could have done that!"

Part of what he said reminded Dolores of a question she wanted to ask. "How long was it?" she inquired.

"Ninety minutes—an hour and a half—altogether," the trooper said. "How far is it in from the ranch, sir?"

"Just under eighty miles—seventy-seven, I think," Mr. Somerton replied. "We lost some time when you stopped us. We might have done better if we'd had a plane."

"I don't think so," the trooper answered. "You'd have lost time loading and unloading."

Dolores wanted to scream at them to stop talking nonsense at a time like that, but she didn't. Mr. Somerton might have set an all-time speed record for driving across the Big Bend at night and Mrs. Somerton might have performed a miracle of contorted heroism, but she was only interested in knowing that they had accomplished their end. She sat on a backless bench against the whitewashed stones of the corridor outside the emergency room and forced her whole being into waiting. Once she discovered that her fingers were pleating folds in her blood-stained skirt. She compelled them to quietness.

The door of the emergency room opened and a woman with captain's bars on the collar of her seersucker uniform stepped into the hall. She was smiling—Dolores could see clearly that the woman was smiling. "We've sent him on upstairs to a private room for the night," she told them. "As soon as he settles down, you can go up and see him. Tomorrow we'll move him into a ward. You can take him home in a day or so, when the heal gets well started and we know there's no infection."

Later—how much later, Dolores was never sure—they all went upstairs and along a corridor, into a narrow white icebox of a room. Jim was stretched out on a bed as high as his wife's shoulders. He turned his head towards them and grinned.

"You all sure went to a lot of trouble for nothing," he remarked. "The patient lived."

"Better luck next time," said his father cheerfully. His mother smiled, too.

"It was just like old times, dear," she observed. "I couldn't help remembering the time you fell off the roof and broke your collarbone and we thought for a while it was your neck."

Dolores was horrified. That anyone should speak so to a sick man—to one who had narrowly escaped death—and his own parents, too. And then she remembered. That screaming rocket flight through the night had not been made to set a speed record. That bending double over the back of the car seat was not simply a test of endurance. These things and the speeches that followed them came from a code and were part of the code. It was her turn to speak, and she perceived that on what she said now depended what her husband and his parents would think of her all the rest of her married life. Something on the floor caught her eye, and she bent down to look at it more closely. It was the belt of the dressing gown, stained with blood and twisted out of shape from being used as a tourniquet. How had it got here in this room? she wondered.

"It's a good thing you were out like a light," she said, recovering the piece of cloth and folding it carefully below the edge of the bed. "Otherwise you'd have found out what I was making you for Christmas."

Jim's eyes were closing and his head was a weight pressing into the pillow, but he managed to play his trump. "Keep out of the shop till I get home," he instructed her, "or you'll find out about my present for you."

6. *This Is the Way We Earn Our Bread*

KANSAS, 1952

GEORGE had always said that when he reached age fifty he meant to retire. Bessie agreed with him; it was a wonderful age for it. They would still be young enough to enjoy life, both children would be through school and college and established on their own, and the ranch, by that time, certainly ought to be able to run itself with a little help from George, Jr. She went along with her husband in making plans and in executing them. When they reached fifty, the ranch was paid out and running smoothly under George, Jr.'s direction, they had money in the bank and their annuity policies were due. They were both ready for a good long rest after Bette's wedding.

The day after George deposited the annuity checks, Bessie first noticed the change in him. He seemed to be sagging all over. He had always been bowlegged. Since his father put him on a horse on his second birthday and went off and left him to manage as well as he could for half an hour, that was not surprising. But now George's legs were more than bowed; they appeared to be bent outward by the weight of his torso. What had been a solid corporation for the support of hard-working levis had become suddenly a pot belly. And the shoulders that had always been broad and straight and flat enough to support any load now had a downward and outward droop like the branches of a fruit tree at the end of a heavy bearing season.

"For the Land's sake, George," Bessie asked him, "what's the matter with you?"

"I dunno," George answered. "I don't feel specially well, is all."

"It must have been that sauerkraut you ate at the church dinner last night. I warned you; Mrs. Perkins never lets it ripen long enough."

"It's nothing I ate," George protested, observing the Epsom salts gleam in his wife's eye.

"It's got to be," Bessie informed him. "You've never been sick a day in your life for any other reason, except that time you broke your hip and collar bone when the old Saltillo horse rolled on you."

"Maybe that's it," said George, chirking up slightly. "I believe that *is* it. My hip and shoulder keep hurting me right along."

"Rheumatism," Bessie decreed. "Well, a dose of salts ought to fix that right up."

She dosed him thoroughly, thereby increasing his misery. He was so unhappy he couldn't take any interest in the travel folders that came in the morning's mail. Bessie spread them on the table before him in an appetizing array of vivid colors and exotic names and betook herself to the bedroom. She was emptying drawers, sorting and discarding her possessions and her husband's, preparatory to giving up the ranch house to George, Jr., and his wife. After all, she and George had always planned that when they retired they would live in town, where they could have a new and efficient and shinily modern house. If they came back to the ranch for any length of time, they could stay in the guest room or the foreman's house the youngsters were going to vacate.

The prospect of smaller space and simplified housekeeping was alluring to Bessie. She hurled away the detritus of half a lifetime with a pleasant smile. She had never been one to cling to articles she had finished with and somebody else could use.

Her keepsakes were sorted from the rubbish and tidily stowed away in boxes of their own; had been, indeed, ever since she was a school girl and first acquired the "Memory Book" habit. She had finished her personal packing for the move by supper time that evening. She told her husband about it at the table, while she put away a nicely browned half-chicken and he uneasily consumed milk toast.

"You leave my things alone," he almost ordered her. "I'll do my own sorting, soon's I feel like it."

Fratchety, that's what he was. Crochety. Well, Bessie's mother had always said that the only way to deal with a sick man was to humor him. If he seemed unreasonable it was because he *was* unreasonable, having been born an unreasonable creature in the first place. You couldn't expect a man to make sense like a woman, Bessie's mother had often observed. They weren't made that way.

Bessie considered resuming packing after dinner. She could just as well start on the kitchen things as not. But George looked so wretched—there was such an indefinable resemblance to a whipped dog about him—that she abandoned her half-formed plan. She would need her cooking things right up to the last minute anyway. She went into the living room as soon as she had finished the dishes, intending to occupy herself with the travel folders that had failed to interest George. At least he had been reading the *American Cattle Producer* every time she entered the living room during the day.

As she stepped across the threshold, she observed that her son was seated across the table from his father, and the sight gave her a distinct shock. She could never remember the day when George, Jr., hadn't come and gone through the kitchen. The thought that he had entered the house through the front door and the formality the action implied jolted her. She was reassured by the trend of the conversation. An old old argument was in process. George, Jr., wanted to drill a well in the north pasture. George, Sr., was firmly convinced, and trying to persuade his son, that the north pasture was no place to drill a well.

"No, son," he was saying as Bessie came in. "It'll never work." He looked brighter and more cheerful than he had all day.

"Dad, I think it will. I'm sure it will. And think of the saving in time and man power. As things are, we can only use that section about four months out of the year, when the buffalo wallows fill up in the spring and fall. Otherwise, to get any good out of that pasture, we have to put a man on to move the stock back and forth to water. With a well there we can use the grass as much as three-fourths of the year, and we won't have to do much more than ride fence to look after the stock."

"That's all right, son. Save whatever you can. But you can't get blood out of a turnip and you can't get water out of hard-pan. I don't see why you're so stubborn and bull-headed about the business. There isn't any water there, and it's money thrown down a rathole to drill for it."

"I don't see why *you're* so sure about it, Dad. I agree that the water probably isn't near the surface. But I had the Soil Conservation Service geologist out there again today and he agrees with me. There's water there. It's a question of going through the surface formation and striking it."

"That's a geologist for you. Hell, there's water—Bessie, stop rattling them papers, you're making me nervous—there's water anywhere if you go deep enough. The whole of West Kansas is resting on water, and under the water they's a layer of sand and then more hard-pan. If you drill for water, you'll likely get it, but you'll mighty soon wish you hadn't, because the sand'll come up along with it and stop your well."

George, Jr., kept his temper. His manner remained amiable and placid, and Bessie rejoiced at his patience with his father. She hadn't always been *sure*, by any means . . . .

"You're absolutely right, Dad, in principle," the younger man said. "It just so happens that north pasture's different. We've got the top of an old earth fold out there, with the hard-pan on top instead of 150 feet underground the way it is most places. If we go through the hard-pan, we'll hit a water-bearing gravel formation at about fifty feet with more shale under that, according to the geologist. We're lucky. We'll probably even get an artesian flow if we hit it right."

George, Sr., slammed his fist down on the table top and then shook his hand wildly in the air to show that it hurt. Serve him right, Bessie reflected. That'd teach him to know his own stren'th, and not go around acting like Popeye in the funny papers.

"Listen to me, son," George, Sr., said, and there was deadly seriousness in his tone. "I never told you the *real* reason why I know that geologist's wrong, but I guess I better. Your grandfather had that pasture dowsed for water when he first took up his homestead here I don't know how many years ago—anyway, long before I was born or thought of. He had the best dowser he could hire—brought him all the way down from Ioway and paid his and his team's expenses besides what he paid him—and they went over this place from start to finish with a willow switch. Your grandfather followed that dowser's advice about every well he drilled, and he never had a moment's cause to regret it. And the one place the man told him never to waste time or money on a well was that north pasture. He never did and I never did, and as long as I'm alive and running this place nobody ever will."

They sat in silence, facing each other across the litter of bright-colored papers; their faces entirely alike in their immobility. George, Jr.'s answer rang in the room as plainly as if he had spoken it. Then he got up, and laid his hand on his father's shoulder. "Go on to bed and get a good rest," he instructed. "You'll feel better in the morning. G'night, Mom." He kissed his mother briefly and was gone.

"Bessie," her husband said wearily, "come and help me to bed. I'm an old man. I'm tired. I can't stand this arguing and going on."

He got up at five the next morning as he was used to doing and tottered out to the kitchen to start the fire and make the coffee. The custom, blissful to Bessie, went back to the earliest days of their marriage. That morning she noticed drowsily that George seemed to be fumbling more than usual and to be making more noise than he ordinarily did. When he brought in her cup of coffee, a good third of it had slopped into the saucer. When she went to the kitchen fifteen minutes later to start break- fast, a scene of wreckage met her eyes. How had her husband, ordinarily as neat as a chuck-wagon cook, managed to make such a thorough mess of things? She cleaned up spilled coffee grounds from the sink, swept the kindling into the dust pan and poured it back in the bin, and mopped up a small lake that had formed in front of the stove, perhaps because the over-filled tea kettle had slopped over.

George seemed brighter after breakfast. Bessie hesitatingly suggested that he start going through his things; just to sort them, she added hastily, not to *pack* anything. George burped profoundly and rose from the table. He departed for the bed- room; then turned with his hand on the door-knob, to say, "I reckon I better not eat any more fried eggs for a while, Bessie. They don't seem to set right with me."

But he was back in ten minutes with the light of battle in his eye. "What's become of my angory chaps?" he demanded. "A fine how-de-do, when a man can't leave his own clothes hang in his own closet and come back and find them a month later. Them was my good chaps; my riding-club chaps."

Bessie turned from the dish pan. "Why, George," she said, "don't you remember what you done with them chaps? You gave 'em to son, when he rode in the rodeo a year ago Fourth of July."

The gleam died from George's eyes; his straightening shoul- ders sagged again. "I reckon I forgot, Mother," he sighed. "I'm getting old." He all but tottered as he left the kitchen. When Bessie finished the dishes and went to see how he was getting along, he was stretched out on the unmade bed, flat of his back and snoring gently.

The sound of the well-rig, rattling past the window at mid- morning, awakened him. He rose and strode out on the front porch, himself again, to see what was going on. The rig con- tinued through the back gate and out on the ranch road, headed for the north pasture. George came back in the house shaking his head dolefully. "Pouring money down a rathole," he mourned. "Good money that my father and I worked hard to make. This keeps on, the ranch'll be broke and sold on sheriff's auction, inside a year."

He did not take kindly to Bessie's suggestion that he spend the afternoon in the north pasture, observing its desecration. He picked at two meals of milk toast and tea. After supper he lighted his pipe, then laid it down after the second puff. "It just don't taste good," he announced.

The next day he lay a-bed in the morning while Bessie made the coffee. It was a lovely day, bright and sunny and warm for early spring, and he finally accepted her suggestion that he go and sit out on the porch. Before doing so, he put on his overcoat and a scarf—George, who had been accustomed to ride out on fence and bring in strays in the teeth of a blue norther, with no more protection than a leather jacket and an ear-flapped cap.

Bessie was seriously alarmed. She left him sitting in the weak spring sunshine and made her way determinedly across the yard to the foreman's house, to take council with her daughter-in-law.

Althea was young, but she was well informed. She had studied to be a teacher. She listened to Bessie's tale of woe and shook her head gravely at the end.

"I don't understand, Mom," she said. "There's something wrong, surely, yet you say he isn't really sick. Maybe he needs a psychiatrist."

"A mind doctor?" Bessie asked. "You try and get him to one!"

"He might be a lot more comfortable if he went," Althea observed. "Why don't you try to get him to go into Topeka for treatment?"

Bessie returned to the house full of thought. The suggestion struck her as a good one, but she hesitated to pass it on to her husband. At last the idea came to her to go herself first, and sound the doctor out. It might be something George could be treated for at home, which would make both of them feel better. She resolutely scouted the idea that he needed the family physician. He wasn't sick, and if he were, she could take as good care of him as old Dr. Watson, who was the only one George would ever go to.

"George," she began, while he daringly experimented with

chicken soup at lunch. "do you think you can manage without me for a couple days?" He raised startled eyes to her face, and she went on relentlessly, "I'm going to need some new clothes for the trip and I thought I'd go into Topeka and give myself a blowout, shopping. Althea says she'll come over and fix meals for you, or you can go over and eat with them if you feel able." She made a mental note to advise Althea of the offer at the earliest opportunity, and waited. Althea often said she'd do anything she could.

"You go ahead, Mother," George replied feebly. "Spend your money if you feel like it. Half of it's yours and always has been, and you might's well enjoy it now as after I'm gone. As for my eating while you're away, I can manage. It's kind of Althea, but she don't have to bother."

Should she shake him or feel sorry for him, Bessie wondered as she got into her navy blue faille two-piece. No use talking, the things from Sears' catalog looked as nice and wore as well as anything she could get in the stores. But George. It would be awful if he really *was* sick and she wasn't taking it right. This mind doctor, this phissy-ky-At-riss, he might could tell her.

The psychiatrist, when she confronted him two days later, proved to be alarmingly young, although his manner was reassuring. Instructed to tell him everything that was bothering her, Bessie told.

"I see," he said when she finished. "Yes. I think we can handle it all right with a patient who is so thoroughly willing to co-operate. Can you arrange to come back two or three times a week during treatment, or would it be more convenient for you to stay in town?"

"You mean for me to bring my husband in?"

"Oh, no," said the psychiatrist, "not until you are further along with your own treatment, please. Later, of course, he should come, but not as long as you are in the early stages of therapy."

"But it isn't me! It's him that sick!" Bessie exclaimed, alarmed.

"Naturally, when one member of the family is in need of treatment, all should receive therapy to re-establish the balance," the young doctor answered matter-of-factly. "You go home and think it over, and when you decide, let me know. Naturally I don't want you to feel that I am putting any pressure on you . . . ."

Bessie went on downtown and went shopping. Then she took her purchases back to the hotel and checked out. Five o'clock in the afternoon was late to be starting for home, but George would worry if she stayed away an extra night. And the silence of the car, the isolation of movement, gave her an opportunity to think, which she badly needed.

The psychiatrist might be right. He probably was. If George went on the way he was headed, she certainly would need a mind doctor—and bad. But somehow that would be surrender; not just surrender of her inner life to another's inspection, but surrender of her own capacity to deal with situations. That was the last resort, and she would hold it in reserve for the time being.

Doctors—medical doctors—were not much more satisfactory. Pricked by her urgings, George, Sr., had had a thorough checkup in the fall. Except that he ate too much and put on a little weight during the winter, there was nothing physically wrong with him. She was still sure of that. A diet of milk toast and chicken soup wouldn't hurt him if he lived on it for a month, she was positive. No, she could do as much for him as any doctor she could get him to see.

Well, then, the minister. A minister ought to be able to help. But still, she hesitated. She and George were Presbyterians—always had been and always would be. A Presbyterian minister could comfort them in their acceptance of the will of God, but he couldn't in good conscience point out the way to change things. Momentarily, Bessie wondered if she didn't feel more like an Episcopalian than a Presbyterian. All things were as God willed, perhaps, but He had given man the power of choice.

That was that. She had the power of choice—it was up to her. She was on her own and she would have to do the best she could. George was tired out, probably; he'd worked hard all his life. The best thing to do was to see that he got a good rest. Considerably cheered, she turned into her own gate.

Since Bessie's earliest girlhood, her mother had observed of her that she was endlessly thorough. Having determined that George should have a good rest, she set about seeing that he got it. She borrowed Althea's three-sided pillow and bed tray, and she lowered the blinds on the bedroom windows. She considered renting a hospital bed, but discarded the idea. She hoped profoundly that George would get rested out and be up and around again in a reasonable time. She cooked delicate meals, capable of nourishing only an inactive canary bird, and she served them to him on what was left of her mother's hand-painted dinner set. She banished the radio and the *American Cattle Producer* and the *Topeka Capitol*. She substituted a copy of *Pollyanna* and one of *Tom Swift's Space Ship,* both left from the children's growing-up days, as the lightest and most cheerful literature in the house.

George was pleased, at first, to have all the attention she could give him. After a few days, when he finally got it through his head that he wasn't going to get either the radio or the newspaper brought to him, he took the books away from her and insisted on reading to himself, on the grounds that there was no sense in her tying herself down every hour of the day to entertain him. Besides, the rocking chair squeaked, and if she lived to be a hundred she'd never learn to sit still in it. Bessie withdrew, rejoicing, to the kitchen, and that night she gave him hamburger instead of boiled chicken for supper. He ate it without comment.

It was two days later that she heard the thud on the bedroom floor and rushed in to discover its cause. George sat on the edge of the bed, his feet planted on the rag rug. *Pollyanna* lay broken-backed, across the room.

"Get me my pants," George commanded. "I can't stand this. A man's got to breathe air sometimes."

She brought him a pair of jeans and soon afterwards she heard the front door slam. Briefly she scouted around the corner of the house. He was firmly established on the porch and in his hand was clutched like a banner the latest issue of the *American Cattle Producer.*

Once recovery set in, it was rapid. He demanded steak for dinner that night: steak and potatoes and french-fried onions. She was out of beef, but it occurred to her that Althea might have a steak in the freezer. She threw a sweater around her shoulders and went across the yard to the foreman's house. The youngsters were eating their own supper when she went in, and George, Jr., looked disconsolate.

"How's Dad?" he asked while Althea stood on her head in the freezer.

"Lots better," Bessie replied. "He's been sitting up all day. He says he wants man-food and not nibblings for supper. I believe he's going to make it all right."

"I hope he does," George, Jr., remarked. "Looks as if he'd better take over the management again."

"What do you mean, son? You haven't heard from the draft board, have you?"

"Oh, I hear from them fairly regularly, but nothing personal yet. No. This is something else. We're down to 182 feet in the north pasture, and there isn't a trace of water in that hole yet."

Bessie hesitated a moment. What she was going to ask would be mighty hard on the boy, but it might save his father's life, not to mention her reason. The question was, was George, Jr., man enough to do it? Well, she could soon find out.

"Son," she said quietly, "will you come over to the house tonight and tell your Dad that? Just that; not anything else?"

For a moment George, Jr.'s knuckles whitened as he tightened them around the handle of his coffee cup. Then his fist relaxed into a hand, and he grinned at his mother. "He shall be told," he promised her.

She could hardly eat her own dinner for excitement; she could hardly wait to wash the dishes before she went into the living room after she heard the front door open and close. But she forced herself to follow the normal pattern of her evenings. When at last she turned off the kitchen light and entered the living room, she saw the two men facing each other across the table—clean now and without any bright litter.

". . . so Granddad's dowser was right and you were right,"

George, Jr., said as she dropped quietly into her rocker. "I guess there isn't any water in that pasture this side of China. The geologist still says it's a freak formation, only now he says it's freakish the other way. The shale formation's on top, all right, and it's on the bottom. It fills up the space in between for good measure."

George, Sr., nodded weightily. "Well, son, I tell you," he began, and Bessie smiled privately, recognizing the ritual opening of a prolonged, man-to-man, heart-to-heart talk. "I tell you," George, Sr., repeated. "A man can spend a lifetime learning all he can about the ranching business and still not know everything. There's some things anybody's got to learn the hard way and nobody can teach him. Seems like where to drill a well must be one *of* them."

George, Jr., nodded wordlessly.

"Now," his father resumed, "I've been promising your mother for I don't know how many years to take her on a trip and buy her a new house. I don't want to go back on my promise, but if she'll meet me halfway, I got a different plan to suggest."

"Anything that's within reason, George," Bessie said.

"Well, Mother, see how this strikes you. Let's stay on in the old house; we're used to it. We'll spend part of the insurance money fixing it up and putting in some of them store-bought gadgets you've wanted so long, and part of it we'll put into a couple new rooms and an extra bathroom and plumbing for the foreman's house so the kids can go on living there in comfort."

Bessie looked across at her son. As he met her eyes, he nodded. "Suits us all right," he agreed. "We're used to the little house and we both like it. What about that trip, though?"

"Well, now," George, Sr., said, and for the first time he appeared uneasy, uncertain of himself. "Well, now. I don't want to go back on my promise to you mother, and Land knows she's earned a vacation. But we always said we'd take the trip when we retired. I've got a kind of feeling maybe I'm not ready to retire and maybe it's best I shouldn't. Question is, will your mother wait till I *can* retire and we can take a real long trip— maybe go abroad—or will she settle for a little short one now?"

He looked across at his wife, and his eyes begged her to compromise.

Bessie rose to the occasion and to her feet. "If that's all you've got to worry about," she said crisply as she got the travel folders out of the desk drawer, "you can make your mind easy. I'd as soon have two or three little trips between seasons as one big one I never got. Now here. We can go most anywhere we want to when we make up our minds where that is. And we don't have to stay a day longer than you want to. We can come home whenever we like." She fanned the folders out on the table before her husband. Psychiatry wasn't a patch on mother-wit when you come right down to it. "Pick and choose," she said. "Arizona? We might go and see how they raise cattle out in the desert. Might come in handy, what with that north pasture . . . ."

PART THREE

What Are Their Houses Like?

BUILDING A HOME *is a slow process, almost as slow as building a life. An old saying has it that no house becomes a home until it has sheltered a birth, a death, and a marriage.*

So there is considerable back-tracking in the section that follows. When three generations have lived on the same place, the roof over their heads acquires its own personality. It is worth going back to the time when the foundations were laid, to understand what came later.

Besides, no part of a woman's life reflects her surroundings as sharply as the roof over her head and the furniture she uses. A house is constructed in a certain way because its environment makes certain demands and supplies certain materials. Nowhere is that more true than on a ranch.

7. *This Is the Way We Build Our House*

MONTANA, 1895–1945

PERHAPS the best and easiest way to describe how a ranch house is planned and built would be to tell a little of the history of a real ranch, the JL on Powder River in Montana. The JL is going into its third generation now, and while it will never build up into a cattle empire, or anything else so anachronistic, it's a going concern and a right good business.

The first JL was Jan Larsen, who came to the United States from Denmark when he was about thirteen. He was the oldest of a big family, and when his parents settled in a Danish community in the Middle West, Jan was already feeling pretty independent. He stayed around home for another year or so, and then he took his foot in his hand and headed out.

Johnny Larsen never told anybody all the things that happened to him on his way west. He managed to eat and he slept somewhere at night. He did odd jobs here and there as he went along, and about the fag end of the eighteen nineties, when he was a husky of sixteen, big as a grown man, he found himself on the Yellowstone, in eastern Montana, looking for a job.

Those were the days when Life in the West was first fashionable. Life in the West is a funny thing. People who live in the West on ranches work harder for less than people anywhere

else in this country. No southern sharecropper would put up
with the hours the average cow hand takes for granted. But
that chivalry business still operates in the West and colors most
activities of the range with bright, attractive hues. The West is
romantic, and it was even back in Johnny's day.

Between the eighteen thirties and the eighteen nineties,
European princelings and offshoots of aristocracy went west for
the big-game shooting. Some of them liked the country and
came back, and a few stayed when they returned. The West
became a good place to make investments, and English and
Scottish capital, particularly, went into cattle lands. Wealthy
Americans from the East Coast made similar vacation trips and
investments. Some of them built the equivalents of Scottish
shooting lodges in Montana and Wyoming and Colorado, and
went out for a few weeks each year for the fall mountain-sheep
shooting.

Johnny Larsen heard of a Philadelphia family that had a
shooting lodge on Powder River, and he heard that they were
hiring hands. The family was putting their place in cattle and
planning to live there most of the year. So Johnny went down
to the Powder River and appeared at the ranch, a long-legged,
broad-shouldered kid, broke and hungry and looking for work.

It happened that that particular hundred-thousand-acre
spread had all the outside hands it needed by the time Johnny
got there. The only job left was that of cook, and it was vacant
because the lady of the houehold wanted a cook who knew about
foods beyond the usual beans-and-bacon-and-sourdough-bread
range menu of the time. Johnny knew less than nothing about
cooking, but he was clean and neat even after his months of
wandering, and he spoke with a European accent. The lady
decided that Johnny, young as he was, probably knew a little
about food on a high plane and also would be teachable. So she
hired him as cook.

Right at the beginning they made a pact. Mrs. Philadelphia
would make out the menus and look up the recipes in the cookbook. While a meal was in preparation, she would stick around
home, within reach if an emergency arose and Johnny needed

help. But Johnny did the cooking. Whether he knew it or not, the boy was following the western tradition that the cook is supreme when he is in the kitchen or near the chuck wagon.

Johnny learned a lot in the years when he cooked for the ranch. He learned how to carve, how to make sauces of all kinds, what wines to serve with which dishes, and how to eat high-powered cheeses without suffocating. Until the end of his life he had Roquefort cheese sent from France for his own use. His family wouldn't willingly go within smelling distance of the stuff.

Outside the kitchen, Johnny learned to read and write English. He learned to read for pleasure. He developed an enormous respect for education and knowledge, but not to the point where he lost his respect for mother-wit. And he learned that a man could go farther and do better as his own boss than he could when he worked for wages. The Philadelphia family sponsored him when he took his citizenship. One thing Johnny had never needed to be taught was that he should be a voting, land-owning citizen.

Not long after Johnny had his papers and was beginning to look around for a place of his own, the homestead law was passed. It marked the end of the open range and of enormous holdings like those of the family from Philadelphia. It also marked the beginning of an era of opportunity for small men like Johnny. With the blessing of his former employers, he took up a homestead down river, and went to work for himself.

The next few years were mighty busy ones. Johnny proved up on his homestead—showed that he had constructed the necessary buildings and fenced his land—and then he began to expand. He leased land from the government and from other homesteaders, and when other little men sold out, he bought their places. He ran cattle, starting with whatever stock he could get and improving it as fast as he could. He bought registered bulls to run with his range cows, and as the cattle generations went by and the stock upgraded, he came to have a very fine herd indeed.

That's all background—interesting as it is—for the story of the ranch house on the JL.

When Johnny first took up his land, one of several things the country lacked was roads. When you wanted to go somewhere, you went, taking off across country and steering a course by the sun around gopher holes. If the way you went happened to miss flash-flooded ravines and go around the biggest buttes, you likely would back-trail on it a time or two. If the process were continued, what had been a trail would become a track, and after a while maybe it would even be a road if enough other people used it.

Johnny could locate without regard for the highway, as far as his building site was concerned. The highway would come by the house in time, if he stayed where he was and drove his stock out and hauled his supplies in, using the same route each trip. If he and his neighbors got in the habit of using one road for several families, the highway would get to them that much sooner. The only consideration, as far as ranch-house communications were concerned, was a location that wouldn't be completely buried with snow in winter.

There was a creek running through Johnny's land, and on the south side of the creek, just above the second terrace and out of flood danger, there was a little rise of land. It made a sort of shelf, and while the acre or so of ground between the curve of the creek and the curve of the hill was open on the north, it had the protection of the willows and cottonwoods that grew along the stream on that side. Johnny, after he had looked the place over thoroughly, decided it was the best location on his land for a house.

He needed shelter for a year or so before he built a real house, and he made it by scooping a dugout in the hillside. Later on he planned to convert it into a bunkhouse—if he got enough land to feed enough cattle to need more hands than were attached to his person. As soon as he could, Johnny went to work on a real house, and he built himself a good one. He was looking ahead to the years when his claim would be a ranch.

Whether or not Johnny built the kind of house he did because he came from Denmark and a log house looked *right* to him we'll never know. True, there were no building stones anywhere within hauling distance. The soil on the ranch, especially along the creek, was clay, and a Southwesterner would probably have built an adobe house. Johnny wasn't used to adobe, and if he thought about the matter at all, he may have thought that a mud house would melt and run away in a spring thaw. At any rate, he paid no attention to the building material that was there ready to hand.

He built a log house and he spent much time and thought on it. There were no logs near by; they had to be hauled from the mountains. It can't have been any easier to snake a load of seasoned fir logs over fifty miles of flats in one direction than it would have been to haul wagonloads of lumber from the railroad fifty miles the other way. In fact, it sounds to most of us easier to haul lumber than logs. Logs did have one great advantage over milled stuff. A log house was stronger and more solid and lasting than a frame house would have been.

Johnny built his kitchen first. For a while he actually had a one-room house. At one end of the space he set up the stove, and beside it he built a table that combined sink and work space and a place for eating. He used a nail keg for a chair. When he had company, the guest got the nail keg and Johnny perched on a cartridge box. He built a couple of bunks against the wall opposite the stove, where they would get direct heat, and he and his hired hand—after he began to hire a hand—slept there. Johnny was always an individualist. He put a plank floor in that one-room log house when he built, and he added windows. No sitting on the dirt and hanging gunny sacks over holes in the walls for him. Johnny was used to a house on the Philadelphia ranch, and he was going to have one on his own.

Another of Johnny's departures from the standard pioneer architecture of that section was his porch. He put a roofed porch on the creek side of the house, and he built a bench for the washbasin right by the door. Lots of ranch houses had outside washing facilities, but mighty few of them had roofs over the bowl, comb, and towel. Johnny had his roof. He wasn't going into his house dirty, and he also wasn't going to stand out in the rain or snow to get clean.

89

The following year Johnny added a room to his house, not a lean-to for cooking, as many ranchers did, but a real, square, sixteen-by-sixteen log room. It was sixteen feet one way because it used one wall of the kitchen, and sixteen feet the other way because that was a convenient length to cut logs for hauling. This room was intended as a bedroom. Like the kitchen, it was constructed with a ridge-pole and a steep pitch to the roof, to shed snow and rain. The first years these roofs were made with planks laid from the ridge-poles to the side walls and stripped poles nailed across the planks. Sods were laid over the poles. The sod roofs were better than nothing, but they were never very satisfactory. Do the best anyone could, sod roofs leaked mud into the food or on the bedclothes whenever there was even a little rain. As soon as he could, Johnny got someone to split shakes for him and covered his roof with homemade shingles.

The house was really nice once the bedroom was added. Johnny had a good year, and he got some furniture: four square-bottomed chairs and a round table so big that the chairs looked lost about it. He got a tin cabinet to hold his flour and sugar and other perishable supplies, and a wooden one to store his kitchen tinware and enamel dishes. He built a fireplace in the bedroom, bringing a rock at a time from the creek whenever he crossed. He had windows in the bedroom, even though he hadn't any mattresses or pillows on the bunks and was still using mail-or-der-catalog suggans for covers—those cheap, cotton-wadded comforts that were always two feet too short for any sleeper: both of them stuck out.

Johnny continued the porch along the front of the bedroom, and cut a door from the bedroom to the porch. He could go from room to room inside or outside the house, which was another architectural innovation. In most houses of that time and place there was only one door for entrance and exit. That kind of con-struction saved time, for it was easier to build a solid wall than one with a doorway, but Johnny was lavish with work and hours in a good cause.

Probably Johnny was too busy to stop and think about in-tangibles, but the fact remains that he was following a practical ranch pattern in building his house as he did. For years country families generally had combination kitchen-dining-living rooms in their houses, for a variety of reasons. In a cold climate you have to shelter your cooking fire and you need a place to store provisions. In a chicken-egg debate that goes on between historians and architects, the issue is whether the kitchen or the sleeping room came first. In most cases a brush shelter over a fire does seem to have been the beginning of domestic architecture.

In Johnny's house, as in most ranch houses, you ate in the kitchen because it was more comfortable and convenient not to carry the food away from the fire where it was cooked. After the meal, you spent what little time you allowed yourself for recreation right there by the same warm stove. It was a lot of work to get another fire started. It was a time-consuming job to saw and split the wood for even one fire. Nobody wanted to sit up late in the evenings. So the kitchen-dining room was the living room as well. It was also the room where Johnny did his bookkeeping and kept his stock records and hence, in a way, his office.

The first few years on the ranch were so busy that Johnny couldn't even think about getting married. He had his hands full getting his business started, even if there had been anybody around to marry. Women had begun to come into the country, but they either stayed in the towns near the railroads or were married when they got there. It wasn't until the JL was a pretty-well-established concern that Johnny got around to serious thinking on the wife subject.

By that time other families had located on Powder River, and there were enough children to need a school. The people of the neighborhood clubbed together and started one. The teacher boarded around, first with one family and then with another. She was a young woman from Illinois, with a college degree. And, yes, the inevitable happened. Johnny was the cowman who married the school teacher.

The next few years were busy times. Johnny added another room and another stretch of front porch to the house right away. His wife was used to a good house, and she was going to have one with a separate living room if he could give it to her. The living room was to have been beyond the bedroom and clear away from the kitchen, but that plan didn't work out. The heating problem was still to be considered, so Johnny and Marian turned the old bedroom into a living room and used some of the heat from the kitchen to warm it. When the weather was really cold—zero or below—they shut the door and continued to use the kitchen on the old cooking-eating-living basis. Then when bedtime came, they undressed by the kitchen stove, took a straight shoot through the living room, and dived under the covers. When they had company and wanted to be impressive and the weather wasn't too cold, they ate in the living room.

As time went on and the Larsen family grew, the family pattern was established. It was easier to cook a meal without the whole tribe underfoot, and more comfortable to eat it when somebody's chair wasn't backed into the cookstove. But the family came and went between the kitchen and the living room–dining room so much, and there was so much talking back and forth between the two rooms, that Johnny took the door off its hinges and hung it between the parents' bedroom and the children's, when he added the new room to the house that fall. By then he could have hauled lumber over the road from town easily, but he stuck to his log construction. He extended the old dugout away from the hillside, while he was in a building mood, and provided his hands with a real, solid log bunkhouse.

When Margie, the oldest girl, was about ten years old, her mother insisted on two major improvements in the place. Johnny had dug a well near the kitchen door the summer after they were married. Having a well was much better than using water hauled up from the creek in barrels. It was safer from the health standpoint as well. However, the dug well was rather shallow—only about fifty feet deep—and the water was raised in a bucket. Every once in a while some animal would wander up close to the house and fall in the well. Even grasshoppers can spoil water in a hurry if enough of them get in a well, and when a dog or cat or calf committed involuntary suicide, it meant a wet, nasty job for Johnny, who had to clean out the well, and a return to dipping water out of a barrel for Marian.

On top of the inconvenience and the possibility of sickness from contaminated water, Marian had another big worry. What if one of the children were to fall down the well? When she was at home, it was probable that she would hear the resulting splash and howl. But sometimes she went with Johnny to the hay meadow, to take him a meal or to lend a hand with the mower. Sometimes she helped out as substitute teacher at the school-house a couple of miles down the road. Or she might possibly be in another part of the house and too busy to hear what had happened or to come to the rescue in time.

After her insomnia seemed to be setting in as a permanent ailment, Marian decided that it was time to take steps about the well. She made Johnny cover it and pipe the water to a pump in the kitchen. They installed a regular sink, now that they had running water, and invested in a cookstove with a water jacket so that they could have hot baths whenever they wanted them. As an extra safety measure, Johnny put a stake-and-rider fence all around the yard to keep the animals out.

A year or so later they got the windmill. There were wind-mills spotted around on the ranch to supply water for the stock, so the animals wouldn't lose time from their eating by going down to the creek and coming back. Marian hinted around, still harping on her health angle, and the day came when a well-driller drove his rig into the yard and started to work on a deep well near the house. He hit a steady flow of good water at ninety-five feet. It came up within ten feet of the top of the well under its own pressure, so the windmill had an easy time boosting the water into the storage tank from which it ran down again into the house.

As soon as Marian had all that water, she decided she wanted a bathroom. They built the bathroom off the kitchen, at right angles to the rest of the house. It was the first time a room was added to the house that wasn't in a straight line across the front. A year later a second room was built beside the bathroom as a storage place. Now Marian didn't have to find a place in her kitchen for six months' supply of groceries at a time.

The Larsens kept on adding comforts, and even luxuries, to

their home. Marian needed a place for her books, so there were bookcases around the living room. They got more books to fill the cases and more cases to hold the books as time went on. As the girls began to grow up, Marian begged for a piano and limbered up her fingers teaching all of them to play. The living room was too crowded to hold the sewing machine, when she got it, so she kept that in her bedroom.

As the three girls grew up, they needed and wanted rooms of their own. Just for general convenience, Johnny added an ell to the house, turning the corner from the old children's bedroom, which remained Margie's. The new wing had a porch along the front, like the rest of the house. Marian had planted grass and flowers in the front yard and a vegetable garden back beside the windmill inside the fence. The girls planted morning-glory vines and clematis and scarlet rambler over both porches. In warm weather they used the porch as an extra living room, but Johnny put his foot down when they wanted to eat out there. He pointed out to the women-folks that he had spent considerable time, money, and effort building them a house to live in. Picnics were all right, when you went out on them and couldn't get back. But when the girls were at home, they would eat their meals in the house like ladies, not out in the yard like a bunch of cow hands.

Nobody who lived there thought of the house as anything special. It was just home. It had grown with the family, to meet the family's needs. Functional architecture was a gleam in the Easterners' eyes, as far as the Larsen family was concerned. The fact that they might be living in an ideally functional house never occured to any of them.

The year Margie got her master's degree from the college in Missouri, she announced to her family that she was going to get married. Old John bucked and reared when he first got the news. All that good money spent on an education—and she was going to throw it away on the first Missouri farmer she met! He was a little reconciled when he learned that Young John's—that was his name, too—family were cattle feeders and finishers, and had been for generations. Old John didn't really give in and provide the youngsters with his paternal blessing, though, until his prospective son-in-law made a trip to the ranch to see him. Young John shot an antelope—first shot—and he asked Old John for a job as a hand, at day wages. Seemed the boy had always wanted to live and work on a ranch and get the cattle started on their way to his father's feed lots.

Margie may have had something to do with this decision, although she said she didn't. She loved the ranch and everything concerned and connected with it. She had a fine education, but she would never have been satisfied as a lady college professor —she had too much of her father in her. She was almost as heartbroken as Old John the night two months before the wedding when the ranch house caught fire and burned to the ground.

Nobody was ever quite sure what had caused the fire. Probably a spark from the kitchen chimney had lighted on the curling old shakes of the roof, and a stiff breeze had taken it from there to the rest of the building. There was just time to get a few cooking utensils and some of the dishes and the piano out of the house. Everything else went, even the bedding. The big old brass bed that had been Johnny's wedding present to Marian was bent and twisted by the heat, and ruined.

Nobody said anything much about the way they all felt, and nobody wasted any time crying and mourning for their home. Old John had been hale and husky and middle-aged when the sun went down. When it rose again, it was an old man who stood in the front yard and told his neighbors, "Put whatever you've got in the barn, boys. We'll have to move in there for a while."

It was a good big barn, and the family moved in. They didn't have any insurance money—couldn't get insurance on a wooden house fifty miles from the nearest town. So the Larsens managed with what they had. They moved the buggy and tack out of the enclosed space that might have been called the carriage house if they'd had a carriage, and put up the stove at one end, with a work table beside it and the dishpan hanging on a nail driven into the wall. They built bunks around the other end, with shelves and pegs to hold their few belongings. In the middle of

95

the room was a sort of table that Young John put together with a few planks and nails, and facing the table on the inside wall was the piano. They all sat on nail kegs and cartridge boxes.

For a while everybody thought Margie's wedding plans might be canceled and would certainly be delayed. They didn't know the Larsens, even after all those years. Young John went right to work on the place, and instead of wages he took an interest in the ranch, with an option to buy it out of his earnings when his father-in-law was ready to sell out. Young John's first job was to haul away all the rubbish the fire had left and get ready to build a new ranch house on the old site. His second job was getting the old bunkhouse ready for his parents-in-law to occupy.

Old John was around, and he made a hand wherever one was needed, but he didn't take much interest in what was going on. For the first time in his life he complained of being tired and of not feeling well. As much to cheer the old man up as for any other reason, Margie and Jack decided to have the big, bang-up wedding people are still talking about, instead of the small, quiet one that seemed more appropriate at first.

After all, it was summer and the flower garden was blooming its head off in spite of the trampling it got the night of the fire. The place was all cleaned up and there was a good stand of grass inside the fence. It was home, and it was still a beautiful place for a wedding.

Old John agreed to cook a barbecue dinner for the guests. He always cooked for guests when the family wanted to make a spread, because he said that no matter how good a plain cook a woman might be, she hadn't the hand with seasonings and the fine, subtle points of cooking that a man had. Johnny was famous for his barbecue, and this time he really laid himself out: a whole beef, and a pig, and a sheep, all roasted over the coals of the barbecue pit he dug well away from the barn so there wouldn't be danger of another fire.

When the day came, the family laid wagon sheets over the grass to make an aisle and a place for the wedding party to stand. They moved the piano out of the barn and set it up on one side of the yard, so that Clarissa, the second girl, could play the wedding march. The day was sunny and the flowers were all there in place, without anybody's bothering with cutting and arranging them. It was the prettiest wedding Powder River had ever seen. There were a hundred guests, and everybody had a wonderful time.

Margie and Jack got busy on their own house right afterwards. They lived in the barn, and Old John and Marian in the old bunkhouse, until the house out of the lumber-yard catalog was ordered and its parts were delivered. The two Johns did most of the work on the two-room house themselves. They built it above and behind the old location, with the windmill in the front yard instead of the back. The house looked bleak and new there by itself, without the graciousness of the old log house, but the youngsters moved into it in the fall, before the cold weather started. Margie used the front room as a combination kitchen-dining-living room and the one behind it as a bedroom.

Old John and Marian stayed on at the ranch another year or two, and then they bought a house in town and moved there. Johnny's heart was bothering him some, and Marian's arthritis was getting pretty bad. Time for them to get near the coal yard and the doctor.

By then the ranch business was good enough to support both families and even provide a few luxuries. Margie and Young John took their time going through the lumber-yard catalog a second time and found the ready-sawn house they wanted. It had a big kitchen and a room that opened out of it and could be used as a living-dining room. Behind those two rooms, across the back of the house, were two small bedrooms and a bathroom, all opening off a hall. And after a few years more they added another big living-room, with a picture window looking towards the creek, and used the old one for a dining room.

Margie remembered her mother's struggles with the storage problem, and she dealt with it before the house was built. The ranch was as far from the highway as ever, although there was a county road along the creek now. So Margie had a cellar built. It was big enough for food storage and to hold an extra bedroom.

97

There was a furnace room, with a shower room opening off it. Jack could clean up before he came in the house, and he didn't have to do it at a bench by the kitchen door.

The little two-room house they kept as a dwelling for tenants, and the old bunkhouse was abandoned. Just in time, too, for the weight of the sod roof became too much for the walls, and the whole thing collapsed. Everybody was sorry to lose the old building and glad they had new houses to replace it.

8. *The Woman's Touch*

THE ranch house on the JL started as a man's shelter from the worst of the winter weather and grew into a family home. It went through many changes, and it added rooms as a young and growing snail increases the size of its shell. The JL ranch house had a kind of accidental quality that was right for it and that reflected the informality and openness of the Powder River country where the house was built.

A great many other ranch houses were built in the same way, being adapted to ranch needs because their growth was an expression and a fulfillment of the environment's demands. But there have also been ranch houses that were deliberately planned and built from foundation to roof tree and that have never been structurally altered.

The Sandhills of Nebraska have a character all their own. They are like no other part of North America. Perhaps the Sandhills have their continental counterpart in the grazing lands of Inner Mongolia. There, they say, the land is never still, but always ripples and moves from horizon to horizon as if the earth beneath it had tides like the tides of the ocean. The Sandhills are like that. They are plains country, but they do not lie in planes. The Sandhills are all curves, and the curves are always, restlessly, moving.

Nowadays the Sandhills are covered with grass, and the grass

99

is something to look at in awe and wonder. This is not grass that forms a carpet; it is grass that sinks its roots into the soil and clutches itself to the earth; that fixes in place the sand beneath it and will never willingly relax its grip. Once, in the mid nineteenth century, the Sandhills were known as the Great American Desert, and no less an authority on the American West than Horace Greeley said that the country there would never be reclaimed. But here and there brave settlers encouraged the growth of the native wild grasses or introduced and planted seeds of other varieties. The grasses grew and came in time to dominate the landscape. The forms of the dunes remained; the grass could not alter the shape of the land. Today in the Sandhills you are confronted with the anachronism of land that once was ocean bottom, and then was desert, and is still carved in ocean and desert forms, covered with grass knee-deep.

Nobody in the Sandhills ever forgets the origin of that land. If there is a drought or a prairie fire or too much rain, or if the wind blows too hard from any one direction, the sand beneath the grass begins to shift. The grass is destroyed or covered over, and the sand repossesses a hillside; unless it is stopped, often a whole hill. When that happens, the stockmen of the region shift their cattle and protect the blown-out area with drift fences until the grass is rooted again. No people in the world are more erosion-conscious than the Sandhillers. Erosion is with them as a living threat all of their lives.

Fortunately there is a layer of impervious rock not too far below the surface of the Sandhills, so the country usually has plenty of water. Put down a well nearly anywhere and an artesian flow results. Stock ponds dot the area and help the grass to grow and hold down the sand. The ponds are thick with birds of many species; nowhere in the West are birds as abundant or as beautiful as in the Nebraska Sandhills.

This was the country, restless and forbidding, flashing with the living colors of birds as other grasslands sparkle with flowers, where R. H. Dawson settled. Here he brought his bride, soon after the twentieth century had got well under way.

Annie O'Neil was a city girl. She had grown up in Omaha.

She had never lived in the country and she had never wanted to. She liked pretty clothes and good food and plays and concerts. Her sister Grace went to college and studied to be a teacher, but that life sounded dull and unexciting to Annie. She found a milliner who would take an apprentice, and she began the tedious business of learning to make hats—in the days when hat-making required a knowledge of structural engineering as well as of style.

Annie's father worked for the Burlington Railroad, and as the railroad moved westward, so did the O'Neil family. That was how it happened that Annie found herself setting up in business in the fast-growing town of Scottsbluff. There she met R. H. Dawson, who had brought some cattle in from his ranch to a feeder, and they fell in love and got married—right away and in a hurry.

Then they went home to the Sandhills; by rail as far as Hyannis and by wagon across country to R. H.'s place. There wasn't a real road out from town, just a general direction. Nobody wanted to risk making wagon-ruts across the Sandhills grass, because blow-outs frequently resulted from ruts. Teams were steered across the dry-land Sargasso by the sun and stars, as boats might have been. Nobody ever went home the same way twice in succession.

R. H. was an Englishman. He never told his wife whether he had been born in England and become a naturalized American or had been born in the States of English parents. The young people hadn't time for much conversation, and such vital statistics wouldn't have made any difference to Annie. R. H. had the upper-class Englishman's respect for fine stock, and he had a feeling that good stock deserved good care. To that end, he had built himself a barn.

The Dawson barn was famous from one end of Nebraska to the other. There is still a story—apocryphal, perhaps, but true as only apocryphae can be—told in the Sandhills concerning an old cowman turned fiddler, who wandered around from one square dance to the next play-party. When he fiddled he drank to loosen his bow-arm, and when he had drunk a certain amount not only his arm but his tongue moved on ball bearings. He was famous for his tall and fancy stories, so much so that occasionally his friends became alarmed and tried to tame his wild imagination.

One night this artist had a few too many at a dance for which he was fiddling, and he began to talk about the Sandhills. He told the usual cow-country windies: how you could see farther and see less; how when the wind blew hard enough in a certain direction the prairie dogs dug their holes ten feet overhead; how when a log chain stood straight out from a fence post, people said there was a fair breeze blowing. Then he got around to R. H. Dawson's barn, and he really began to spread himself.

It was the biggest barn in Nebraska, he said. He wouldn't be surprised if it was the biggest barn in the United States. Why, for all he knew, it was the biggest barn in the world. How big *was* the barn? demanded a a heckler.

The old windy swelled out his chest and threw back his head, ignoring the calming gestures of a near-by friend. "That barn," he proclaimed, "is four hundred feet long———"

"Watch it, boy, watch it," his friend besought.

"Four hundred feet long," the speaker reiterated, "and one foot wide!"

The barn actually was four hundred feet long, but its width was nearer seventy. The barn towered to the height of a three-story building. It was constructed of whitewashed brick on a framework of steel girders, every ounce of the material having been hauled from the railroad siding at Hyannis. The gabled roof was tiled, and the concrete floor was built with a drainage trough through the center, so that the floor could be cleaned by hosing it down. The barn was a copy of the great dairy barns of Pennsylvania and Wisconsin, but in those days barns for beef cattle were unheard of in the West. So were the purebreds that R. H. Dawson raised. Mighty few people in those days were interested in the ancestry of animals that were headed for the slaughter pens.

Cowering before the barn was the house. It was meant to be the bunkhouse eventually. It was a small frame structure, painted white, neat enough in appearance, but not to be compared with the barn in any way. The house had been good enough for R. H. Dawson and his hands to live in, and it was all he had to offer his bride in the way of a home.

They lived in the bunkhouse all that first winter, and Annie had her hands full most of the time. She cooked for her husband and herself and the hands, and she kept the books and the stock records, although she hated paper work. Once in a while she ripped an old hat to pieces and remade it, to keep her hand in. When she had nothing else to do she drew plans for a house, the kind of house she wanted to live in and was going to build—some soon day. There was a baby on the way before spring, and Annie spent more and more of her time planning the house.

R. H. Dawson died of pneumonia a couple of months before his son was born. Annie still didn't know for sure whether her husband had been born in England or the United States—as she put it long afterwards, they were both too busy to get really well acquainted in that way. She found herself with the ranch and the barn and the purebred stock, in total ignorance of what to do with the combination.

Annie was never one to waste time. She wired her sister what had happened, and Grace came out to lend her a hand for a few months. With time out every once in a while for school teaching, Grace stayed on at the ranch. She kept the books and the stock records and tutored her young nephew when he needed help. When they found time to sit down quietly for a moment, the sisters worked on the house plans together.

What both women wanted was a house that would match the barn in size and splendor. They worked steadily towards that goal, but it was four years before the house was built: of brick, with a tile roof and hardwood floors and an open fireplace in the living room.

In certain ways, Annie anticipated architectural fashions. A mind for style is a mind for style, whether it be applied to a hat or a house. She built her living room to extend the full depth of the house on one side, and she built it on two levels, with Grace's grand piano on a raised dais at one end. There were clerestory windows in the wall behind the piano and the other end of the room was almost entirely glass. The great window looked out on the rolling Sandhills and the south pasture where the purebreds grazed. The walls of the room were of blond brick, neatly laid and unmasked with plaster, for the rough texture was planned to contrast with the blond smoothness of the oak floor.

The kitchen was equally well arranged, with a recess for the stove and a corresponding alcove on the opposite side of the room. Originally the sink was built into this niche; later, when electricity and electric refrigerators were available, the icebox was placed where the sink had stood and the sink was moved to the end wall of the kitchen. From the beginning there was running water in that house. With all the water there was underground, Annie saw no reason to be without it in her kitchen.

The front door opened into a square hall, with the big living room on one side and the dining room and kitchen on the other. Facing the door was a flight of stairs. Upstairs Annie really let herself go. Doors opened from the second-floor landing into bedrooms for young Harris and for Grace. Another door opened to a tiled bathroom, almost as large as the bedrooms, and a fourth door entered Annie's own two rooms. Across the front of the house was a porch, divided so that the two sisters shared its sleeping space and looking out on the south pasture and its purebreds.

The guest rooms were on the third floor, away from the movements of the family. This floor could be closed off when—if it ever happened—there were no guests in the house. Everywhere there were hardwood floors and walls paneled with walnut or maple. Everything that two intelligent women could think of to make a house attractive was built into the place; nothing they thought they might enjoy was omitted. When it was finished, the house stood forward, as if it were on a promontory overlooking an ocean. The barn was not dwarfed—it could never be dwarfed—but it was relegated to a place in the background. It became a cliff behind the headland where the house stood.

Annie was faced soon enough with the ranch woman's eternal problem: send the children away to school, take them to town and live there while they are in school, or try to bring the school to them? She solved it by leasing her ranch and taking her son to town to live until he was ready to enter university. Then, for the first time since she had left it, Annie returned to her house. She hadn't had the heart to go near the place before.

From the day of her return to the ranch, Annie kept herself busy. She not only raised purebreds, she raised purebred bulls for sale and to improve her own herd. She was active in community affairs, to such an extent that she was elected to important positions in political administration. In fact, as soon as he could, Annie insisted that Harris take out a pilot's license. She could save a lot of time by flying on her trips away from the ranch. And then, once the ranch was equipped with its own planes and landing field, they didn't have to worry about getting supplies and equipment in if the road blew out or washed out.

Annie did a lot of traveling, one way and another, always with her house in mind. The winter she spent in Mexico she had the weavers in the city of Saltillo make rugs for her, with her brand woven into every rug. She had her portrait painted, to hang above the piano. Her Irish face emerged looking, by some magic of time and place, that of a Spanish *señora*.

Annie's interest in housekeeping extended beyond the walls of her home. She had the first electrified kitchen in the Sandhills, not in her own house but in the bunkhouse, where the men's meals were cooked. When the help problem became acute, Annie solved it in her own way by putting innerspring mattresses on the maple "Early American Style" bunks in the bunkhouse. She supplied her hands with a recreation room, complete with ping-pong tables and a good radio, and she saw to it that there were chintz drapes at the bunkhouse windows.

No woman can do a man's work without encountering problems even more complex than those she meets in her own field. Annie was determined to succeed in both fields. She pondered the matter in the days of her early widowhood, and she developed a formula that was a success, for it worked.

"When I had something to do and didn't know how to do it," she said once, "I thought over all the men I knew until I decided which of them was best at solving that particular kind of problem. Then I went to him and asked him for his advice. After I got it, I followed it. I didn't go to anybody else and then start comparing notes and wondering which way was best. I did as I was told, and I never lost by it. How could I? I had the best advice I could get for whatever I did. And every time I did it, I made a new friend."

9. *The Kitchen*

THE house on the JL was started from scratch. Annie Dawson built hers for a reason. Each was intended to fill the needs of the family that occupied it, as is the usual process with ranch house-building. Even on a ranch where the house is there to begin with, the structure will be changed about and reshaped to meet the needs of the family.

The Higgins ranch has been through a lot of ups and downs since Bill Higgins' father first homesteaded the land. The original homestead is still part of the ranch, but 160 acres are lost in the shuffle nowadays. The Higgins family controls almost a hundred thousand acres as of now, what with ownership and leasing and government grazing permits.

The house where the family lives today is about centered on that spread of territory, located, as would be the capital city of a state, in the heart of the land to be governed. The ranch headquarters is a capital in more ways than one. It is the center of operations; cattle raising, schooling, church-going, shopping, selling, bookkeeping, communications (both by road and by telephone), entertainment, and the hundred-and-one-other-things that are part of ranch life all head up at the ranch house or in one of the adjacent buildings. There is constant coming and going around the capital, and Mrs. Higgins has been known

107

to say breathlessly that she wouldn't know what to do with a dull moment if she had one.

Probably not. The chances are, too, that she wouldn't recognize the dull moment as anything but a chance to catch a small nap if it did come along. After all, the lieutenant governor of a state is pretty nearly as busy as the governor, especially if the governor is subject to being called away at odd hours and all seasons.

Rebecca Higgins has one great advantage over some other women who hold similar positions of authority. She was born on a ranch and she grew up on one. She married a rancher and she has raised her family in a ranch house. This is the life she knows and loves, and she can hardly imagine herself living any other kind. Like many ranch wives, Rebecca knows that a series of bad seasons, even now, could throw the whole property into bankruptcy and mean starting over again. Not for the first time.

So when the house has needed alterations, when family growth has made new living space necessary, or when time and dry rot have affected the foundations of the frame building, Rebecca has given matters careful thought and then done her own planning to correct the damage. Taking capital out of the business to repair or reconstruct the house has always been something to think twice about—and then think once again. Rebecca usually has felt it safest to go ahead with the construction work more or less on her own with the money she has in hand herself, without bothering Bill about it. In that way she has been sure of getting what she wanted, without arguments. The formula perfected with time, she has passed it on to each of her daughters as the girls married.

At one time the four-room frame cigar-box was the show place of the Big Horn Basin. Frame houses were all but unheard of there when this dwelling went up. Lots of big trees grow on the southern slopes of the Big Horn range, and most people used logs as building material.

The reason for the house was considered even more remarkable than its construction at the time the building was completed. Old Mr. Mattson was what the northern cattle country bluntly calls a squaw man. He married a Crow Indian woman, of whom people now remember only that she was right good-looking and incredibly shy. She had been educated in the East—probably at Carlisle Indian School—she dressed like a white woman, she spoke good English, and she was an unexceptional cook and housekeeper. But she was also exceedingly timid, and whenever company came, she withdrew to her kitchen and stayed there until the strangers went away.

Mr. Mattson built the frame house to prove to the neighbors who were scattered at thirty-mile intervals along the creek that his wife was as good as anybody else's, that she deserved the best there was, and that he intended that she should have it. So he built the little yellow box with two bedrooms, a living room, a dining room, a front porch, and a lean-to kitchen just like a house in town. He moved his wife out of the old log house next door and into the new one.

As it happened, the log house was better than most town houses in the West in those days. Mr. Mattson piped water into the building from an artesian spring a hundred yards away up the hillside, so there was running water in the kitchen. He installed the same kind of plumbing in the new house when the time came.

It could have been because she was overwhelmed by the running water, or it could have been because the frame house was harder to heat and required more and steadier wood chopping than the log one; it could have been because the Indian woman was just plain homesick. At any rate, Mr. Mattson sold out to Bill Higgins a year or so after the house was finished and moved with his wife back to her people on the reservation. And Bill and Rebecca moved into the yellow box because it was in the middle of their property.

What with six children coming along at fairly regular intervals, getting them to the doctor and dentist when necessary and to school as soon as they were old enough, the Higginses were pretty busy from the time of the move on. They were much too busy to think of their house in any but the most elemental way. The house was a shelter, a roof over their heads. As long as the roof didn't leak, they were satisfied. They added a bedroom and turned a closet into a bathroom, but those alterations were the strictest necessities.

They hit a run of hard luck, too, after they had been on the place a few years. There was drought all over the West, and cattle died where they were pastured. The Higgins' stock was just as informal about it as their neighbors'. It was the purebreds, bought at heavy expense to upgrade the rest of the herd, that were hit the hardest. Nothing, Rebecca Higgins often said, can die as fast as a purebred bull unless it's another purebred bull. The Higginses were just about wiped out in those bad years. If it hadn't been for a banker who was a born gambler and bet his shirt on Bill, they never would have pulled through.

Once the worst struggle was over and Rebecca knew they'd keep the place and live there the rest of their lives, she sat down and took stock. It was right to reinvest their profits in the land and in improvement of the herd, she could see that. If they let the place run down, they would lose everything they had put into it. Upgrading herds and repairing fences were high-priority matters—she realized that as clearly as her husband did.

But nobody could run a factory with a defective power plant, and Rebecca saw the ranch-house kitchen as just that. Bill and the boys came home to get their batteries recharged with good, square meals. If the men weren't properly fed, neither they nor the place could run right. The ranch house, and especially the ranch-house kitchen, was the dynamo of the whole spread.

The kitchen especially was anything but adequate to the demands made on it. The lean-to was dark, with only one small window, rather high in the wall opposite the stove. There wasn't a real sink, nothing but a bench for the dishpan with a faucet bobbling at the end of a pipe that was angled above it. There was not a smidgin of storage space; everything except the current day's supplies had to be kept in another lean-to, built on behind the kitchen.

The kitchen roof was low and sloping, and the roof of the storeroom was even more so. To reach supplies at the back of the storeroom, Rebecca had to get down on her hands and knees and crawl, or send one of the children in for whatever she needed. A good big kitchen with adequate supply space was the next most necessary requirement of her part of the ranch.

Rebecca's biggest problem was where to get the money for her new kitchen. Before she seriously considered ways and means, she had to know what a new kitchen would cost. On her next trip to town Rebecca consulted old Mr. Burnsides, who did carpentry here and there up and down the slope for anybody who needed a building job done. Mr. Burnsides calculated that, by scrapping both existent lean-tos, reusing the lumber, and adding the barest minimum of new secondhand stock, he could get by under a hundred dollars and still build Rebecca a decent kitchen.

"You got to remember," he cautioned her, "there won't be nothing in it that ain't in the kitchen you got now. I can't build nothing but the walls for that." Rebecca didn't argue or protest. All she wanted for the present were good solid walls enclosing adequate space. Bill and the boys could add cabinets when they had time.

Rebecca puzzled herself considerably over the best way to raise the hundred dollars. She dared not figure on less. She had no office or business training or experience, even if there had been an office or business within fifty miles to offer her that kind of job. Women made money by selling homemade jams, jellies, and crocheted doilies, but they seemed to be women who didn't mind selling the things neighbors normally exchanged. Rebecca's family ate up her jams and jellies as fast as she made them, and her crocheting time usually went into mending socks and patching jeans. Women wrote books and magazine articles about how to make money at home in your spare time, but writing seemed to require a special kind of mind as well as a knowledge of typing. It also required a chance to sit down and remain uninterrupted for five consecutive minutes. Writing a book or an article probably sounded easier than it was.

Therefore it seemed to Rebecca like an answer to her prayers when Bill announced he was going to add sheep to the cattle they ran. "Sheep are mortgage-raisers," he declared, laying

111

down the *Wyoming Stock-Grower* with a bang. "You've got two crops a year to market—meat and wool—and the sheep won't hurt the pastures if you handle them right and rotate them on grazing. We've got the mortgage. We'll give the sheep a chance to lift part of it."

"What are you planning to do with the bum lambs?" Rebecca asked.

"Bum lambs?" Bill hesitated, evidently considering the matter for the first time. "I don't know. If the mothers won't own them, you can't get other ewes to take them. And if the mothers are dead, the lambs never suck other ewes. Kill them, I guess."

"That means losing part of your crop—part of both crops," Rebecca reminded him. "Can I have the bum lambs if I'll raise them?"

"Sure," said Bill, and they considered the discussion closed.

That was in October. The next month Bill brought the first sheep on the place, late as it was. He and the boys built brush sheds to winter the woolies, on a lower pasture not far from the house. They had an open, easy winter that year, and the sheep did all right. Nobody paid much attention to them except when it was time to take feed or salt up to the sheep pasture.

When the frost went out of the ground, late in April, Rebecca got her garden plowed. It was always understood that she would have a man for a day to do the plowing and that he would show up once every two weeks during the growing season for cultivating. Otherwise, Rebecca was on her own as far as the garden was concerned, except for such help as the younger children gave her.

There was a fence around the garden to keep out the deer. The fence wasn't 100 per cent effective, but it was still better than nothing. It provided a place to tie the fluttering rags that were intended to drive the animals away. Anything low enough, phlegmatic enough, or well enough informed to ignore the waving strips of cloth could work a way through the fence and get to the planted rows.

The garden was in but not up when the first bum lamb was delivered to Rebecca. Its arrival was not the pretty pastoral proceeding portrayed on church calendars. A wet, tired, and disgusted husband rode in at the fag end of a hard day of lambing, and fished a leggy, sprawling, bawling creature out of a fold of his slicker. "There you are, Mother," he said without tenderness, "take the damn thing and raise it if you can stand the smell of it." Sheep might be mortgage-raisers, but Bill Higgins had been born, and all his life he remained, a cattle man.

Rebecca had prepared for the event by finding the baby bottles she had stowed away eight years before. The rubber nipples had dried out and cracked through. When she tried to squirt warm milk on the back of her hand, to test its temperature, the nipple split and went to pieces. She fell back on the time-honored expedient of a rag wick in a pop bottle.

Much to Rebecca's surprise, the first lamb survived and throve. So did the others Bill and the boys brought in, one at a time, in the course of the next few weeks. At the end of lambing she had eighteen little bums, all alive and endlessly blatting. By establishing a schedule and making all the lambs conform to it, Rebecca managed to get them fed without starving her family.

By that time the garden was far enough along to need weeding. The lambs were beginning to nibble the grass in the front yard. Bill promised that on some future Sunday he would rest up from the week's work by building a fence around a grass patch near the house and making a lamb pasture out of it. But that Sunday was still in the future and seemed likely to remain there for a while.

Rebecca came out of the house with an old straw hat of Bill's on her head and a trowel in her hand. The lambs were interested immediately. As far as their little knowledge went, she had never come outdoors without feeding them. They rushed towards her, bleating, their pink-lined mouths wide, stumbling a little on their blunt hoofs with haste, and clustered around her to examine the object she held in her hand. Trowel was a new flavor to the lambs and they tasted it experimentally. They wrinkled their noses and decided they might like it if they got used to it. Rebecca shook her apron at them and shooed, before she crawled under the fence into the garden. The lambs, with their eyes riveted on her, paid no attention to the fluttering rags above their heads. They crawled right under the fence behind her.

Rebecca scolded and shooed again, and the lambs withdrew from her skirt to watch her from a distance, all standing bunched together beside the fence that was supposed to keep them out of the garden. Now it apparently served to keep them in. When Rebecca scolded again and brandished her trowel at the creatures, the lambs looked around them and suddenly perceived that they were hemmed in on all sides by horrible dancing nameless things. They fled to the far end of the garden, paying no attention to their footing, trampling on and rolling over young lettuce and spinach plants and the beginnings of pea vines. By the time they had finally been bunched together and driven from the garden, Rebecca was too worn out even to estimate the amount of damage the bums had done.

But she stuck to the job of raising them all that summer. She had to have a vegetable garden for winter canning, and she was determined to raise the lambs in order to have a decent kitchen to can in. Bill built the fence around the lamb pasture—by request—the following Sunday. He used four strands of barbed wire, set close enough together to discourage any four-footed creature. So he thought. On Monday morning Rebecca went into town and invested her dress allowance for the next six years in chicken wire to put around the garden. It was a feeble effort to save what were left of her plants after the lambs' all-night revel up and down the rows. If Bill were unable to fence the lambs in, she was determined to fence them out.

Bum lambs are supposed to be delicate and difficult to raise. This supposition is based on the fact that most bums are incorrectly fed, Rebecca Higgins declares. Give bum lambs enough fresh garden vegetables—preferably directly off or with the plants—and they will thrive mightily. She lived all that summer to shrieks of, "MOTHER! The lambs're in the garden!" She and the girls took turns dashing out and driving the lambs away from what was left of the family's winter food supply.

Usually sale day is a sad day at the Higgins ranch. To outsiders it seems that after all the time and work that have been invested to the sole end of raising cattle to salability it would be absurd to display any but joyful emotion when the beasts leave the ranch for the railroad. But Rebecca was never able to watch the stock driven away down the road. She knew, too, that Bill refused to watch his own cattle loaded for market at the railhead.

Even so, Rebecca was perfectly sure she would be able to see the lambs leave without a trace of regret. The summer had been sickeningly hot, and its whole daily succession had been a series of frustrations. She had had to can at night—partly because the coal stove made the lean-to unbearable in the daytime, partly because her days were broken into by the battle to keep the lambs out of the garden. A new kitchen had become, in her mind, not merely a desirable addition to her house, but a necessity if she were to remain sane.

Yet when the sale day came, Rebecca stood with the buyer's check in her hand while he loaded the once-bum lambs into the back of his pick-up, and was shocked to discover that she was crying. It wasn't until the truck had clanked across the cattle guard and its dust had drifted off the road and on to the last sunflowers that she looked at the check. The lambs had brought her enough for the kitchen and enough more to cover Mr. Burnsides' estimate of the cost of the cabinets.

Rebecca didn't have him build the cabinets for another five years. In the interval she invested her surplus in a hog-proof fence around the garden. She reasoned that if she didn't raise the bum lambs, the poor little things would die. And letting any part of your investment die was poor business—if you came right down to it.

PART FOUR

What Is Their Biggest Problem?

WHEREVER THEY LIVE *and whatever their houses are like, ranch women face one great emotional and economic problem. How are they to educate their children?*

The alternatives are equally unhappy: to send the children away to school and miss sharing in their most interesting and formative years; to take them to town and abandon the ranch and the family's means of livelihood; for the mother to take the children away while the Father remains on the ranch and the family is—sometimes—permanently divided by unshared experiences; to bring the school to the children.

Each ranch wife solves the problem in her own way; each wishes for some other solution for each approach has fallibility; each does the best she can to give her children what they need both within and without the family. But if anything in the ranch wife's existence is hell, facing this problem is it.

10. *This Is the Way We Go to School*

MONTANA, 1950

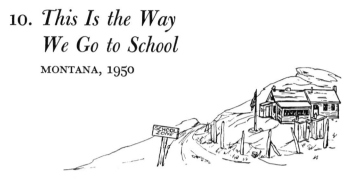

A normal morning on the JL contained a certain amount of bustle. Jack had to have his breakfast and get started; the Jerseys had to be milked and the milk strained and set to cool. The children had to be wakened, given their breakfasts, and directed in dressing themselves. Margie had to wash her face, the milk pans, the inside of the refrigerator, and the spot where she spilled milk on the floor, in addition to supervising the activities of the other members of the family. This could all be accomplished in fair time if there were no deadline hanging over their heads. On school mornings, when time imposed a rigid limit on each duty and its accomplishment, confusion, as Jack said, not only reigned, it poured. Margie forgave the pun on the occasions when she noticed it. Certain of Jack's puns were so time-ripened as to pass unnoticed by his self-protecting hearers.

The school was only three miles away down the creek. It was in a pleasant location in a bend of the stream, where willows and cottonwoods shaded the play-yard in the warm months. The schoolroom was at the front of the building, looking out towards the road and across it to the steep buttes of buff and yellow sandstone spread with their covering of silver-green sage.

The teacher's quarters—living room, bedroom, kitchen,

dinette, and bath—were at the rear, looking across the fenced play-yard towards the trees and the water. Jack and the Dennisons, who composed the school board when the building was constructed, had decided on the arrangement as least disturbing to study and most agreeable for the teacher. The fence around the school yard, Jack patiently and repeatedly explained to visitors, was not there only to remind him of his old home in Missouri. It was there to keep wandering stock from using the teeter-totters as back-scratchers.

On the morning of the first day of school, Margie turned off the alarm clock at five. She noticed when she reached the kitchen that her husband had not only lighted the fire and made the coffee, but had milked. He must have the same feeling she did, that for the next nine months they would be more or less on their own. Little Jack made a hand now, and he had worked all summer with his father. Dorothy had worked in the house with Margie. School was the children's full-time job during the winter months. Their parents managed without help except over week ends.

By six the milk was put away and the kitchen cleaned up. Jack and Margie had had their breakfast, their dishes were washed, and the table was reset. Margie called the children and set them down in night clothes and dressing gowns to their hot cereal. Dressing came later. While the children ate, she buttered bread, sliced ham, and opened a new jar of peanut butter for their lunches. The radio blared the "Early Riser's Program," a mixture of news, cowboy music, gossip about local personalities, and coaxing, encouraging advertising. Margie listened with half an ear while she mentally listed the lunches, books, pencils, tablets, and wraps to be packed in the car in an hour.

She had all three children settled in the car by a quarter of eight. Little Fred had to go along for the ride; he had ridden to school with her since he was three months old and he was not going to be left behind just because he had passed the age of three years. He shared the front seat with Margie. Dorothy and Jack were settled in the back with their schoolbooks piled between them.

The edges of the morning were crisp with frost and its heart was as warm and spicy-sweet with sunshine as a fresh ginger cookie. There was a little white frosting on the crest of each rut in the road, but the rime melted and ran as the sun rose and warmed the air and the earth. The willows were brittle-brown, the cottonwood leaves were honeyed gold. The car turned into the school lane and stopped beside the gate in the fence. Margie got out with the children, and they swung the gate open and walked to the door together.

Inside, the building was freshly painted and its floor was newly sanded and waxed. The knocking of steam and the smell of cooking paint showed that the furnace had been lighted and the first chill was being taken off the radiators. The blackboards had been washed and the Spencerian alphabets that made a dado above them had been rewhitened. The children's desks were ranged in order, and the golden oak table and chair of the teacher fronted them at an angle, slightly turned away from the window so that the light could come over her shoulder.

Everything was ready for the first day of school, Margie thought, as her eyes adjusted themselves from outside to inside light. She focused, at first blurrily, then more clearly, on the woman coming towards her.

"Good morning," Margie said. "I'm Mrs. Brooks. We're so glad you're here. I'm sorry I haven't been over to welcome you sooner, but I knew Mrs. Dennison—both Mrs. Dennisons—would do that better than I could."

The woman laughed a little, deprecatingly. "Don't worry, Mrs. Brooks. After all, I got here only night before last. And I know that with three youngsters you must be busy. Can you sit down a minute, or must you go right back?"

Margie chose a seat in the front row of desks, watching the woman welcome the children, watching the woman herself. Neat, well-dressed, really smart in her appearance. A tailored suit and a silk blouse were a little surprising to see here, at eight-fifteen in the morning. But the woman had been teaching in town and undoubtedly she was wearing the same work clothes she had worn there. They weren't at all unsuitable for a professional woman. Probably the children would enjoy seeing somebody dressed up. They would certainly like looking at the carefully arranged hair, the fresh make-up, and the bright junk jewelry after seeing their mothers in blue jeans and cotton shirts most of the time.

The teacher turned back from the children to Margie.

"Mr. Brooks is chairman of the school board, isn't he? I'm looking forward to meeting him."

"You will, a little later," said Margie. "He's getting his fall cattle ready to ship this week and next, and then he will have a minute to get over and see you. A stockman never apologizes for putting cows ahead of people, you know. They have to come first." Heavens, she thought, that *sounds* awful! I don't want to insult the woman! She'll think we haven't any manners at all. I'd better shut up before I make things worse.

The teacher did not appear to be aware of possible rudeness.

"He painted such an attractive picture of the country," she said, smiling. "He made me quite eager to see it. He must be an old-timer here; he's so enthusiastic about everything."

"Mr. Brooks is a Missourian," his wife replied. "Sometimes the old-timers think he overdoes his enthusiasms about this part of the world. But he loves it out here and he wanted to settle here as soon as we were married." Worse and worse, she thought. I don't have to let the fact that she's had a manicure and I haven't make me start clawing.

"Well, he made it sound perfectly charming," the teacher insisted. "I was crazy to see it. The doctor said it sounded like just the place for me: fresh air and sunshine and a simple outdoor life and all. I showed him the letter as soon as it came from the teachers' agency, and he said it was perfect and the job I ought to have."

"The doctor? Have you been ill? I hope this won't be too much work for you. Please let us know if you find taking care of the furnace or anything else too heavy, and we'll get someone to help you."

"I've been in the hospital the last few months," the teacher said quietly. "Nothing organic, just a sort of general letting-go.

I'm fine now; I can do anything I want to. And of course it was wonderful to find everything all spick-and-span clean when I got here. That made me feel as if I were ahead on my work already."

What was it about the way the woman spoke that, as Margie's father, Old John, used to say, tickled? Something here was vaguely wrong, out of key. That was silly. She didn't have to discuss her ailments with a stranger if she didn't want to, and coming from a small town in Iowa she probably wasn't used to the western custom of saying whatever you had to say right out to anybody who would listen. This eastern woman was probably used to keeping herself to herself. She certainly had every right to do so. Margie rose as another car stopped before the school.

"We want our teachers to be happy," she said. "We'll all do anything in the world to keep them contented! We want our children to go to school, and at the same time we don't want to send them away from home to live while they're growing up. That's why, with only ten families and eight school-age children in the district, we advertise in the states with the highest stand-ards for teachers and try to pay the highest salaries possible." There I go again! she thought despairingly. I stand here, prac-tically telling the woman I hired her and I'm her boss! Why don't I learn to keep my big mouth shut?

"Oh, it's a very good salary," the teacher agreed quickly. "Two hundred and fifty a month for such a small school, with the quarters and utilities included and everything in the world to work with in the way of equipment—it's a wonderful oppor-tunity."

"You're on the fence-line telephone, you know," Margie re-minded her. "Let us know if you need anything or if you want company. And we'll be calling up and dropping over to see you. Outside school hours, naturally. Good morning."

She hurried out and she and Olive Dennison passed each other on the path. Margie gathered Fred up out of a knot of playing children. Olive would come by the house for a cup of coffee on her way home, and they could talk things over then.

Olive seemed to take the teacher as she was, a pleasant woman, a little overdressed, ". . . but she'll get over that when she really has to stoke the furnace," said Olive. She hooted at Margie's slight feeling of unease. "Don't be silly," Olive said robustly. "You've been out on the range too long, that's all that's the matter with you. You've forgotten how people operate outside the cattle business."

"You're boasting," Margie grinned. "Just because you went to the National convention in San Francisco three years ago . . ."

"Well, if you'd rather stay home and have a baby . . ." Olive retorted, and they both laughed, and commenced the endlessly fascinating topic of what the children said and how their remarks compared with the sayings of other children.

Jack asked about the teacher at supper that night, and Margie let the children answer. They were enthusiastic. The woman was pleasant, and she taught well, "As well as mother," Dorothy remarked.

Little Jack was not quite so exuberant. "She teaches all right," he agreed. He was naturally conservative, and Margie reflected that she might have spoiled him, unknowingly, when she taught the children at home.

But after the first homework of the year was finished and the children had gone to bed, Jack repeated his query, more pointedly. "What do *you* think of the teacher?" he asked, laying his pipe aside to show that this was the beginning of a conversation, not an idle, isolated inquiry.

"She's very pleasant," Margie replied slowly. "I'm a little worried because she told me she'd been in a hospital last year with a general breakdown. She's always lived in town, and this kind of life is hard sometimes for a well woman who's used to it. I only hope she won't get sick again."

Jack picked up the pipe and deliberately reloaded it.

"I didn't know she'd been sick," he observed. "Naturally we did know she was a town woman. But she was the only one with a record and standing we liked who was willing to come out here. We didn't make it sound too good, either. We told her the place was isolated and she'd have to do some of the heavy work because we couldn't get a janitor. We'd already arranged that

124

each member of the school board would do heavy cleaning a week in turn and that one of us would always be on call if she needed extra help. But she didn't mind the idea of doing her own work—didn't seem to, anyway. Said she loved the country and country life, and she knew she'd be happy here."

"Jack," demanded his wife, "do you remember your father's farm, and what the life there was like?"

"Sure."

"Was it anything like life here?"

"Well—no."

"Well," said Margie, "*that's* what most people mean by life in the country; that kind of Grandma Moses Christmas card atmosphere. *This* is still the frontier, as far as most country-lifers in the East are concerned."

"Oh, she'll get used to it. Everyone does."

"If they don't they leave, and that's what I'm worried about."

"Don't you want to go back to schoolteaching, Mother?"

"I will if I have to," Margie answered thoughtfully. "I'll do anything to keep the children at home till they're high school age and still have them educated. I've got all the State Department of Education forms and records for isolated ranch-home schools this year, in case I need them. But I've got my hands full as it is. And I'd like the children to be able to remember something more about mother after they're grown than a streak of blue jeans going by."

Jack laughed and held another match—the seventh—to his pipe and picked up his paper. Margie took up her book. The new Book-of-the-Month Club publication stood on the shelf behind her with thirty-six companions that had arrived since Fred's birth. Margie dutifully promised herself each month that she would start reading them, but she never seemed to get around to it. After all, she was *used* to *Pickwick Papers*. She didn't have to strain her mind or attention figuring out what would happen next. She knew in advance.

The fall continued normally. The two older children went to school in the morning, riding their ponies when the weather was good. When it was bad, Margie loaded her offspring into the car and drove them over. They brought their homework back in the evenings and conscientiously studied on either side of the cleared dining-room table after supper. Jack got the stock gathered and shipped to his father's fattening pens. They had the satisfaction of hearing two weeks later that the load had arrived in good shape. Thanksgiving began to move from the background of family life to the foreground. Margie, taking heed of her social duties, left the car at the schoolhouse gate one morning and walked up the path with the children.

The schoolroom, when she entered, was not quite as she remembered it. The floor looked as if it had not been cleaned for some time, and there were dust kittens rolled in the corners and beneath the teacher's desk. The atmosphere was close, frousty, as if the room had not been aired in several days, and it was warm—almost tropically warm. There were long, dusty eraser streaks on the blackboards. The teacher's desk had been turned so that the teacher sat with her back to the window, in profile to the class.

The teacher herself seemed a little frousty, too. She still wore the tailored suit, but it looked now as if it had not been taken off even at night since the day that school opened. Her nails had grown to claw-length, carrying the chipped and streaked enamel outwards towards the ends. But her hair was still neatly—even elaborately—dressed, and she still smiled when she spoke. She accepted Margie's invitation quickly, rather eagerly.

"I'll try to be on time," she said when Margie told her the hour. "I may be a little late. I have to walk."

"I thought you had a car," Margie said.

The woman waved her hand and let it trail off to one side.

"I sold it," she said indifferently.

"Mr. Brooks will be glad to come and get you," Margie offered briskly. "Good-bye for now." She left the schoolhouse hastily. Something was wrong.

How wrong was apparent when Little Jack got out of school that evening. He confronted her anxiously in the car. He had put Fred in the back seat with Dorothy and had established himself beside his mother without any argument. He and his sister must have made their plan earlier in the day.

"Mother," he asked, "do we have to have her for Thanksgiving?"

"Why, Jack, what do you mean?"

"Do we have to have that old teacher for Thanksgiving dinner at our house, with us?"

"We don't *have* to," Margie answered, her attention divided between his question and a porcupine that had chosen that moment to decide to cross the road. "We don't *have* to have anybody. But it always seems to me that Thanksgiving is a time for making people welcome to your home, especially people who are away from their own homes and who might be alone otherwise. That's how the Indians treated the settlers and the settlers treated the Indians when Thanksgiving started in this country."

"Well———," Jack hesitated. "I know, Mother. But, gosh, why can't we have somebody we like? Somebody we don't have to see all the time? It isn't any fun having her."

"We have to think about what will be pleasant for the other person as well as for ourselves, Jack," his mother said. "We are the only family around here that hasn't entertained the teacher already. I'm ashamed of myself because she's been here two months and hasn't been in our house yet. Now, remember she's a stranger here and make her have as good a time as you possibly can, so she'll know what we mean when we talk about ranch-house hospitality."

"Well, if she's visited one week end with each of the other families, she hasn't had a chance to get to see us anyway," said Jack stubbornly. "And besides, she hasn't sold her car. It's out in the garage behind the schoolhouse. All four tires are flat and the battery won't turn over, but it's there."

"John," said Margie sternly, "it's wrong to gossip about your teacher. Maybe she has sold the car and the person who bought it decided to leave it where it was until spring. Naturally she wouldn't want to drive it if it belonged to somebody else."

"Why doesn't whoever it belongs to get it fixed then?" Jack

queried. Margie, stopping the car in their own garage, avoided answering by pretending not to hear him.

She repeated the story to Big John after the children were in bed. He laughed at her. They said nothing more on the subject until the Friday after Thanksgiving. Then, peeling an apple before bedtime, Jack observed,

"I don't think there's anything wrong with her. She acts all right to me."

"She was all right," Margie agreed. "She'd got her hair done right and filed off some of the fingernails, and that was a beautiful dress."

"I wrote back to her home town in Iowa," Jack said, "and asked a few questions of the school board there. It's kind of pitiful, what they told me. She's a widow, although she calls herself Miss. Her husband was a railroader and was killed in an accident about four years ago. He did a lot of night work, so she kept on teaching after they married, and when he died, she stayed on the job. But about a year and a half ago she broke down and had to go to a hospital for some time. When she came out, she didn't want to stay there where everything reminded her of her husband and all, so she looked around for a new job. People said she's always been nervous and kind of dressy, but there wasn't a thing in the world really wrong with her before she had her breakdown."

"Jack," Margie demanded, "was that a mental hospital?"

Jack busied himself with his pipe. "A private one," he said when his head was satisfactorily misted in smoke.

Margie looked at him. "Do you think an isolated schoolhouse out on the flats is the best place for a woman with that kind of medical history? What did she do when she broke down?"

"Oh, they said she sort of neglected her appearance, and thought people were picking on her. That's about all. I believe there was something about thinking she couldn't walk for a while . . . ."

"And now she thinks she's sold her car and she hasn't! Oh, Jack!"

"Now, you don't know she hasn't."

"I'd know if she *had*. And so would you."

"Well, what can we do, Margie?"

"I don't know. You can't fire her for incompetence—the children seem to be learning as well as they did when I taught them at home. And unless they show signs that something's wrong, there's nothing you can take hold of."

"She may be cured, for all we know. Let's hope so."

Over the week end, Margie made excuses to check with the children on their lessons. They seemed to be progressing satisfactorily. Dorothy was no further behind in arithmetic than usual, and her spelling had improved. Jack, always a steady plugger, was about where his mother had expected him to be. He was having some trouble with geography, and Margie got out the globe and gave him a general review.

"You listen to the news broadcasts from now on, and make lists of names of places," she instructed him. "Then look the places up in the atlas and on the globe the way you did last year. It's important to know where things are in the world."

"Gee, Mother, you make things interesting," Jack said. "I wish you were teaching us at home, like last year."

"Don't you have more fun going to school with the other boys and girls than staying at home and seeing nobody but your sister and brother?"

"Ye-es. I *guess* I do. But, gosh, Mother, I sure don't learn as much as I did when we were home and you were teaching us. Why can't you teach us and the other children, too?"

"Because my job is really making the home nice for you and Dad. If I taught school, things wouldn't go so well here because I'd be too busy to take care of everything as well as I'd like to. Schoolteaching and homemaking are both full-time jobs, Jack."

"I'd rather have you for the teacher," her son muttered under his breath as he put the globe away.

On Monday morning Margie wakened to see the world dead-level under a night's thick snow. The glisten and sheen of it as it covered sage and bushes and the smaller inequalities of the ground reduced everything to flatness. The sun was intense now, but there was a feel in the air that heralded more snow later in the day. When she drove the children to school, Margie left the car and entered the building to speak to the teacher.

"Isn't it wonderful!" the woman exclaimed. "So beautiful! I never saw anything like it."

"I'm glad you don't mind it," Margie replied. "It's very late for a first snow and the chances are we'll see it from now till May. Any time you get bored with life here at the schoolhouse, come home with the children for a night or a weekend, won't you?"

"Thank you," said the teacher. "I don't think I'll mind, though. It's so beautiful. And I've gotten very fond of my little home here . . . ."

"Just remember," Margie insisted, "we're always glad to see you."

She made a point of mentioning her invitation to the children that evening. Snow was coming down in big, splashy flakes, clogging the windshield wipers, and Margie had to raise her voice to make herself heard above the clacking beat of the blades.

"I bet she won't come," Little Jack said. "She didn't even go out in the yard at recess."

"She probably didn't want to get her feet wet," Margie said, absentmindedly. Was it her imagination, or had the schoolroom been even closer and untidier than she had remembered it?

The snow continued to fall uninterruptedly for the next week. Its whiteness shut in the world and bounded them on all sides. All sounds were hushed by the enfolding closeness of the white bandage that wrapped the world. Movement seemed slower and more difficult in the moist atmosphere than it would ordinarily have been. Little Jack came out of the schoolhouse on a Tuesday afternoon, his face as white as the snow around him, his eyes blazing.

"Mother!" he gasped as he opened the door of the car, "Mother!"

"What is it?" Margie cried, her own breath clutching the walls of her throat. "Are you sick? Is Sister all right?"

"Mother! She said something *awful!*"

130

"Sister did? What is it, darling? What, Jack? Tell Mother." Dimly, Margie was aware of Dorothy climbing into the back seat, of Fred round-eyed and startled beside her. "Get in the car, Son, and close the door so the others won't get cold. Now. Who said what?"

"The teacher. She said something *awful!*"

"To you? Or Dorothy? Or one of the other children?"

"Not *to* anybody. She just *said* it. She was looking out of the window, and she said it."

"What did she say, Son?"

"She said, 'This isn't America. Some people may think it's America, but it isn't. This isn't America. This is Siberia; it's Russia.' Mother! What did she mean?"

Margie drove faster than she had ever driven on snow before. She had to get her boy away from the sound of the words, although the words still sounded in the car, in her ears as they must in his. She had to get home, had to talk to Jack, had to see what was the best thing for them to do.

Jack, when she told him, was rock-calm. "Let's go back to the school, Margie," he suggested. "That poor woman must be in trouble."

They found the teacher seated at her desk with her back to the window. The room was cold and seemed piled with litter and dirt. There were no eraser streaks on the blackboard; words were written over arithmetic problems and problems scrawled over words in an indecipherable palimpsest of learning.

"Excuse me for not getting up," the teacher said when she saw them. "Something seems to be wrong with my legs. They don't want to work. They've gone flat, like the tires on the car." She laughed throatily, abstractedly. "What does it matter?" she asked them swiftly. "You can't ever get out of Siberia. When you're in there, you're sentenced for life."

"Help her up, Margie," Jack said gently. "We'll get her to bed and send for her folks, if she has any, in the morning."

"I can stay here and take care of her until they come," Margie answered, holding her voice steady. "We won't have any school until they come to take her home. By that time, I can get things ready so I can teach for the rest of the year."

131

11. *She Needs Certain Advantages*

ARIZONA, 1952

LOUISE WHITSON closed the suitcase and shoved it aside. She pushed herself up off the floor with one hand and pushed her hair away from her eyes with the back of the other. Deliberately she smiled at her daughter, although smiling did not altogether erase the down-drawn parentheses that framed her mouth.

"Sweet Briar will be proud of you, and so am I," she said.

Judy swung her feet over the edge of the bed and tried to smile in return. "Mother," she asked, "do you think I have the right clothes? Going away to school and all—and the blue jeans and plaid shirts and everything—just what I wear every day right here on the ranch. Are you *sure* I'll be dressed right?"

Louise struggled—and held down the desire to toss her arms in the air. This discussion—you really couldn't call it an argument—had lasted for three months now. Ever since they had decided to send Judy back to Virginia to school, there had been just such a period of soul-searching over clothes each day.

"Judy," Louise said, "when I was your age and went to Sweet Briar, a girl wouldn't have dared let anyone on the campus know she'd ever owned a pair of jeans. It was thought daring for girls to ride astride, and they had their choice of side saddle or hunting saddle in the equitation classes."

Equitation! Good Heavens! And she herself had chosen the side saddle! Now she grabbed a rope and snagged whatever horse came handy in the corral, and if she had to ride bareback she could do it. Sweet Briar was still a little behind the Arizona times by equitation standards. She went on with what she hoped would sound to her daughter's ears like a clenching argument.

"If you had only my word to take, naturally you'd question it and be right to," she declared. "I haven't been East since I graduated myself. But after all we're going by what the *Mademoiselle* Magazine college board says. If we'd just read the magazine, we might be a few weeks behind the times, even so. But you wrote them yourself, darling. You have their personal letter telling you what to pack. Remember?"

Judy reached behind her on the bed and picked up the letter. She had read it so constantly and persistently for the past month that the stiff, smooth paper was roughened and slightly stained with wear. Judy consulted the letter and its enclosed list when she rose in the morning and before she turned off her light at night. It was more to her than the Bible to a Fundamentalist—she regarded it with the reverence a True Believer accords the Koran. She read from it now:

"Four pairs of jeans, and they shouldn't be too new."

Well, Louise thought, they weren't. They'd been thoroughly broken in on the ranch during the course of the summer. "At least four plaid cotton shirts. Six are better, because you can wear them with a tailored suit as well as with the jeans." That was practical. Louise remembered her own stiff-starched white blouses—Sweet Briar had just discarded uniforms when she enrolled. They still discouraged originality in dress, even so, and all the girls wore plain white blouses and looked as much alike as if uniforms had been required.

Louise patted the top of her daughter's head and went into the kitchen. There she found her husband pretending to read a week-old newspaper.

"You got everything all ready, Lou?"

"All packed and ready to go, Bill."

"Seems kind of a shame all around, the way things are working out."

"I don't think so. I believe it's the best way possible."

133

"You going down to the train tomorrow, honey?"

"Why, Bill! Of course I am! Naturally!"

"Well, all right. Don't get upset about it. I just thought—it's going to throw school here one day late, that's all. I wondered about the school board . . . ."

Louise washed her hands at the sink-table and threw the water out of the kitchen door. "I'll be glad when we get the drain cleared," she said absentmindedly. "I don't know anything that makes me feel poor white except throwing used wash water out in the yard." She caught her breath, appalled at what she had said. She turned towards her husband, giggling a little, a silly feminine giggle. "If anything ever *could* make me feel poor white, that would be it," she said, and rubbed her hand along his cheek. The red that had been rising from his neck to his forehead subsided. He smiled at her.

"You always could tease me, Lou," he said, "and that lisp of yours makes things sound so little girl—I know you ain't serious, but sometimes I get my back up still yet."

She got out the mixing bowl and started hot biscuits for supper. Judy loved them, and while Judy would get plenty of hot biscuits where she was going, they wouldn't taste exactly like home—her mother hoped.

"It's all right with the school board, Bill," she said, resuming the important conversation at the point where he had interrupted it. "I spoke to Mr. Browning yesterday."

Bill had picked up his paper again, and now he looked around the edge of it. "That's all right, then," he said. "Some of the folks seems to think it's kind of odd for the school teacher's kid to be going east to school, as it is. I wouldn't want them to think we didn't think this school was good enough for her."

Louise paused in her mixing. "It isn't," she informed him. "Whether we admit it to the neighbors or not, Bill, we might as well be honest with ourselves. Judy's too bright for me. She's gone beyond what I can teach her."

"That's an awful way for a kid to feel about her mother! I won't have a daughter of mine . . ."

"Listen, Bill," Louise said quietly as she patted the dough

on the floured board. "Don't fly off the handle. Judy doesn't feel that way—yet. But she would if she stayed here another year. Judy has a future ahead of her. She wants to act and she can act. If she stays here, all the acting she'll ever get to do will be for an audience of steers."

"Let her go to the state university, then! Why has she got to go east to some high-toned girls' school? Just because *you* went there?"

"Partly," Louise answered with the tranquility she had taught herself long ago. "It's the right school for her, or I wouldn't send her there. What I learned at Sweet Briar has stayed with me all these years, and it's been all I had to go on with here at the ranch. Bill, don't you realize that? I wasn't trained to be a ranch hand; I wasn't even trained to be a cook. I was raised to be a young lady, to teach school in a pretty little country town—like the ones back home—for a year or two, and then marry the banker's son or some young minister—whichever came along first."

Her husband laid down the paper and faced her across the kitchen table. "Sorry you didn't, Lou?"

"I'll never get over being glad. I answered that ad for a school teacher in the Superstition Mountains on a dare—I never told you that, Bill. I hadn't any more idea than a jaybird what Arizona was like, but I was young and healthy and curious. The best way I knew to find out about the rest of the country was to get a job out here, instead of in a town in the Blue Grass."

"You could still have married the banker's son or a young minister, at that," Bill remarked thoughtfully. "They were both courting you the day after you stepped off the train. I never have understood why you didn't take one or the other of them."

"I could have married a horse thief or an Indian or an old nester back in the hills who'd worn out three wives already, too. But I didn't marry any of them because I fell in love with a cow-man."

Bill hid behind the paper, abruptly, and the voice that issued from its screen was hoarse. "You fell in love with a cow *poke*, honey, and try the best you can, you'll never make any thing but a hand out of him."

135

Louise shut the oven door. "I don't want to make anything out of him," she observed. "I want him the way he is. But one thing Sweet Briar taught me was to face the facts. And the fact of the matter now is that Judy needs teaching I can't give her. The school has a fine drama department. When she finishes her two years there, she'll be ready for college. She can come back and go to the state university at Tucson, or she can go on to school in the North. That will be for her to decide, with the school's help, after she's been there."

Judy emerged from her room to set the table. She paused with the knives and forks in her hand. "Is Jim coming, Mother?"

"Oh, my goodness!" Louise exclaimed. "I forgot about Jim. Why, I suppose so, Judy. Better set a place for him."

"I bet he doesn't come," Bill said. "With Judy going off to school, and all."

Judy giggled. "Why, Dad! You know he comes to see Mother, not me."

"Surely to Goodness, Judy," Louise began. A knock at the door interrupted her.

"There he is now," Bill remarked. "Let him in, Judy."

Jim stooped through the open door and silently peeled his hat from his head. Nobody hurried him. He would speak when he was ready. He hung his hat on the visitors' hook by the door and deposited himself on a chair in the exact middle of the room. It became apparent that he was in labor with words.

"Good evening, Miz' Whitson," he finally produced. Judy snickered and Bill grinned. One of Judy's famous imitations was Jim entering the house and uttering the first words of the evening.

"Good evening, Jim. Have you done any work for me?"

"Yes, ma'am. I sure have. I been working right along . . . ." Jim was started now. Louise motioned her family and guest to the supper table and began to serve the meal. She handed Judy the hot biscuits folded in a napkin and followed them with a plate of butter and a jar of wild honey. She started the cold fried chicken that was left from their noon dinner on its way around the table, with the potato salad and cold canned tomatoes in pursuit. She got up and poured coffee for everyone and passed the canned milk and the sugar. She and Bill and Judy accomplished all necessary actions and invited each other to partake of various dishes in pantomime. It was a standing joke in the family that Jim had a chance to speak only once in every two weeks and that he should be allowed to make the most of each opportunity.

Jim held forth during the entire meal. The consumption of food was not essential to him if he could talk. He piled food on his plate, blindly serving himself whenever he was handed a dish. When Judy started to pass him a fourth biscuit to add to the pile that was growing beside his plate, Louise shook her head sternly. The signal was familiar to them all. Jim stopped his talk in full spate and looked down at the food before him. Judy got busy with her own meal, and Louise took her turn talking.

"We're taking Judy down to the railroad tomorrow, Jim," she said as her guest at last began to eat. "Is there anything we can get for you in town?"

"Answer yes or no," said Bill, grinning.

"Yes," said Jim. He had a literal mind.

"What is it?" Louise inquired. "Don't tease him, Bill. Give him a chance."

"I need some more drawing paper," Jim said, "and some of those pencils you lick to paint with."

"All right," Louise said. "If I can't get them, I'll send an order off to Phoenix. What's the trouble, Jim?"

For suddenly Jim looked stricken. "Oh, gosh, Miz' Whitson. I forgot all about Judy going tomorrow. I shouldn't-a come tonight. You want this evening with her."

"Now, don't worry, Jim. Judy and I have had all summer vacation to say whatever we wanted to each other. I'm sure she'd rather remember her last evening at home as being like a regular one, after she gets away, than look back at her Dad and me sitting around, trying to think of things to say to her. If we have any parting shots, we'll fire them tomorrow on the way to the train."

"How long you going to be away?"

"Two years," Judy answered. "Two years if I can stand it."

"Two years," Louise repeated firmly. "We can manage train fare once each way! She can stand it and the school can stand it." She did not say, I don't know whether I can.

Bill spoke deliberately. "Judy couldn't go at all, if her mother didn't have the teaching job. That's what's making the trip possible. The last eight years Mrs. Whitson's been saving for this. Twice I had bad luck—most of the stock wiped out in the freeze in forty-eight and then that flash flood got half my steers in fifty. So Judy's school money had to go to restock the place both times. Otherwise she'd have gone three years ago. That's what happens to kids whose dads are failures."

Louise intervened swiftly. "And that's what happens to wives who marry Irishmen, Jim. Their husbands squeeze the last drop of dramatic blood out of any old turnip they find lying around. People ask me where Judy gets her talent. They ought to know what an actor her father is when he wants to be!"

Bill looked at his wife, and many expressions struggled on his face. He looked simultaneously like a dog who is patted when he expected to be kicked, an elephant suddenly discovering his intellectual superiority to a tapir, and a cat who has topped an elegant meal of canary-bird with a sardine sundae.

"Women!" he said profoundly. "I never will understand them!"

"Jim's got more talent than I have," Judy said unexpectedly.

"Jim has different talent," her mother corrected her. "You have the kind of talent that needs to be trained and disciplined. Jim has the kind of talent that needs to be released."

"Yeah," said Bill from the head of the table. "Jim's all right. I bet if he'd got to go to your mother for art lessons sooner, he'd have been another Charley Russell."

"Jim can become another Frederic Remington," Louise said quietly. "All he needs is time and the things to work with. I can't teach him, but I can give him a chance to teach himself."

"Oh, for Goodness' sake," Judy interposed. "You folks quit talking about him like he wasn't here."

138

"As if he weren't here, dear," her mother corrected her, and her father added under his breath,

"The Sweet Briar touch."

Judy rose and began to clear the table. "Ding, ding!" she said. "Art school will now take up. Come on, Dad, We'll wash the dishes."

Jim did not stay late that evening. He had been known to keep his teacher up past eleven o'clock and to spend most of what was left of the night riding home to the other side of the mountain. Louise wondered after she got into bed how many nights Jim had not slept at all, but had gone right to work on the day that followed an art lesson.

How many of the children who came to her for teaching every year actually had talent? The question plagued her now as it had many times before. When the talent was as clear and strong as it was in Judy and Jim, there could be no missing it. Room to expand and develop and the most elementary tools were all that were required.

But where some special ability was less evident, where there was a chance that she might miss it—did she miss it? Did she fail to give any other child the chance she worked to secure for her daughter, that she lost sleep in order to supply to her neighbor's son? Of the six who would enroll with her day after tomorrow, might there be one who had in some hidden degree what Jim and Judy had?

Six students and six different grades. If she couldn't sleep, she could work out the year's teaching schedule now. It would keep her from thinking about tomorrow. This must be the way people who were going to be executed felt, she supposed. Fear could be a physical pain—fear not of the pain you inevitably would feel, but fear of showing your pain—that was pain itself. She wouldn't—she-would-not-think about Judy's leaving and what it would cost in loneliness and boredom to have no one to whom she could talk, no one who knew what she meant if conversation went beyond the quality of feed in the south pasture.

Jim, of course. But he was different, too. Jim did not need her except as a means towards an end. Jim's talent was so great, it was so near to genius, that it transcended and encompassed the dwarfing influence of the gigantic world of the West. Jim could be as interested in the hay in a given meadow as Bill, not only because the quality of the hay would determine the amount of drawing paper and Aquarelle crayons and sable hair brushes he could buy in the coming year, but because the color of the hay would be one thing near the creek and another way from it; the texture of the hay would be light in a dry year and dense in a wet one—oh, for many reasons the hay in the meadow was and always would be as important to Jim as to any other rancher —and more so.

Whereas Judy was always *here*. Had always been here. Judy was part of the mechanics of her life, one of the profound, unrecognized because profound, necessities of it. And Judy was going away—she was sending Judy away. She wanted Judy to know that there was another kind of life before she came back to Arizona and married a rancher and had babies of her own.

For Judy would come back and marry a rancher—Louise was sure of that. Girls who grew up on ranches almost always did. They might go away, but they seldom got away. Never admit that to the neighbors—never admit it to Bill. Never say, I know that if Judy finishes college after she graduates from Sweet Briar, her real life will be on a ranch. Bill would scream aloud like a panther about the waste—the waste of Judy's time and her mother's money. She was a little afraid of what Bill would say if he realized as clearly as she did that at the end of her education Judy would come home and marry a rancher.

That was Judy's business; Judy's, and, to some smaller degree, her mother's. Let Judy know first that there was a world beyond; let her know that choice was possible, before she had to choose. Louise had known. She had known her alternate choice so well that ranch life had seemed to her escape from something about to enclose her. And now she knew what it was that she had escaped into, she would choose the same alternative again, and choose it gladly. Judy also should have the chance to choose; to choose knowingly. All that any mother could do was provide the chance.

140

Don't think about it—any of it. Plan the school schedule, work it all out in her mind, every bit of it. Six children and six different grades—but they all could read. No real beginners this year. The youngest was in the second grade. And with the oldest already started in algebra she could really coast—it would be downhill all the way—downhill into sleep—

She stood beside Bill on the station platform the next afternoon. Judy, already all atwitter with the push-button gadgets in her roomette, stood on the Pullman steps above them. The train finished taking on water. Blue-serge arms waved, voices clarioned, "All aboard!" antiphonally from one end of the train to the other. Slowly—noiselessly, at first—the wheels turned. Then, the chuffing and rattling and spurting dust were gone, and Judy with them, her arm still waving stiffly out from the half-closed vestibule door.

Louise turned to her husband. Never before in their married life had she so wished to lay her head on his shoulder and sob. The tears on his cheeks stopped her. She laid her palm against his cheek and swiftly manufactured an imitation smile.

"Two years isn't so long, sweetheart," she said exaggerating her lisp. "Just a couple of calf crops, and your baby will be back."

PART FIVE

How Do They Live?

IT IS IN DETAILS *that the ranch woman's everyday life differs most sharply from that of the town-living woman of the mid-twentieth century. Most ranch homes are supplied with electric power now; most of them have long had reliable water supplies. The time of water hauled in barrels and of homemade candles is long past.*

Yet the ranch wife, while she deals with much the same housekeeping and shopping problems as any other housewife, must be prepared to deal with them in wholly original ways whenever the need arises. Constant preparation to meet emergencies, without possible foreknowledge of what the emergencies may be, makes the ranch wife a woman of infinite resource, infinite capacity, and unbelievable flexibility of character.

Life on a ranch is never dull; by its nature it cannot be. Nor can a woman live on a ranch without good humor—and a good sense of humor—in addition to the more conventional virtues of courage and fortitude. The combination of elements—with humor usually on top—produces women whose very conventionalities are unconventional.

12. *The Roundup*

MONTANA, 1950

JACK was already pulling on his boots, standing on one foot and balancing himself against the foot of the bed, when the alarm clock went off. Margie reached for the switch and flipped it down, silencing the clamor before it could rouse the children at the end of the hall. She wrestled briefly with an entangling sheet Jack had thrown across her when he rose, swung her feet over the edge of the bed, and yawned dazedly.

"Wake!" Jack whispered, trying to be urgent and dramatic at the same time. "Wake! The morn that gilds yon dewy mountain tops——" His boot heels banged on the floor as he started towards the door.

Margie tried to suppress a shriek and still make her whisper as urgent as his. "Shut up——!" She pulled a robe over her pajamas while she started for the kitchen. There she added a coverall apron to the rest of her costume and began breakfast.

Any dawn that came around gilding mountain tops at two in the morning was making a sad mistake, she reflected as she lighted the stove. The oatmeal was soaking in the double boiler, and she started it heating. Canned orange juice was in the refrigerator, and it could wait to be opened until the coffee was on the way. She dug out the juice can and balanced it on the fingers of her left hand, with the butter resting on her palm. She grabbed a milk jar and hesitated over the eggs. No, to try to add

145

them to her load would be to tempt the fates. She deposited the
first load on the work table and went back for bacon, eggs, and
the sourdough crock. That had been her father's idea. "Never
try to run a ranch without sourdough," he would say, and whenever anything went wrong, he declared it was because the wom-
en folks had let the sourdough supply get low.

Now Margie measured flour, salt, soda, and baking powder
into a crock, added a spoonful of sourdough, hesitated, and
filled the tablespoon again. She ran her finger around the inside
of the milk crock and brought it out with a sheet of heavy cream
clinging to it like a bandage. That went into the pitcher to be
used in coffee. The second layer of cream she lifted with her
mother's old aluminum ladle that had grown gray and dull in
service, and dumped into the batter. Cream made the pancakes
a little rich, but there was no question that it made them good.
She beat the dough again and then thinned it with top milk.

Jack came through the kitchen door and set two foam-topped
milk buckets on the sink table. "I'll see to it," Margie said. "You
pour the coffee and sit down."

He filled two of the old white china mugs, crazed by the fire
that had burned the old ranch house to the ground, and set one
of them on the back of the stove for her. His own he took to the
cleared end of the kitchen table and drank gulp for gulp with
his orange juice.

Bacon on the griddle and bacon in the frying pan. Thickish,
pinkish slices of home-cured meat, sent from Missouri by Jack's
family. Then eggs in the frying pan and dough-cakes on the
griddle. Margie finished her coffee, turned eggs and cakes in a
quick series of movements, and reached for her orange juice. As
she set her refilled mug on the table, she reached again for the
spatula. This was a quick and easy breakfast, when there were
only two people to eat it. Just for a moment she strained away
from the kitchen, her mind reaching down the hall, listening to
be sure the children slept.

Half-past two. Breakfast on the table. Milking done. Everything was running smoothly and on schedule so far. Jack wrapped
himself around oatmeal, bacon, four eggs, and a stack of griddle

cakes. "Anything more?" Margie asked. He shook his head as he finished his third mug of coffee.

"Plenty for now," he answered when his mouth was free. "You'll meet us at Half-mast Butte?"

"I'll be there with the fire going by seven," she replied. "You men can have breakfast as soon as you get there with the stock."

Somewhere outside there was the ghost of a sound, the faintest whisper of a chink of metal against metal, as it might be a link chain touching a bit. "Fred," said Jack. He bent over and kissed the top of her head. "You've got syrup on your chin," he informed her. "I've got to get going."

She looked at her watch, mopped at her chin, and then followed him outside. Ten minutes of three, and already the first stars were showing yellow instead of white against the first alteration of color in the east. Night was not paling yet; only the sky quality changed as she watched. A little cool wind ran along the ground and she could feel all the creatures of the earth stir with it; the old cat coming from the barn to rub against her ankles, the waking dog yawning and stretching first his forelegs, then his hind ones, the horses dipping their heads and snapping them up again. The cattle would be rousing and stirring in the big pasture, preparing to wake fully and drift down to the coulee for water. Time—full time—for the men to ride out on the spring roundup.

Now was the coolest hour of the day or night, the time when temperatures sank, when sleepers at home reached for another blanket and patients in hospitals rang for nurses and ordered hot water bottles. Now was the time, if there were a time, to feel low and draggled and droopy; but if you were awake and watching men gather their reins and mount, watching horses gather their feet under them and prepare to move, it was an exciting time. When the men rode away—Jack and Fred and the two Dennisons, father and son, from down the creek, and Mr. Mathers from Wild Horse Butte and his friend who ran the Ford Agency in Miles City and always came out for the roundup—it was exactly three o'clock. Margie turned back into the kitchen and prepared to get busy.

She went directly to the bedroom and dressed for the day. Clean checked shirt, blue jeans, anklets, saddle shoes. Boots looked better with the rest of the outfit, but they weren't so easy to get around the house in. She brushed her hair quickly and tied it back with a ribbon. Lipstick, then, and a dab of powder. No need for rouge! She'd be in a fine, fiery glow in half an hour. Then back to the kitchen, back to work.

She gathered up the breakfast dishes and washed them swiftly. According to the rules of the family she should have left them for Dorothy to wash after the children had their breakfast, but Dorothy would have plenty to do when she got up and her mother needed space. The food Margie left out on the kitchen table, ready for Dorothy to cook when she and the boys wakened.

With the kitchen in order, Margie went to the barn. She had everything ready there, for Jack had loaded the heavy things in the car for her the night before. But she had learned long before this that something was always forgotten if she didn't go through this last-minute ritual of checking up.

The old chuckbox was in the turtle-back of the sedan, with the flap dropped over it. Margie raised the metal hood, and released the catch of the box. The table-door fell, its leg falling beneath it and supporting it. Her father always made a joke of having a chuckbox with a trained leg so the table was in place and ready to work on as soon as the box was open.

Everything inside the box was orderly. The big roundup coffeepot was fastened to the back of the box, with the big skillet hanging in place behind it. The two two-pound cans of coffee were there, and the five-pound can of sugar, and the half-gallon can of maple syrup. The pancake turner, a husky iron utensil, not an effeminate spatula this time, was in its place beside the butter knife. Three pounds of lard waited in a tight-lidded bucket. Ten pounds of flour in the old enamel container. Jack had loaded two five-gallon cans of water into the back seat of the car the evening before. She had the staples; now she needed only the perishables.

There was a real change and a brightening of the sky as she

148

returned to the kitchen. She took a can of sourdough batter, pre-pared the evening before, from the bottom shelf of the refrigera-tor. There was a can of coffee cream beside it. The two made a considerable load as she carried them to the car and set them in their places in the chuckbox. She went back to the house for the eggs—somebody always asked for eggs at the second break-fast and that always started the others off—and the crock of beans that had been baking in the oven for the last two days. She left the oven burning while she carried the beans and the eggs to the car. She went back to the house again and took the steaks from the refrigerator. She wrapped the meat in extra waxed paper, and then in a heavy layer of newspaper. She had every-thing ready to take out to the men. Everything but butter, she suddenly recalled. They all said they didn't need butter and that good rich hog grease did just as well, but they were all dis-appointed if she forgot it. She took two pounds from the icebox, hesitated, considered, and added a third. She could bring it back and use it for cooking if they didn't eat it. And at this time of the year with the milch cows on fresh pasture, getting the but-ter used up could be a major housekeeping problem.

Once again she returned to the kitchen, and this time, as she looked at the sky, she found herself repeating poetry: "Wake! For morning in the bowl of night/Has flung the stone that sets the stars to flight . . . ." The rest of the stanza fled from her mind as she stood again in the electric light of the kitchen.

She poured herself another mug of coffee, then emptied the pot and rinsed it before she set it back on the shelf above the stove. She sipped quickly, then bent down to get the big roaster from the cupboard under the sink. Holding it in one hand and the coffee mug in the other, she went downstairs to the basement storeroom. There, on a shelf in the zinc-lined storage cupboard, wrapped professionally in brown paper, was the roast Jack had cut off for her when he butchered last week.

Twenty-five pounds of beef made a considerable weight. She unwrapped the upper part of the roast and rolled it off the shelf into her pan; then jerked the paper away from the rest of the meat. She wadded her empty mug in the paper and tucked the bundle under her arm. With the laden pan held before her in both hands like an offering, she went back up the stairs to the kitchen.

Emma was there, already refilling the coffeepot. Margie kissed her lightly on the cheek and wondered how many times in her life her mother's sister had been—just *there*—there, wherever it was you needed somebody with a level head and a steady hand. Often enough, at any rate. Emma had never failed her. Things in the kitchen would run smoothly now. She could get started for the roundup without worrying about a thing.

"I've got the oven hot," she told her aunt, "and the roast can go in right away. I boiled the potatoes and eggs for the salad yesterday. There's another pot of beans in the oven—that makes beans twice in one day, but the men would rather have them than anything else. I haven't done a thing about the biscuits. There's sour cream in the storeroom, if you can get Dorothy to settle down long enough to churn it—which I doubt. You can't even think about coffee for dinner until I get back with the big pot. I've got the mix made for the pumpkin pies and the shells partly baked—they're in the storeroom, too. That's about all, I think . . . ."

"It's all right," Emma said soothingly. "I can manage. You've got two-thirds of the work done as it is. You go ahead and get started; it's a quarter past four now. You can't drive too fast with the chuck-wagon load. Give yourself plenty of time to get the fire going right."

"Jack and the boys went up there yesterday and got plenty of firewood and piled a fire up ready to light," Margie said. "I didn't want Jack to go—he was tired out. They gathered both the Dennisons' herds yesterday, and Mr. Mathers' the day before, and he had all the planning to do about getting ours in today. The children and I could have managed it . . . ."

"You've got plenty to do today, and you were busy all day yesterday, too," Emma reminded her. "And don't think I'm going to let you off doing a full day's work for me tomorrow. You haven't had much time to spare for firewood piling." She gave her niece a small, neat spank on the seat of her jeans. "Go on, now, get started, or you'll have the men waiting around for food and finding fault with everything you do. Feed them before they have time to find out they're hungry, and they'll think everything's perfect."

Margie walked clockwise around the car to look at the tires before she opened the door. That had been a ritual of hers ever since her father had first tried to teach her to drive and the car couldn't be used because a tire was flat. That had been in the days when a flat tire was a tragedy, necessitating a trip to town on horseback, with the tube hung limply on the saddle horn. Nowadays there were two spare wheels and tires in the barn in addition to the one in the turtle-back, and tire-changing was a simple matter. Today there was no need to change; the tires stood securely under the car, firmly inflated.

The motor turned smoothly when she touched the starter. She let it catch and run and warm, then backed out on the gravel turn-around outside the garage, and shifted. Easily and quietly, still without waking the children, she hoped, she turned down the driveway and headed away from the house.

"The year's at the spring/And the day's at the morn," Margie found in the front of her mind. This was certainly the Brooks family's poetic morning! "Morning's at four-thirty," she continued to herself, and stepped on the gas in a determined effort to reach Half-mast Butte and get her fire started in good time. The men could be expected any time after seven, and she wanted to be ready for them.

Old John had built the corrals and the branding pens out on this flat, away from the house, for several good practical reasons. The place was near the road and almost at the center of the ranch. There was a spring flowing from the base of the butte, and water could be piped to a stock tank without the expense and bother of putting up a windmill.

The Butte itself threw a long blue-violet shadow across the bleached whiteness of the earth and the bleached green-gray of the sagebrush. The spindly pinnacle of rock, from which the Butte took its name, stood sharply against the sky at the north end of the stone bulk. Long, long ago Old John had said the spire

151

looked like the mast of a ship. And Old Mr. Philadelphia, for
whom Old John had worked when he was Young John, had
corrected him and said it looked like only half a mast. So Half-
mast Butte the formation had become even on government survey maps.

Now the Butte was insubstantial, floating delicately in the
still-early light, looking solid only by contrast with the drift-
wood-silvery-gray of the weathered cedar corral bars. All this
land had been an ocean bottom once, and its light and wind and
air still weathered wood as waves would do. Pale and delicate,
wind-carved and sunlight bathed, the corral bars looked inadequate for the work they were meant to do.

Somehow, with the desert landscape returned to its beginnings, it seemed right and proper to Margie that as she stopped
the car and sat for a moment gazing about her a curlew should
begin to sing. Piercing-sweet, sharp-sweet, an uncloying ringing
sweetness like no other sound filled the air. She sat still and
looked intently at the grass before her until she saw the bird. It
was dusty-silver in color, brown-barred, equipped by Nature to
hide itself equally well against the dim color of this semiarid
pasture or the muted tones of the shore line from which its ancestors had come. The curlew still had the long, thick-jointed
legs of a shore bird and the long, spiked beak could pick up insects from any kind of sand, wet or dry. Now the beak was
parted in the ecstacy of song, and the long, smoothly rounded
body, shaped like a duck's body, swelled as it filled itself with
music and shrank again as the sound poured forth. So the curlew
sang while Margie listened and forgot about roundups and
breakfasts until the bird finished its recital and flapped rather
heavily away.

The lark had better not get to winging around here, Margie
thought, suddenly intent on her work. I'd be sure to stop to
listen to it, and I plain haven't got the time. She scratched a
match on the seat of her jeans and grinned, remembering Jack's
boast. She had overheard him one day in the Harvester show-
room, saying, "My wife's as good a hand as a man any day—if

you don't believe it, watch her light a match when she's got her pants on."

The fire caught easily and well and flamed steadily—not too high, but with the heat dry sage and greasewood and cow chips have long been famous for. The cow chips were Jack's concession to the roundup ritual. Old John always said that food cooked over a cow-chip fire was better than any other, and Young John saw to it that there were cow chips on hand to start the fire, even though most of the real cooking would be done over a flame from pine and mountain oak wood.

Coffee was the first chore. Margie poured a pound of coffee into the pot and half-filled it with water from one of the five-gallon cans before the fire was ready to cook on. Then she stacked the tin cups on the front fender of the car, so the men could reach for a cup and fill it first with water, then with coffee, with a minimum of effort. She set the skillet, with a pound of lard in the bottom, near the fire to start heating. She got out the old black griddle from the chuckbox and laid it on the ground to warm for the cakes. Last of all, she put the bean-pot, still too hot to lift bare-handed, in a hole Jack had dug for it, and raked ashes and live coals over it.

The coffeepot began to steam—a little. The lard snapped and crackled in the pan for the first time, and then began to bubble and give off little pops of fat. The surface of the griddle began to shine like the face of a woman bending over a fire, and Margie got out the crock of batter and beat it down. She laid out knives and forks and spoons—steel-tined and -bowled and -bladed, with twisted horn handles—old eating tools, part of the first equipment to go in the chuckbox. The coffeepot was really boiling now, and Margie pulled it back from the fire and filled it with cold water to within an inch or so of the top. Let it steep—and let the men come on whenever they liked. She was ready for them now.

She wasn't consciously listening, and yet she knew she heard the first possible sound—the running murmur along the ground that was the concerted movement of the herd. Almost at once she heard the first bellowings, the first shouts of the men. Then she was conscious of the lighter foot-falls of walking horses making a counterpoint against the heavy bass beat of the cattle. A dust cloud dimmed the north horizon. The men and the animals were coming in to the corrals.

They came slowly, never breaking the walking pace that was almost a drift of movement, yet never letting the animals stop moving. Here and there a cow caught at a wisp of grass at the edge of the herd, or a calf ran and caught up with its mother and sucked a mouthful of milk before both were carried on. Solid, steady, the cherry-red wave speckled with the white crests of the Herefords, washed towards the corrals. You would never think that these cattle could run. Yet give them the slightest alarm, the barest suggestion of sudden movement, and Margie knew they could sweep over anything that got in their way. After which, she and the breakfast would be scattered to the four winds together.

Easy, easy, easy. Margie called the words in her mind, and the men called them aloud to each other. Easy, Jack. Easy Fred. Easy, Tom and John Dennison, easy. Two on each flank and the rest of the men riding trail in the dust; the horses knowing their work as well as the men, if not better. Then it was done. The corral bars slid home and the herd milled and tossed inside the enclosure. The cattle were water behind a dam, washing up its sides and down again, noisy as a millrace.

The men were afoot now. The horses were tied to the hitching-rack, away from the corral with its noise and dust. Girths were loosened and men spoke to one another in normal voices as they worked. Then they came in a group across the hundred-yard space between the corral and the fire, to grab up the tin cups and fill them at the water can. The day was on them now, and with the coming of the day, its heat was added to the heat of movement. Water first, as Margie had foreseen, and after the water, coffee.

They drank it scalding, right from the pot, and while they drank Margie dropped the steaks into the deep bubbling-hot fat and poured the first blobs of batter out on the griddle. By the time the cups were emptied, the first round of meat and cakes was ready. She yelled, "Come and get it!" because that was part of roundup, but she knew she didn't need to. The men picked up their tools and took their enamel plates from the stack. They lined up without being told.

She cooked another round of steaks and piled more cakes in readiness while the first portions disappeared. The men ate neatly, without words and without waste motion, as all men do who are used to eating out of doors. Almost before the meal was cooked, it was consumed, and the men had settled back with refilled coffee cups to heap praise on the cook. There had been no time for them to discover that they were hungry and to find fault, as Emma had warned.

At a quarter to eight Margie finished her own breakfast and began to gather things together. The men took over the cooking fire and moved it on shovels into the branding corral ready to start their own work. Jack came over to speak to his wife.

"We ought to be back at the house by two," he said. "We didn't have any trouble, and if things go all right here we'll finish up in good time."

Margie nodded. "I'll have dinner ready when you get there," she informed him. She swiped out the last plate with the last used paper napkin, dropped all the papers on the final coals of the fire, and watched it flare up and die down. "You put out this fire?" she asked, and Jack nodded. That was part of his work and he would have done it anyhow, without her speaking of it, but it made her feel more secure to ask.

She watched him empty the water can on the coals, and lift the unused can from the car to the ground. The men would drink every drop during the day. He would leave the empty can there until someone could drive out and get it. That, too was part of their roundup pattern.

Back at the house, Margie glanced at the car clock as she switched off the motor. Nine. Four cars were already parked before the gate. That meant that the women of the other families were there, doing their part to prepare the dinner and visiting. The ranches along Powder River were too small and they ran too close to the edges of their budgets to hire many hands, even if there had been hands to hire. Roundup and branding and driving to the railroad to ship were all co-operative jobs in this community. Everybody shared the work on each ranch in turn, and they decided on the turns by drawing lots. It was the only fair way to do things.

The day was hot now, and the kitchen was hotter than it ever was at any other time. But the women gathered there did not seem particularly to mind the heat. Emma was at the sink, washing every dish and utensil as fast as it was used. Dorothy was beside her, drying, and Little John went back and forth, returning each article to its place on the shelves. They would keep that up all day so that the dishwashing never piled up or tempers frayed because of soiled spoons or knives.

The two Mrs. Dennisons, seated at the kitchen table, were peeling the potatoes Margie had boiled in their jackets the day before. Mrs. Mathers, seated facing them, was peeling onions for the potato salad. Small Fred sat among their feet under the table, out of the way. The wife of the man who had the Ford Agency—Akers, that was their name, Akers—was cutting pickles into the big yellow crockery bowl. The potato salad, evidently, was well under way.

"Jack said they ought to be through by two," Margie announced in answer to her guests' greetings. All the women nodded in unison, and she laughed at them. "You look like machines," she observed.

"I feel like a machine—a potato-peeling machine," Olive Dennison declared. "I've done nothing but peel potatoes all week. Everywhere I go, whoever has the roundup even when it is our own herd, people look at me and say, 'Oh, Olive, you were only married three years ago; you're practically a bride. You mustn't do any of the heavy work. Just sit down here and peel the potatoes.'" She giggled and the others laughed. Nobody would dream of saying so, but the truth was that no one was quite sure how Olive would cope with the other details of a meal for thirty or so people. Before she married, she had always lived in town.

156

"Come and sit down for a minute, Margie," Emma said. "Have a cup of coffee and draw a deep breath. Then you can get going again."

As she sank into the rocker and accepted the mug Dorothy handed her, Margie wondered a little madly how many cups of coffee she had drunk that morning, and whether, if she offered her blood to the Red Cross, pure coffee might not flow into the jar. Then she decided not to worry as long as the coffee still tasted good. When the sight of it began to make her sick, it would be time to stop.

"How many coming out from town, Margie?" Mrs. Dennison inquired.

"Just the family," Margie answered. "I counted eight of them last night."

Emma took her hands out of the dish water and counted drippily on her fingers. "Nine, with your mother," she corrected. "Six of us, and six husbands. Twenty-one. And your three and Mrs. Mathers' three are twenty-seven, and the three younger Dennison boys. Just thirty. We've got plenty of time and plenty of workers. It's easy."

It was easy; the work seemed to run itself. Nobody was straining; nobody was trying to do everything, nobody wanted to do too much at one time. Olive's three young brothers-in-law came over from their garden work at noon and helped Margie set the long trestle tables out under the trees. Mrs. Akers and Mrs. Mathers carried out plates and cups and utensils and paper napkins. The children loaded trays with sugar and cream, salt and pepper, bread and butter. Margie stood by to direct them and to cover the food with paper napkins to keep off the flies.

It was all done and ready at three o'clock, and fifteen minutes later Margie saw the first dust puffing up along the river. The men were coming in. The members of the family who had come out from town had not tried to run things. They had all recognized a well-ordered system when they saw it. Mother and town-living sisters had sat in the living room and entertained the children and whoever else was not working until dinner time.

Margie watched the men unsaddle and turn their horses into the lot to roll and shake and rest. She watched Jack herd all the men downstairs to the shower room, to clean up and get into the fresh clothes their wives had brought for them. She went to the kitchen on a last inspection trip. The roast had been sliced and laid on the platter, ready to serve. The potato salad was piled, yellow and spicy and redolent of onion, in the yellow bowl. Emma was lifting the bean-pot from the oven. The coffee-pot—the big, old, roundup coffeepot—brought in from the chuck wagon, was steaming cloudily on the back of the stove.

Margie poked her head around the corner of the basement door. "Come and get it," she yelled over the last splashing drips of the shower, "or I'll throw it out!"

13. *The Auction*

NEW MEXICO, 1951

MARTHA brought her nephew west with her because he said he wanted to see America. Secretly she suspected that he wanted to see America because he was unable to get passage to Europe that summer.

Whatever Lochinvar's reason for wanting to go into the West, Martha, who was an Easterner by birth but a Southwesterner by conversion and conviction, felt that his desire should be fulfilled. She loaded him into the elderly, respectable, substantial family sedan, equally useful for transporting guests and dogie calves, and drove him purposefully across two-thirds of a continent.

Tom, her husband, had never met this member of her family. Briefly, on her way, Martha dreaded the first encounter of the two men. She was reassured within the first half-hour. No two so completely unlike one another in backgrounds, interests, and achievements could be antagonistic.

In her seventeen years of marriage Martha had come to take the Southwest and the Southwesterner she had married entirely for granted. Here was her chosen world. Her annual trips to the East, to visit the other members of her family or—later—to put her sons in school, had been ventures out of her own world and into another, not unfamiliar but totally different. Now in her nephew's person that other world had penetrated hers. Now for the first time she saw her world through another's eyes.

159

Familiar, accustomed facets of life took on new sharpness; sparkled with new brilliance. Her nephew announced, suddenly, at breakfast, that he would write The Great American Novel, and that it would be about The West and The People Who Lived There. Martha welcomed his decision, not only because the work would keep him busy and happy, but also because it would give her, through his manuscript, an opportunity for continued reappraisal of herself within her surroundings. She was astonished as time went on to observe how quickly and completely she came to see herself and all about her through her nephew's fresh and newly awakened eyes.

Summer was definitely over when Lochinvar came to the high valley, and the talk of summer was folded up and put away. Only one remark he overheard from a late afternoon visitor seemed to have been left over from an earlier season.

"How's your young dude getting along?" this person had asked his host and hostess.

Later Lochinvar referred to the question. He was earnestly searching for a vocabulary of the West and frequently requested definitions of words that were too often used in the household to need defining. "I thought dudes were all on dude ranches," he said tentatively.

"Well, yes, usually they are," Martha answered absently, "but now and then one of them gets off the reservation, as you might say. Dude ranches really *are* like Indian reservations, come to think of it; they're there to protect the dudes. He meant you, of course. But you're safe enough here. Tom and I will protect you!"

Lochinvar was sure that Tom could protect anybody who needed it, although why he himself should need protection escaped him. Tom was a typical Westerner only in his wife's definition, expressed one day in his absence, of being absolutely himself at all times. He did not resemble the Westerner of eastern folklore in any way. He was not a lean and lanky type, physically; there was about his short body and deep chest absolutely no suggestion of Gary Cooper. Tom's somewhat bowlegged, waddling walk did not summon to mind the panther-like grace of Gregory Peck on the prowl. Nor was Tom silent. He talked whenever he had an audience; when he lacked one, he whistled, or hummed to himself, some of the more complicated passages of the music of Johann Sebastian Bach. When he was neither talking nor discoursing what he believed to be sweet strains, Tom was usually to be found near the record-player, listening attentively to the works of his favorite composer.

Much of the time Tom was busy outside the house. He rose before dawn, and long before Lochinvar. Martha and her nephew customarily ate breakfast together, at first in the patio; when the weather grew colder, by the living room fire. At about eleven-thirty Lochinvar, deep in the agonies of his work, would hear the plugging of hoofs along the road and smell the fresh cloud of dust that heralded Tom's return from whatever mysterious work had occupied him. Presumably his labors were connected with cattle. Lochinvar sometimes dimly wondered why it was he never saw any cows around the house—not exactly like dogs, not underfoot, of course, but why were no cows visible when he was told repeatedly that he was living on a ranch?

Tom's return to the house was announced by a rush of water in the shower-stall of the bathroom separating the two bedrooms and then by Tom's voice, shouting incoherencies to Martha. She was, presumably, seated at her writing-desk in the further room. The shouts would die to mumbles, increasingly incoherent, while Tom shaved, his mouth obligingly twisting itself for the razor around misshaped words. Then water would run again —in the washbasin, this time—and smaller splashings would tell that Tom was washing his razor. A whistle, its shrillness just escaping sweetness, would invoke, "Jesu, Joy of Man's Desiring," in a rhythm the late eighteenth and early nineteenth centuries had not quite imagined. Pleasantly beckoning smells would begin to issue from the kitchen, to be followed by Martha's voice, summoning her nephew to lunch.

After lunch Tom withdrew to his office, as he called the flat-topped desk and flanking filing cabinets in a corner of the living room. There he seemed to be endlessly busy with papers and record books during the afternoons. At half-past five he emerged from his office, leaving his revolving chair to swing aimlessly from side to side behind him, and departed to mix cocktails in the kitchen before he joined his wife and guest in the patio or before the fire. His cocktail-mixing left the kitchen strewn with bar-tenders' guides, half-squeezed lemons and limes, trails of spilled sugar, and drippings of bitters. The elaborateness of the preparations was not always justified by the results. Martha once remarked, when her husband had ecstatically withdrawn to mix a second round, that her married life had been one long succession of bar-tenders' mistakes.

It seemed to Lochinvar that Martha and her husband saw little more of each other than they would have if they had lived in a New York suburb, with Tom commuting to a downtown office. Tom's business was Tom's business, and it seemed to affect Martha no more than to produce a certain flexibility about meal hours. For days at a time Lochinvar could set a clock by the man of the house. Then a day would come when Tom's work kept him late at noon, and lunch was delayed or even eaten in his absence. Martha never seemed to worry if her husband did not appear for a meal, not even when he missed dinner as well as lunch and returned to the house late at night.

"He'll eat with the men," she said the first time this occurred during Lochinvar's visit, and on another occasion, "That's all right. He's working with Maclovio, and they'll eat together."

Maclovio appeared and was introduced late one afternoon. He refused a cocktail in favor of a glass of port which he drank formally, standing, in one swallow. Then he sat down, lighted a cigarette, and announced, "I guess is time for roundup."

Tom agreed. "We ought to get the cattle down from the range soon," he added. "It snowed on Truchas last night, and it'll get to the pastures before long."

"I tells the mens," Maclovio said. "Next week all right with you?"

"Fine with me," Tom said. He turned to Martha. "All right with you?" he asked.

"Certainly," Martha answered. "This is Saturday. If you leave Monday, you ought to have them down at the sale pens by Sunday, shouldn't you?"

"Ought to, if everything goes right," Tom said. "Can you call the buyers?"

"Of course," Martha assured him. "Leave me the list, so I won't have to guess, like last time."

"I'm sorry to hand you all the dirty work," Tom remarked, anxiously. "This snow came earlier than I expected . . ."

"That's all right," Martha insisted. "You go ahead, and we'll meet you at the pens for dinner Sunday."

Tom nodded, and Martha turned to her nephew. "This is the busiest time of the fall," she informed him. "The men who raise cattle and live in the Valley don't try to graze them here. They lease grazing land in the mountains from the government and pay for it on a pro-rata basis, so much for each head of stock, because they haven't enough pasture of their own or enough head apiece to make leasing worth while. They work everything on a co-operative basis, although each man owns his own herd and takes his own profits and pays a fee to the group for maintenance of pens and for clerical work.

"When the fall comes, they all work together to move the cattle from the high pastures in the mountains down to the open grazing land along the river for the winter. Halfway down are the selling pens, and the men try to move the cattle so they get there on a week end. Buyers come from Albuquerque and Amarillo and Denver and pick out the cattle they want. Those are left behind for shipping to market, and the others are moved on down to the winter pastures."

"Have the cattle been out on the mountains all this time?" Lochinvar inquired. "I wondered why I didn't see them around. Who stays with them?"

"The men take it turn about, a week at a time," Martha informed him. "Each man stands guard two weeks out of the summer, usually. Tom went up while I was away; he'd just got back when we came home. But they all have to go when roundup time comes because it's a big job and takes every able-bodied man who can turn out."

Maclovio eyed the visitor speculatively. "We don'ts makes you go this year," he commented. "Next year, maybeso . . . ." He chuckled, as did Tom.

"He hasn't been on a horse since he got here," Martha reminded them. "You're not going to do one of your dirty, put-up jobs on him, either. I won't let you. No mustangs, no burrs under saddles, no nothing. Remember."

"Yes, ma'am," Tom said, and Maclovio rose hastily and took his departure before the feminine influence became too strong.

The house seemed strangely quiet on Monday. Tom and Maclovio left long before daylight, a leaving that was accompanied by the smell of bacon and eggs and coffee, the jingling of headstalls, the thud of blanket rolls on the pack saddle, rushes of yellow light through suddenly opened doors. There followed a brisk thudding of hoofs down the road and a rising, penetrating, momentarily all-enveloping scent of dust. They were gone, and for the rest of the day there was no sound of the rushing shower, no shouting from room to room, no whistled Bach. Martha put the B-Minor Concerto on the long-player during dinner, but it was not the same thing, not the same thing at all.

The quiet persisted during the week. Martha deserted her desk for Tom's and worked over the books and letters in his stead. "It's the one chance in the year that I get to really check the breeding records," she said wearily on Thursday evening. "Tom has the only purebred stock in the Valley, and he hopes in time to upgrade the whole community, but it's slow work. It's hard to convince people they can get more money from fewer head if the cattle are better. They're used to thinking that the more steers the more dollars, and they haven't figured out the difference yet. They're conservative."

Lochinvar nodded as gravely as if she had spoken comprehensibly. He refrained from asking questions; he decided to work this series of definitions out for himself.

On Friday, Martha set the books and records aside and began to cook. She produced an enormous roast from the freezer and mixed a baking of bread. She constructed pies—apple pies, with thick, durable crusts. "Tom gets so tired of bacon and beans," she remarked, sprinkling the pies with cinnamon. "He pretends he loves them because they're traditional he-man food, but a week of them upsets his stomach for a month. I can't take something for him without taking enough to go round. It wouldn't be polite."

She was up on Sunday before the sky was even tinted with dawn, and breakfast was on the table at what Lochinvar had previously considered an impossibly early hour for rising.

"I want to get out there good and early and see the cattle come in," Martha said. "I haven't seen them all summer, and I'd like to find out what shape they're in." Her blue jeans and lighter blue sweater fairly blurred as she raced around the kitchen, drinking coffee, washing dishes, wrapping food in foil, and directing Lochinvar's activities in a simultaneous whirl of movements.

"Bring your camera and notebook," she commanded as he finished his meal. "This is research on the hoof. You could spend years in the West, and unless you knew someone who could take you to one of these roundups you wouldn't even know they went on. This is tradition, boy. This is where you see the thing really happening."

The road they followed when they left the ranch house crossed the highway at right angles and led off into the mountains. The air was crisp, blue-stained, and perfumed with piñon smoke from the chimneys of adobe houses; the Valley was ringed by a rim of white-crested mountains surmounted by piled white clouds. Dust trailed behind them, close to the ground and almost parallel to its surface. More dust rose above the road ahead of them, where it had been stirred up by earlier cars. Martha sneezed, and drew her neckerchief up to cover her mouth and nose. Presently Lochinvar pulled his own handkerchief out of his pocket and imitated her. Within this shelter he found that he could breathe more easily.

The road was uphill, seeming to climb at only a slight angle until he looked back and saw how steep the slope actually was. Then Martha swung the car on to a side road, and for the first time Lochinvar understood why light station wagons were un-

suited for southwestern travel. This surface needed a solid car
—the kind of substantial sedan Martha and her neighbors drove.
This road was not merely rough; it was active, viciously trying
to tear the tires off the wheels and the wheels off the axles. It
was full of chuck holes into which the sedan thudded and from
which it leapt. Martha clung to the wheel and Lochinvar clung
to anything he could reach.

"This is a secondary road," Martha panted once. "It says so
on the map."

"In fine print," Lochinvar muttered and was silent again,
hoping that if he kept his mouth shut, his teeth could not be
knocked out of his head.

Suddenly they reached the crest of a rise, and another valley
spread below them. This was oval in shape, like the valley from
which they had come, and mountains framed three of its curves.
On the fourth side—the west—the frame was a fringe of chrome-
yellow trees, growing so thickly they threatened to choke one
another. "The Río Grande," said Martha, in response to Lochinvar's lifted eyebrows. "Cottonwoods grow all along it."

In the center of the valley were the selling pens—a series of
squares, divided from one another and set off from the curving
land around them by posts and barbed wire and by boards set
on end in the ground and held together by horizonal planks. A
cluster of cars edged a clump of piñons, off at one corner of the
pens. Tied along the fence rails on the south side of the square
a bunch of horses drooped on three legs apiece. Never had Lochinvar seen horses look smaller or less interested in their surroundings. Away to the northwest, parallel to the river, dust rose and
devoured the cottonwoods like smoke from a forest fire. Slowly,
with great deliberation, the cloud rolled towards them.

"They're coming!" Martha exclaimed. "We beat them!"

She hurled the car into a miraculously small space between
a huge red truck and a souped-up Ford roadster and sprang to
the ground, leaving her keys swinging from the ignition switch.

"Aren't you going to lock the car?" Lochinvar asked in horror.

"Why?" Martha demanded over her shoulder. "We know
everybody." She ran to the corral fence and somehow scrambled

166

up it, using as rungs the cross-strips that connected the uprights. More slowly, and much more awkwardly, Lochinvar followed.

Except for the discomfort involved in sitting on the thin edge of a one-by-twelve-inch board, the top of the fence was a fine grandstand. The series of pens was neatly arranged before their eyes. They overlooked the tied horses and the clump of trees, where Lochinvar could now see people moving around what were evidently cooking fires. The smoky dust was nearer, now, and he could sense movement behind it, steady, forward movement as of a mass of bodies. Beside the forward press there was a flickering, broken movement like that of sharks swimming beside a school of whales. Then a rider broke through the dust for a second, and Martha cried, "There he is! There's Tom!"

"Where?" Lochinvar exclaimed. A moment before he had mentally rebuked his aunt for raising her voice; now he was shouting himself. Somewhere in the movement towards and beneath them was communicable excitement. Now he could hear other men shouting, too; hoarse cries, short from dust and weariness, that guided and never checked the flow of the herd towards the pens. He tried to find Tom in the turmoil, and was unable to identify anyone.

Now one man rode ahead of the others and reached from his saddle to open a corral gate. "Maclovio always does that," Martha said. "He's president of the stock growers' co-operative, and he won't let anybody else take the risk." Maclovio's horse backed, the rider swinging the gate steadily open, and the heads of the first cattle appeared in the gap. The beasts hesitated, then, with a rush, urged by the men and the pressure of the animals behind them, they entered the corral. They stood in its center, tossing their hornless heads, looking about them with more curiosity than alarm, and snorting.

"Those are ours," Martha exclaimed happily. "Aren't they beauties? Look at the bloom on them!"

An indefinite number of creatures had followed the first cluster. They all looked exactly alike to Lochinvar, as did the dust-coated men who entered the corral behind them. One rider circled the herd and pulled his horse to a stop before Martha.

"Give me some tailor-mades," he croaked in a semblance of Tom's voice. "I've had nothing but Durham to smoke for the last three days."

Martha tossed him a pack from her pocket, and he caught them handily, saluting her with an upraised arm in the same gesture.

"See you at dinner," he said, and then, as he turned away, "They came through all right, didn't they?"

Now the movement in the pens became purposeful. Gates were opened and closed; selected groups of cattle were driven through them and separated from the main herd. The horses seemed to move without commands, always taking the men where they wanted to go. No one gave orders, and the occasional shouts seemed to do no more than guide the stock. Presently even Lochinvar could see that the cattle were roughly graded according to size. The biggest beasts—three of them—were in a small pen by themselves. Cows with calves were in another. The intermediate sizes were again subdivided, on what basis he was not always sure. An inner emptiness spread through Lochinvar as he watched and the board on which he perched cut into his rump, but still he sat fixed and absorbed, with the sun on his head and the wind cold against him, until the work was done.

"Dinner time," Martha said finally. The men were leaving the pens and tying their horses to the fence away from the first bunch. Lochinvar and Martha descended stiffly from their grandstand and limped side by side to the car. There Martha gathered up the food she had brought, and they joined the groups around the fires among the piñons.

Now there was time to notice that many cars had driven up and been packed tightly in the parking area. Boards on trestles had been set up to serve as tables, and fifty-pound lard cans were being lifted from the fires and carried, each by two men, to one end of the table. All the work was done by the men, and the women and children, whom Lochinvar had not noticed until that moment, armed themselves with paper cups and plates and formed a line to be served. Martha's packages were distributed along the board, the wrappings turned back so the men could help themselves. The spectators contented themselves with the stew and beans that filled the lard cans.

Everyone ate sitting on the ground. Tom joined his family and they were surrounded by other family clusters, each intent on supplying the needs of the man who was the center of attention. There was little time for conversation. Now and then Tom or Martha glanced at a group of men who sat a little apart from the others, solemnly consuming their coffee, stew, and beans. These men were dressed with a certain elegance; the fawn-colored whipcord suits that clothed them were unmarred by the dust of the roundup.

"Those are the buyers," Martha said, interpreting Lochinvar's gaze in that direction. "The sale starts as soon as everyone gets through eating."

"Why doesn't anybody go over and speak to them?" Lochinvar demanded. "They must be pretty important. I should think people would want to get acquainted with them."

"It's not polite," Martha replied. "Naturally, everybody knows them, but they won't talk till after the sale's over. Otherwise it might look as if they were trying to influence them—make a sale."

"But isn't that what they're here for?" Lochinvar queried.

"Oh, yes, but it isn't ethical to pressure them." Tom grinned and rose. "I've got to get back to the pens," he announced. "I'll go home with you, if our stuff and Maclovio's sells. I've been standing night guard, so I can get away if we're cleaned up."

"Oh, good," Martha said. Neither put into words any thoughts they might have about the silence and emptiness of the house in the Valley. That, too, would be impolite, Lochinvar perceived.

There was a general loose-jointed cleaning up going on around them. Everything that would burn was dumped into the fires; everything else was fed to half-wild dogs that had appeared from nowhere to scavenge the camp. The men drifted across to their horses, tightened girths, checked headstalls, untied lines, lighted cigarettes, and finally mounted. The large red truck was driven clear of the crowd and stationed by the gate of the first corral. Some of the buyers climbed to the roof of its cab;

others went on foot into the pens. Nowhere in sight was there a man without boots and a wide-brimmed hat, and Lochinvar blushed for his low-heeled shoes and bare head. Martha scrambled back to the top of the fence. Lochinvar lamely but gamely followed her. For a moment a question crossed his mind: What would he do on the morrow? He was sure he would be equally unable to stand, sit, or lie down. However, the life of the moment gripped him immediately, so he forgot his nascent aches and pains.

Below him was a herd of medium-sized cattle and around the edge of their pen a fringe of men. Maclovio stood before the corral gate, his eyes fastened on a yardstick in his hand. "International Harvester Company," Lochinvar read on its ferule. Maclovio raised the stick and pointed it at the cattle. A buyer raised *his* stick—courtesy John Deere Company—and also pointed. He called a figure. Maclovio repeated it, politely, questioningly. Someone else called a higher figure, and again Maclovio repeated it. Again the figure was raised.

"Oh!" exclaimed Lochinvar, light dawning. "It's an auction."

Martha solemnly turned to look at him. "Yes," she agreed, "it's an auction—just like Parke-Bernet's. And those," she crooned lovingly, "are our little Rembrandts."

"They're nice cows," Lochinvar assented, and Martha glanced at him in some surprise, but said nothing.

The figure that won was two-twenty, and Martha seemed extraordinarily pleased. Two-twenty, she explained in answer to her nephew's plea for information, did *not* mean $2.20, but $220. And it was paid for each *calf*—she somewhat stressed the word—and not for the whole penful. "All those nice little beefsteaks running around," she murmured. "It's a shameful price if you have to buy meat, but my, doesn't it look nice on a check?"

Two-twenty, it was presently apparent, was the highest price of the afternoon. No other penful brought so much, although some came close to it.

"That's because we've got purebreds," Martha stated as casually as though it were a complete explanation. "They fatten up quickly when they get to the feed lots, and it doesn't take so long to get them ready for slaughter. That's why the buyers can afford to pay more for them than for grade stock. They have to spend more money feeding and fattening the others."

"That's why it pays to have purebreds, then," Lochinvar observed, and his aunt smiled at him and said, "Go to the head of the class."

The afternoon wore on in a play of blue and gold, always misted by the tan foam of the dust. Maclovio turned over his duties as auctioneer to the vice-president of the co-operative, and he and Tom came and stood in the crowd that pressed close around the edges of the pen. Dark clouds gathered over the horizon to the north, and once Tom glanced backwards and upwards and observed, "Glad I'll have a bed instead of a sleeping-bag tonight."

The last lot of stock to be driven into the sale pen was composed of the three huge beasts that had been penned by themselves all day. The final price for them, after much coaxing from the auctioneer, was two-seventy-five. Lochinvar was horrified.

"Why, they're terrific! They're several times as big as those that brought two-twenty," he protested. "I'll bet you could slaughter them right now, without feeding them at all."

"You could," Martha agreed. "They'll probably do just that, as soon as they get them to the yards at Albuquerque."

"For steak?"

"Oh, no," Martha said. "For boloney. Those are old bulls, you see, and they're worn out and tough."

"What are those others, then?"

"Yearling steers," Martha's surprise showed in her voice.

"But what's the difference," Lochinvar persisted, and his voice rose high and clearly audible in the hush that had fallen over the crowd as the bulls were driven away, "they're all cows, aren't they?"

Martha sat riveted to the top of the fence, and the blush that spread itself over her face and neck seemed to rise from her toes. She looked frantically around her. "Tom," she quavered, "Maclovio———" The men's backs were turned, and they were moving, shaken, away from her. "You come back here!" Martha shrieked in desperation. But the men continued on their way. The crowd was drawing back on every hand; Martha and Lochinvar sat exposed and shivering and lone on top of the high board fence.

"What *is* the matter?" Lochinvar inquired.

"Look," Martha said, "men in the cow country are polite. They just don't talk about such things with ladies—or before ladies. And the most prudishly polite of all are the Spanish Americans. You just said a dreadful thing."

"But what thing? What are you talking about?"

"Look," Martha began again. She searched her recollection of the world to the east and its vocabulary. To Lochinvar's strained eyes it seemed that she visibly searched. "Look. You know what a eunuch is? A castrated male?"

"In the Chinese Empress' court?" asked Lochinvar, "Oh, yes."

"Well," said Martha carefully, "a steer is a eunuch. And a bull—a bull—a bull—well, a bull *isn't*. A cow is a mama and a bull is a papa. And you mustn't—NOT EVER—mix them up. You can talk about cows and bulls and steers, as long as you call them by those names, but you mustn't talk about the differences or how the critters got that way. Why do you think I have to wait till Tom leaves home to check the breeding records? After seventeen years of married life and with two boys old enough to leave home to go to school, he'd still be embarrassed to discuss such matters with me."

"Oh," said Lochinvar. Then he said, slowly, "I guess, if I have any other questions, I'd better take them up with Tom or Maclovio."

"Yes," said Martha, "that's what you'd better do."

She slid down from the fence, and Lochinvar followed her, stiffly, deliberately, but less painfully than he had feared. They walked without words to the car. Tom and Maclovio leaned against its front fenders, smoking tailor-mades, their faces alike in their complete lack of expression.

"Ready to go home?" Tom asked Martha.

"I'd like to wait a minute," Martha answered.

"To say good-bye?" He put his arm around her and pulled her up against him. Maclovio politely looked away from this demonstration of affection. "So would I."

And so they waited in the thickening dusk. Little spurts of rain fell around them from the black clouds over their heads, and the dust began to settle as if it, too, were tired. There was the sound of a motor churning. The big red truck lurched past them, crowded to the tail-gate with two layers of bawling calves.

"There they go," said Tom, his voice hoarser than ever, and he blew his nose resoundingly. Martha was crying openly.

"There they go," she repeated. "Oh, Tom, let's don't raise any more. I can't stand to see them go."

"That seeley," Maclovio remarked. "Eees good money you get there for good stocks. Next year you see, you raise 'em and they be better than this year."

"Oh, I know it," said Tom, getting into the car and jabbing at the starter with his boot heel. "I'll keep on upgrading till I go under the sod. But all the same, I always hate to see them go."

14. *This Is the Way We Wash Our Clothes*

MONTANA, 1951

W HEN Old John Larsen moved into town, he remarked that the best Christmas present a man could give his wife was an electric washing machine. Then she could not only spare her back from bending over the tubs; she could support him if she had to. Marian remarked that many a true word was spoken in jest, and most of the family forgot all about it.

Not so Margie. She had a feeling—inherited or learned from her mother—for the meaning of words and their nuances. She had liked puns ever since she was a small child; in fact, her first was produced at an age when she was so young everyone but Marian thought it was an accident. So her father's remark about the washing machine stuck in her mind.

Wash day was a tough time on the JL at best. The house had no laundry, so washing took place in the kitchen in bad weather and out in the yard in good. Margie could dry clothes on the back-yard line in summer, but as long as there was frost she dared not hang things out; the cold froze the water in the wet garments in the winter, and the wind was often strong enough to snap them from the line after they were stiff. Jack remarked that the old negro woman who had washed for his mother always said that freezing bleached the white things out and was better for them than any chemical you could buy, but that remark did not comfort Margie when she mourned for a dozen sheets that had been what her husband called, "broke plumb in two in the middle." Drying in the basement gave her a clammy-damp, depressing atmosphere throughout the house. No, wash day was not pleasant even with an electric washer.

So on the Monday when Jack came in for breakfast and announced that the well was low and washing would have to be delayed a few days, Margie did not feel particularly saddened at first. In fact, she felt about the way the children did when she gave them a holiday from their lessons the year she kept them all at home and taught them herself.

"Why is the water low, Daddy?" Little Jack demanded. He was at the age when he not only asked specific questions, he wanted them answered in a definite, informative way. His father encouraged him. The only way to become a rancher was to ask questions, Big Jack declared. Nobody was going to take time to stop and deliver a lecture on any subject for your especial benefit unless you asked for it.

"The water is low, my son," Jack said now as he sugared his oatmeal, "because there is a drought on the runoff. And there is a drought on the runoff because last year the cattle didn't graze on the mountain and in the fall there was a fire, and all the grass and timber that should have held the water back was burned off. SO we had flash floods down here in the bottoms this spring. *Therefore* we have a drought now. *Hence* your mother can't do her washing for Goodness only knows how long."

"Why did the cattle not grazing make a fire?"

"Margie," said Jack, "there's no getting around it; this boy's going to be a scientist, not a rancher. He never leaves off worrying the one main point."

"He comes by it honestly," Margie said. They rarely mentioned Jack's M.A. in biology, or hers in human geography any more. Time had been when the attainment of degrees was the most important thing in the world to both of them, an end in itself. Now the framed diplomas lay wrapped in an old quilt on the closet shelf. Margie hesitated to hang them, for few people knew what they were, and explanations took too much time.

"*Why* did the cattle not grazing make a fire, Daddy?"

Jack set aside his oatmeal bowl and devoted himself to the education of his son. It might delay his start on the day's work, but it came first, ahead of any other interests. He and Margie had decided on that policy as soon as they knew for sure that Dorothy was on the way.

"Listen, Jack," he began. "You've got to know about this sometime. You might as well start young. Ranch life is a pretty good life, as you've probably noticed already."

"Sure, Dad."

"Well, son, nobody ever gets anything for free. No matter how good it is, there's always a string tied to it somewhere. Like ranch life. We get all kinds of wonderful things, but along with them we get the U. S. Forest Service, and that's the fly in the ointment and the sting in its tail."

"What's wrong with the U. S. Forest Service? Our school geography book says it does wonderful things—it preserves old ruins and keeps people from getting lost and cutting down trees and prevents overgrazing—oh, gee, Dad, all sorts of things."

"I often wonder," Jack said with notable restraint, "who writes the schoolbooks. I'd like to take him around the place with me and show him a thing or six."

"But *why* . . ."

Jack was rapidly becoming so angry he was incoherent. Margie took over. After all, she was the school teacher. If anyone were going to correct the schoolbook, she had better be the one. She hoped she remembered exactly what it said, and that she could deal with the matter impersonally—unemotionally.

"It's this way," she began. "When the cattle are grazing in the National Forest there are bound to be men with them to watch them, aren't there? And when the men are there, naturally, they watch out for fires all the time. They have to. It wouldn't be safe for them or the cattle, if they weren't very careful."

"Sure," said her son.

"And when the cattle are there they go through the brush,

176

and they make paths and break and trample down the dead stuff. So it gets packed and hardened, and finally broken to dust and blown away. That makes it harder for a fire to get started. Even if one does start, there are the cattle trails already there for the men who fight the fires to follow. You can always get a horse through on a cow trail, and usually you can take a jeep over one, because cattle will pick the easiest, openest walking. So fighting the fire isn't difficult. Do you understand?"

"Yes."

"But three years ago the Forest Service closed off part of the forest and forbade any more grazing there. So the trails weren't used, and a lot of brush and young stuff grew up in them. And rocks rolled down from above———"

"*Were* rolled down———" her husband corrected her.

"——— were rolled down, and the trail was hard to get through on a horse and impossible with a jeep. Then, when that big thunderstorm came along last August and lightning struck in the brush and loose stuff, a fire got started. And because the fire-fighters had to cut their way through and roll rocks out of the way and even blast them to get through in some places, the fire got out of hand and burned a big patch of timber and grass on the runoff. *That's* why we had flash floods in the spring and why we're low on water now. Do you understand?"

"I guess so," Little Jack said soberly. "It's pretty bad, isn't it, Mother?"

"It may get worse before it gets better, too," his father observed, rising.

"Mother," Dorothy inquired, returning the conversation to its starting point, "what are we going to do about the laundry?"

"Well," said Margie, "it's all gathered together and sorted and ready to go in the tubs. I guess the best thing will be for you and me to load it in the car and take it into town. We'll stay overnight at Grandma's, and I'll do the washing at the Laundromat and the ironing after we get back home."

"Why don't you put the sheets and towels and things through the mangle?" Jack asked, his hand on the doorknob. "It won't take you much longer, and it'll mean that much done when you get back. Jack, son, do you want to go into town with Mother, or stay here and work? You're getting man's wages, remember."

"I'll stay here," Little Jack decided. "I'm taking my pay in calves like you said, remember yourself? I'll stick with my herd."

"What can I do?" Fred piped up.

"Another county heard from! What do you want to do, old man? Go with Mother and Sister, or stay here with the other men of the family?"

"Stay here!"

"I think you'd better go with us in case we need a man," Margie suggested. "After all, if Daddy and Jack are both here, they can look after the place."

Fred considered gravely, while a stream of egg yolk coursed down his chin. "All right," he said at last, "I guess I go and take care of the girls, Daddy."

"You do that," his father advised him. "Ready, Jack? Let's get started. Uncle Fred brought the sprayer over last night. Think you can work the underline while I take the back spray?"

It was all rather like the old nursery rhyme, Margie considered as she gathered pajamas for the two children and herself and stowed them in a suitcase. "The rat began to gnaw the rope, The rope began to hang the butcher, The butcher began to kill the ox, The ox began to drink the water, The water began to quench the fire, The fire began to burn the stick . . . ." She stopped herself there with a shiver. It was time. Not for anything in the world would Margie have admitted aloud the fear of fire that was always with her. It was difficult enough to admit the panic to herself. The fear had always been there since she was less than Fred's age. The night the old ranch house burned had set and hardened her terror until it became something to haunt her, to wake her at night from blazing dreams and make her, trembling, clutch at Jack.

Of course they were safe enough from a forest fire down here on the flats. The nearest they ever came to the potential hazard was the belt of National Forest they drove through when they went over the crest on their way in and out of town. And that belt was so narrow—only three miles wide—that it was nothing to worry about. The loss of water on their own place was much more serious. Undoubtedly they were in for a series of flash floods in the spring seasons, and all the dirt and isolation floods entailed. The only way to get from the ranch house to the road was across the plank bridge above the creek, and if the bridge went out every spring—as it probably would—they might save themselves time and trouble by moving the family and its goods and chattels across to the other side of the stream and building there.

At the worst it would probably mean only a series of inconveniences, like this business of taking the laundry into town. And that was a pleasant inconvenience if you looked at it in the proper, Pollyannaish way. It was fun to have a visit with her mother and sister, fun to take Dorothy and Fred on a little trip, fun to get out of drying problems. It might be worth while to plan such a trip every other week for the rest of the year—or for as long as the ranch road was open for the car. If she taught school again that winter, she might even consider sending some of the washing in by Jack to the steam laundry. Mrs. Dennison always did that—always had done it. Of course, it meant outfitting everyone in the family twice, so that they had clothes to wear while others were being washed . . . . She abandoned the idea, although she was charmed by it. At the rate Jack and Dorothy were growing, they wouldn't need clean clothes, they would need new ones, by the time the washing got home. And it was all she and Jack could do to keep them clad now.

With the laundry in the turtle-back of the sedan and the children beside her, she drove by the spraying chute to say good-bye. Little Jack was operating the underline most efficiently, timing its upward jet to coincide with the mist his father directed at the backs of the beasts. These were yearlings and particularly susceptible to blow-flies. They were also skittish and skeptical about the benefits of spraying.

"Have a good time," Jack said, waving the spray at her, and she turned the car and headed it towards the road, feeling cheerful and even a little gay. It was a lovely, clear morning—no novelty, for there had been six weeks of them—but still a pleasure. The late summer storms were almost due, but they would probably hold off for another week or ten days. The car motor hummed most agreeably, taking them all forward; the mud tires Jack hadn't got around to taking off in the spring hummed on the gravel beneath them, and Dorothy hummed beside her. Margie puzzled a little over the tune, and then identified it. "Three Little Words." They had heard it on the radio the night before. That was turning back the clock! She and Jack had circled to that at college dances the year before they were married.

The heat seemed to grow as they went along, and in town it was intense. That was strange; this wasn't a city with tall buildings to cut off the breeze. The most anyone could say was that it was a small, pleasant town. But that night seemed stifling, as if the trees that grew along the streets were a roof to hold the heat down against the bodies of the town dwellers. Back at the ranch, Margie knew, the curtains were standing straight out into the rooms, free of the window frames in the breeze. But here in town the night was breathless. Dawn brought no relief; waking fully, she still found herself unable to cast aside the blanket of still, dense heat that had weighed upon her all night long.

"This is a weather-breeder," her mother said at breakfast.

Margie laughed and quoted a saying that is local everywhere in the West, "Only a tenderfoot or a damned fool will prophesy weather."

"I've lived here longer than you have, young lady," Marian reminded her, "and I'm not scared that anybody will call me any kind of a fool. This is a weather-breeder. You'd better plan on getting an early start back."

There was a kind of uneasiness in the atmosphere. It was something that made Margie restless. Much as she enjoyed her mother's company, she found she was in no mood to linger. As fast as she could, she piled her laundry and her overnight bag in the car, with the extra supply of fresh vegetables in the portable icebox—the spring garden had gone downstream with the bridge that year—and she and the children started for home. The air, put in motion by the sedan's movement, seemed cooler as soon as they were out of town. The sun still shone intensely, but the sky on the western horizon was a cold steel blue, and the color was edging slowly towards the north.

"Now I feel at home again," Dorothy said suddenly, when they were ten miles out of town.

"What makes you feel that way?" Margie asked, as much amused as puzzled.

"You see that little butte over there? And you see those little trails going around it like a corkscrew? Well I know those are cow trails going up around the hill, like the spiral staircase in the Little Colonel books, and they always make me feel good, like going home."

Margie smiled. "I always felt the same way, honey, when I came home from college. Only they were game trails as often as they were cow trails, then. Animals are naturally smart. It took farmers in this country years and years to learn how to terrace land and get the most out of what they had on a slope. If they'd watched the animals, they'd have learned about soil conservation a whole lot sooner."

"Are there fewer wild animals now than there used to be, Mother? You said the terraces used to be game trails."

"There are more game animals now than there were when I was your age," Margie said, slowly. "They live differently now. Back when I was growing up, things were more—more natural, I guess. In those days there were still some timber wolves around here, and there were a lot of coyotes and eagles and big hawks. There were even some wildcats. Nobody had got around to offering bounties for natural predators then. After a few years men began to kill off the coyotes and the other predatory animals. The idea was to protect the cattle and sheep at first. Later, a lot of people said it was to protect the wild grazing animals: the deer and antelope and elk. It didn't work out that way, though. The grazing animals increased until they ate all their own food and began taking the pastures away from the cattle and sheep. Believe me, the stock suffered more from the gentle little deer than they ever had from the coyotes. And then sick animals that would have been killed in the course of nature before they could spread their diseases lived on and on and infested whole areas, so that not only the deer but the sheep had to move out or die. Then there had to be open seasons for hunting, to get rid of the surplus game, and that meant a lot of shooting accidents when dudes came out to go hunting. Not only men were killed. A lot of stock was wiped out." She paused to draw breath.

"Mother," observed Dorothy, "you know as much about these things as Daddy."

"Mother's mad," Fred commented, looking at the flush on Margie's cheek.

"I love this country," said Margie, staring through the windshield—what *was* that across the road ahead of them?—"and I've studied about it. And the two things go together to make me get excited—not mad, Fred boy—about anything that hurts it. Erosion gets me worked up. But there was natural erosion long before there were cattle here, so I only got really mad when people say the cattle caused all the erosion."

She slapped her foot on the brake pedal, and the car jarred to a stop. A young man in a trim Lincoln-green uniform stood beside the black-and-white-striped barrier that closed the road ahead of them. He was completely impassive as he stood looking at Margie and the children in the car.

"Sorry, ma'am," he said to her unasked question. "Road's closed."

"Is there a fire?"

"Not here, no, ma'am."

"Then, why———"

"We've had word of one higher up the mountains, spreading downhill and coming this way. It started in the old forty-mile pasture on Baldy———"

"But that's twenty-five miles away! This strip is only three miles wide! I can get through it in fifteen minutes if I crawl."

"Sorry, ma'am. Forest Supervisor says no one across the fire lines. There's a thunderstorm announced as coming this way and the air's full of static electricity. No telling what might set it off."

"But my husband and elder son are at the ranch, expecting me home! I haven't any way to get word to them. They'll be frightfully worried about the younger children and me. I'm sure we can get through without trouble———"

The young man left the barrier and advanced to the side of the car. He leaned his arm on the window sill and looked down at Margie. His eyes were the precise shade of the thunder-colored sky and as unrelenting.

"Lady," he said, "I don't care if you and your husband have to wait and worry for a week. The Forest Supervisor says you aren't going in there, and you—aren't—going—in. They've got every able-bodied man they can find on the job already, clearing trails and brush, and it's no place for a woman. I wouldn't let my own sister in there." Wildly, for a moment, Margie wondered what he *was* capable of letting his sister do. "Now, you turn the car around and head back for town, or I'll have a state officer out looking for you when you do go. Go on."

This was fascism, Margie thought, as she wrestled the car around in the width of the road. It was not democracy; it had nothing to do with democracy. Every able-bodied man could mean Little Jack as likely as not—she had heard of twelve-year-old Boy Scouts being taken along to cook for the men on fire crews, and he was almost eleven. It almost certainly would mean Big Jack—she should have kept her mouth shut about their being in there. She could have cried with frustration and anger. If she had been a man, she almost certainly would have sworn steadily all the way back to town.

Her mother did the best she could to comfort her. "Fire's an awful thing, dear," Marian said, looking off towards the mountains. "Is that a cloud there to the south, or is it smoke? You know yourself how dreadful it can be. You wouldn't want another fire up there in the forty-mile pasture, would you?"

"I don't want fires anywhere," Margie said furiously. "But I don't see why they had to close the trails last year. If they'd left the cattle trails open, they could have got a jeep crew up there right away, before the fire really got a start."

"Go on in the kitchen and start your ironing, Margie," her mother said. "You can work it out on that."

Margie ironed. Then she baked. Then she went down to the creamery and bought cream and churned and worked out sweet cream butter. She went to the grocery and bought two lugs of plums and made jam. She put in the week as well as she could; when all else failed, she took her mother and the children to the drive-in movie. She felt that she was a long way ahead on both the winter's work and its arrears of entertainment when the news broadcast brought the word that the road over the crest was open again.

Nothing much was changed on the drive back. The thunderstorm had come and gone, and the air was neither hotter nor cooler than it had been before the clouds began to gather. The gashes in the earth beside the road were possibly slashed a shade deeper than before—after all, the runoff from half a mile of road was about equal to that from a sloping section of pasture land —but the change hardly showed.

The three-mile stretch of forest on the crest was exactly as it had been when Margie saw it last, except that the barricade and its guardian were gone. There was no trace of smoke in the air, nothing to show that there had been a fire within twenty-five miles. And experience had taught Margie that you usually knew it if there were a fire fifty miles away.

She asked Jack about the fire that night, after the children were in bed. No use scaring them, or trying to explain everything to them.

"Well, there was a fire," Jack said reflectively. "Lightning struck that patch of standing pine on the south slope of Baldy, and the fire got started up there. The Dennisons and I took the community bulldozer up as soon as we heard about it. The Forest Service didn't have one within a hundred miles—the nearest was in Sheridan. We broke through that second-growth stuff without any trouble, and got to the blaze in a couple of hours.

Then we piled dirt around it—it was still small, most of the growth up there is green—and after we had it banked, the jeep crew that had trailed us went in and put it out. The whole thing was over as soon as it got started, matter of fact."

"I knew you'd be in it," Margie observed. She shivered. "Jack, where was little Jack? You didn't take him with you, did you?"

"Hell, no," said Little Jack's father. "I left the kid at home. Somebody had to be here to look after the place and the stock."

15. *The Shopping Trip*

MISS Annabelle Wilson sat with the letter open before her on the desk, and gravely and systematically considered its contents.

"In consideration of your interest and activities in the work of improving farm life and developing rural communities," the letter began, and continued in a spate of polysyllables. Boiled down and rephrased into something resembling spoken English, what it all meant was that Annabelle Wilson had been awarded a trip abroad because she was a leading ranch woman and a rural sociologist.

During her years at the State College and her later years in Washington, Annabelle Wilson had been aware of the fact that there were people even in her world who regarded trips to Europe in about the same light that she regarded her own dashes to and from Austin. They spoke of "Popping over to Norway to study Conditions," and they solemnly assured each other that the only satisfactory method of transatlantic travel was by air—you *lost* so much time if you went by boat. They were generally the kind of people who made you wonder what they could possibly do with the time they *found* by flying.

But Annabelle had never considered Europe as a possibility for herself. Certainly it never appeared to her to be the necessity it seemed to these others. Her business was ranch life in the southwestern United States. The southwestern United States was an area wide in geography and complicated in problems, and Annabelle devoted herself to southwestern complexities with no feeling that she lost anything by not encountering at first hand the bewilderments of the rural Swiss. If she could persuade her mind to run parallel to the mentalities of rural Spanish Americans, she felt that she was doing well indeed.

Perhaps Switzerland and Norway—even possibly England or France or Italy—might have had a bearing on her work while she was working. Now she had retired; first to nurse her mother through six years of illness that exhausted her own strength, then to take over the operation of the ranch by herself after her mother died. A trip abroad, with all expenses paid, presented itself now in the light of a totally unnecessary luxury. Annabelle tapped her fingers on the desk. That was the way to take it. She had done her work sufficiently well during her working years. Now that she was independent, she could afford to allow herself a few frills and frivolities. Very well. This voyage—she was fond of slightly formal language—should be one of them.

Also, she reflected, it might be useful in connection with the 4-H girls. She had always enjoyed having a hobby; hooking rugs in her Washington apartment and knitting argyle socks on trains in her traveling years. Here at home the 4-H girls were in the same category. They came dutifully to the house every Thursday afternoon at four, and from four to six Annabelle revealed to them the mysteries of canning or cooking or cleaning— of almost anything domestic but dressmaking.

At six o'clock they all ate a pot-luck supper in the kitchen or by the barbecue pit on the lawn—depending on the weather. When the dishes were disposed of, she rigidly played the upright piano for half an hour, and they all sang 4-H songs and selections from the book of *Old Favorites*. At eight the girls went home and Annabelle went to bed with a sick headache. Nobody enjoyed the encounters particularly. But 4-H was Annabelle's duty —aside from its value as a hobby—and she did it. She was uneasily certain that the girls' mothers explained to them weekly that it was a great opportunity and privilege for them to do their 4-H work under An Expert.

The only phase of 4-H work on which they all held back was clothing. Annabelle was uncomfortably aware of the fact that the girls regarded her severely tailored suits and blouses as "hopeless." She knew that to them she must look old-fashioned. For her part, she had no taste for sweaters knitted of neon yarns or for thigh-confining skirts slit halfway up the calf. She thought such garments hideous, however fashionable they might be, and only by grim force restrained herself from saying so.

Well, she pondered as she deliberated over the itinerary, both she and the girls might feel differently about clothes after this trip! Four days in Paris, two in London, four in Rome—she remembered a recent issue of *Life* Magazine which had contained a feature article on the eminence of Rome as a dressmaking center and how the girls had gazed and twittered over the illustrations. She would have to look—dutifully—at foreign clothes, or the girls would never forgive her. Meantime, she ought to consider her packing.

Her next idea was a corollary of the one that had preceded it. Why pack? She was going to the clothes centers of the world—*Life* said so and offered convincing evidence to prove its point. She hadn't really been shopping or near an urban shopping center in the years since she returned to the ranch. Why not take with her the absolute necessities of travel and wait until she got abroad to buy her wardrobe? It would be fun to go on a real shopping spree and doubly fun to do it in a place where she had never been before. And if she were to travel with a group of women, she could probably get someone to go with her and help her choose. The letter said a group.

The question of shopping in a foreign language did not dismay Annabelle. You could always get an interpreter from somewhere. Her experiences in rural Texas and New Mexico had demonstrated that. As for money—what if she were cheated occasionally? All Americans who went to Europe expected to be exploited. The last calf crop had sold at what seemed to her an immorally high price, and Europe needed dollars for recovery. She would simply regard the whole business as a contribution to international good will and let it go at that.

Annabelle flew to New York at the end of a month, stopping overnight in Washington on her way. It was pleasant to see again some of the people she had worked with in the office, pleasant to drive from the National Airport around the Tidal Basin under blossoming cherry trees that residents of the Capital had decided to refer to diplomatically as "imported," pleasant to sit in the ample, dignified dining room of the Grace Dodge Hotel and be offered hot rolls by a white-gloved Negro waiter. Remembering how she solemnly cautioned the 4-H girls against the dangers to digestion of hot bread, Annabelle sighed luxuriously and accepted a second piece of Sally Lunn.

New York the next day was fun, too; even the smell of sewer gas and manure, incongruously mingled, that scented the streets forever was fun. Annabelle took a taxi from La Guardia all the way to the Barbizon Plaza, solely for the pleasure of looking at windows from their own level. She didn't need a taxi; her single bag was sufficiently small and compact that the airlines had regarded it with beaming approval. But this trip was to be a luxury for Annabelle, and that included taxis instead of airport limousines and subways.

After she had checked in at the hotel and inquired for Miss Schubert, who, a later letter had informed her, would head the traveling group, Annabelle went to her room, bathed, and sat down by the window overlooking the park to consider matters. This was not the room officially assigned to her—she had taken an outside one and paid the difference herself. It was part of her luxury mood. She realized that she would have to subdue that mood presently, in order not to be conspicuous in the group. But while it lasted, she would enjoy it.

Now she debated getting another taxi and going shopping. Perhaps the one bag was a little too limited in its wardrobe possibilities. Mentally, she listed the garments she had with her: the well-tailored dark-brown suit and its accessories; three nylon blouses, all tailored; one long skirt that could be worn with the blouses for evenings; a waterproofed tweed topcoat with a zip-in-and-out lining; two pairs of oxfords and one of pumps; terry-cloth mules. Underwear and nightwear of nylon; six pairs of service-weight nylon stockings. The top-coat could be worn as a dressing gown until she got to Paris. Naturally, she would buy lingerie and a negligee in Paris. And perfume. She looked at her one small bottle of "Tweed" toilet water and wondered if she would be able to stand herself if she smelled differently.

Well, she could get by in a crowd with a push as she was. There was no room in her bag for anything else. She would, of course, buy new luggage when and as she needed it. For a moment she debated going down to Mark Cross and splurging on a matched set to start out with. The thought of starting out with more bags empty than full restrained her. What if her bags didn't match at the end of the trip? So much the more traveled and worldly—so many more stories to be told about where and how she had obtained each one.

The telephone rang, and Annabelle answered it. Miss Schubert speaking. She would like to meet the group in the lobby in fifteen minutes. Could Annabelle be there? She could and would.

Looking around the lobby when she reached it, Annabelle felt a personal pride in ranch women generally. You simply could not pick them out with the naked eye. These women had come from the West, and from the most remote sections of the West. They ought to be conspicuous in the lobby of a New York hotel, but they were not. She remembered Clotilda Schubert vaguely from other rural life conferences: a big, bosomy woman, always dripping red foxes over tailored suits; a woman with a warm, glowing laugh like an open fire. Annabelle saw her on the opposite side of the lobby, crossed, and shook hands.

Miss Schubert, to Annabelle's surprise, was to head the group because she had been to Europe before, not once, but a number of times. That was like Clotilda, when you came to think about it. She was too busy putting her knowledge to use to waste time talking about how she got it. Now she was deftly explaining the intricacies of shipboard life to her followers. They clustered around her and took notes in leather-bound notebooks with ball-point pens, six alert and intelligent women, determined to know before they went aboard whom to tip how much, where and when and how to take their baths.

After the briefing, Miss Schubert looked around her and smiled. "Class dismissed," she said. "Go on out and do what you like for the rest of the day. You can't get lost in New York. It isn't big enough. If you aren't certain where you are, ask a policeman. He'll tell you how to get back here."

Three of the women—the little, dry one from California, the rugged one with craggy features from North Dakota, and the young, blonde, efficient Nebraskan with the voice that could saw through granite—produced maps of the city. The Coloradan and the Missourian announced that they had friends in town and would visit them. Miss Schubert looked at Annabelle and raised her eyebrows. "Well, Miss Texas?"

Annabelle smiled a little. "I used to come here for week ends. I can find my way around all right."

After brief consideration Annabelle decided that she would do two things. She would go to the Tailored Woman and get a dressing gown, and she would go to Mark Cross and buy a new handbag. Here was the beginning of her shopping spree.

The dressing gown was tailored, naturally, and was, gratifyingly, of navy blue nylon. The bag was really two bags in one; a small dress bag that was attached as a pocket to a capacious object of hand-stitched saddle leather. It was a magnificent bag, with not only multitudinous pockets but a real filing case. Annabelle cheerfully paid seventy-five dollars and tax for it. This was the bag she had been looking for all her life.

She emerged from Mark Cross on the Fifth Avenue side and stood considering her next move. It was three in the afternoon, and she was only a block from the Museum of Modern Art. She would go over for half an hour and see whatever show was on the walls. Then she would have tea—or perhaps a cocktail—at Hicks and Sons, and return to the hotel.

The placard at the museum entrance announced a show of Mondrian paintings, with sculpture by someone else. Annabelle was half-way around the galleries when she recognized the group of women ahead of her, and caught up with them. "Well," the Nebraskan was announcing in her penetrating voice, "all I can say is, I like my kitchen linoleum better."

191

The Californian laughed. "Many linoleum designs are based on these paintings," she read from the museum catalog in her hand. "Can't you think of it as research—getting back to the source of something?"

"I can, but why should I?" demanded the Nebraskan. "The next time I'll take my own advice and go to the Metropolitan: I get upset every time I come near this kind of picture."

"Why come?" inquired Mrs. North Dakota practically. "I never was here before, but I saw some of the exhibitions this museum sent out. I must say I liked those and I'm disappointed at this. The electric irons were beautiful, and there were some wonderful toasters. But I'd just as soon this man kept his research notes to himself and sent me the linoleum. Hello, Miss Wilson. What do you think of these things?"

"I don't like these much," said Annabelle, "but sometimes they have exhibitions here that I do like."

"I don't like them and I'm going to leave them," exclaimed the Nebraskan. "Where's the nearest place we can have a cocktail?"

Annabelle piloted them to Fifth Avenue and the tables at the back of Hicks and Sons. "A general store!" said the Californian, laughing. "Here we are, ranch women away from home, and we go to a fancy grocery store to get a drink!"

They all laughed over that and then they all began to talk: about their families, and their ranches, and their families again. By the time they had decided to go to dinner together and had divided the check and the tip four ways, they were all good friends and a cohesive group. Annabelle, unwrapping the new dressing gown in her room that night, decided that the trip would be worth taking even if nothing happened to her but meeting other ranch women from other parts of her own country.

Three months and several thousand miles later, Annabelle had arrived at the conclusion that country women were country women wherever you found them. She had reached Rome in a state of breathlessness. They had landed in England and had toured England first, with a brief side trip across the border into Scotland, where the Ayreshire and Aberdeen Angus cattle were beyond Annabelle's belief sleek and cared-for. They had crossed to Ireland and seen green fields whose color was so intense that it seemed almost poisonous, but where Annabelle was convinced that if you thrust a bare twig in the ground it would grow.

Then there had been a somewhat rough and unpleasant voyage that ended on the Scandinavian peninsula. Here Mrs. North Dakota acted as interpreter, as Miss Schubert did when they reached Germany. Between Sweden and Germany there had been France, including the long anticipated visit to Paris. But somehow in Paris there had been so much to see and do that nobody got around to going shopping.

Annabelle was still traveling with one suitcase and her Mark Cross bag. Into the bag she put the small things that were given them as souvenirs; bits of Irish lace and Scandinavian textiles, a small sample of linen from Normandy, and a tiny vial of perfume from the mayor of Rouen—all kinds of things. She considered getting more of the same kind of perfume in Paris, but was restrained by the fact that she didn't know how it smelled—she hadn't had a moment to herself to get the cork out.

Wherever they went, the group visited rural communities. They saw folk dancing. They inspected model farms and run-of-the-mill farms. They went down the Rhine in a boat and looked up cliffs at castles. They watched brown Swiss cows grazing in green, flower-spangled Swiss meadows. At last they went over the Alps in an air-conditioned bus, pervaded by what sounded to Annabelle like Music by Muzak, and through the Apennines and into Rome. This was the last lap. From Rome they were to go by chartered bus to Marseilles, and so home.

Annabelle realized that she was once more in a fashion center and that she should go shopping. If she intended to shop at all, this was the time to do it. She was restrained by two important considerations. In the first place, even in her well-fitted Gold Cross shoes, Annabelle's feet hurt. In the second place, she was the only woman in the group, not even excepting Miss Schubert, who had not once had to worry about where her luggage was or whether she would be able to get her clothes washed at their various stops. Getting soap had been a minor problem compared with getting laundry done.

She had not had to worry about whether she had on the right or the wrong clothes for any given occasion. If they went somewhere in the evening, she wore the long skirt; if in the daytime, she wore her tailored suit. Thus she was delivered from unnecessary bewilderments. She had been neat, clean, and comfortable for the whole trip, and she felt that she had profited from that fact.

For Annabelle had been able to concentrate. Since she was at last in Europe, she felt that it would be a shame, as well as base ingratitude to the International Rural Life group that had sent her, not to see and do and learn all there was around her to be observed. She had plunged into the business of the trip as systematically as she went into haying when she was at home. Her feet would not hurt now, she reflected, if she had waited to get her shoes half-soled when she got home instead of having the work done by a cobbler in a village in northern Italy. Everybody she had ever known had talked about the craftsmanship of hand-cobbled shoes, and no cowman would think of wearing ready-made boots if he could get them made to order. Annabelle reflected that she had also heard people talk about the divine imperfection of handmade articles. For her part, Annabelle thought, easing her toes against the bare floor, she could do with a little less divinity and a little more machine-produced perfection.

There was a knock at her door. She limped stocking-footed across the room, and opened it. A page handed her a note, accepted a suitable tip, and disappeared down the corridor. Annabelle hobbled back to the easy chair and dropped into it. Probably, she thought, she would feel better when she got back to a country where stockings were made to fit feet and not blocks of firewood. She missed the nylons she had brought with her; she had walked through their toes. She opened the note and examined its contents. She sighed. Miss Schubert wanted to meet the whole group downstairs in her room.

It was the business of customs, Miss Schubert explained when they gathered. So far, because they were tourists traveling from one country to another, they had not had to worry about the matter. Now they were on the home stretch. They would be landing in New York far sooner than now seemed possible. They would have their imports to declare, declarations to fill out, possibly duty to pay. She wanted them all to be ready, in order to avoid unnecessary complications and delay.

That settled it for Annabelle. This was her vacation. She had enough bookkeeping to do at home at the ranch. The souvenirs she had received did not need to be listed, for they were gifts. She did not feel like going shopping and she was not going shopping. Instead, she and Miss Schubert and Mrs. North Dakota pooled resources and rented a car. For the three days that they remained in Rome they allowed themselves to be driven luxuriously from place to place. They did their sightseeing sitting down.

While they drove, they talked. With the most magnificent buildings and the most appalling slums of the world before their eyes, they agreed that life was better in the country than in the city, whatever one's nationality. Remembering farmlands plowed by shells and trees bulldozed by mortar fire, they also agreed that war was as destructive to farm as to city life and that a country without farms would be a country in a desperate state indeed. All things considered, they decided, the country women of the United States should work more strongly and more determinedly for peace, for they stood to lose more than any other people in the world in the event of another war.

This world around them was not their world; its ways were not and never could be their ways. Even the two women whose parents had been immigrants, who had grown up speaking their parents' native languages with their own, found themselves foreign to the ways of thought and to the ways of life around them. For Annabelle there was only direct comparison. Things were one way in the life she knew; they were another, totally different way in the life she now saw around her. She could not say, and lacked the arrogance to say, that one was better than the other; only she could decide which one she preferred for herself.

"But I *am* glad I saw it," she said finally. "Unless I had, I would never have known what it was like." Then she laughed. "I know that sounds silly and obvious. But it is the way I feel. I've listened to so many people talk about their trips to Europe and say so little, that I don't hear them any more. Now I know, and I'll be able to listen to them and make sense out of what they're trying to say."

"You may even talk some yourself," said Clotilda Schubert.

They all talked on the return trip; talked and talked and talked, although they came to no new conclusions. Peace—and the responsibility for peace—rested in their hands, as nationals and as individuals. Their duty was clear; to teach peace and the need for peace. It was as simple, as obvious, and as un-believably, impossibly difficult as that.

But teaching—even preaching—peace was not going to be enough for the 4-H girls, Annabelle perceived when she thought about them. By that time she had checked into the Barbizon Plaza again, and the room she sat in could have been the one she had left in the spring. Now the leaves in the park were brightly colored, and there was a tingle of woodsmoke to prickle the nostrils, underlying the perpetual smell of sewer gas and manure.

Now it was September, and she was going home. Systematically, Annabelle had kept accounts of her personal expenditures on the trip. Looking at them now, she saw that she had spent less on herself in the last four months than she would have at home. And this was to have been her wild, free time—her extravagant splurge! She could never go home and face those girls without one new garment to show for the trip but a tailored dressing gown.

Suddenly a number of things were clear to Annabelle. She had been indifferent to other people's European trips because the people themselves had made at once too much and too little of them. Too much, if they talked about things they disliked in the United States and compared them with things they liked in Europe. Too little if they, like herself, did and said nothing in Europe that they wouldn't have done or said at home. You could take boat trips on innumerable American rivers and look at castles in California that were grander than those in Germany. You could see art museums at home that set the world's fashions and shaped its ideas of visible beauty. You could hear music that was as good as any anywhere. There was no point in traveling for any one of these things alone.

But what you could see and hear and have from Europe—and the thing that somehow those returning travelers had never given Annabelle—was a feeling of wonder and mystery and adventure. You should be moved and stirred and changed by what was meant to be an enormous experience—returning to the roots of your own culture. And people who returned and talked only of tips and plumbing and air-conditioned buses were cheating their audiences. They weren't giving their hearers what they needed to hear if they were to respect the speakers—or Europe.

All right, then, Annabelle decided, she would be different. If you were going to produce any effect beyond repeating dreary statistics at Grange meetings, you had—again—to get to the roots of things. Having gone to the roots of your culture, you had to go to the roots of humanity. You had to give people what they wanted before you could expect them to turn their thoughts to your interests and to take what you wanted to give.

Annabelle rammed her feet back into her painfully half-soled shoes and picked up her Mark Cross bag. She went downstairs and asked the doorman to summon a taxi. She went as straight as traffic would allow down Fifth Avenue to Saks, and there she began her shopping.

Afterward Annabelle wondered how she went through it all, from specially fitted corsets to two trailing and fluffing evening gowns, without a qualm or a quiver, knowing as she did that she probably would never wear a tenth of the things she was buying. But she shopped as efficiently as she did anything else and as rapidly as fittings and adjustments would allow.

Her last gesture before she left New York—the last of the group to head west—was a trip to Rockefeller Plaza and the small bright shops, of many nationalities, that rimmed it. There she bought reckless and extravagant presents to take back to the

4-H girls. Laces and linens and perfumes, but on a large scale, impressively, each item chosen as an individual gift. If sometimes now she wondered about next year's calf crop, the thought was rapidly covered by the practical consideration that the duty on her purchases had already been paid by the importers. She did not have to waste time filling out customs declarations. Her last afternoon in New York could be—and was—leisurely spent at Elizabeth Arden's.

Annabelle stepped off the train at Amarillo enveloped in an almost visible aura of Chanel's "Ivoire." Her Palter de Liso pumps had four-inch heels, and few hats like hers—from Schiaparelli—had decorated Panhandle heads. The porter who lifted her set of matched bags—from Mark Cross' English department—from the Pullman, staggered under his load. Annabelle twitched herself inside her waist-nipping corset and reflected that she knew how a horse must feel when it was cinched up for riding. Then she crippled across the platform to a taxi and asked to be driven to the garage where she had left her car.

By the time the 4-H group met on Thursday, the word had got around. The girls were not merely on time for the meeting, they were early. Annabelle, got up regardless, dared not face herself in the mirror. Clothes that had seemed only mildly extreme in New York looked plain freakish at home. But the girls were enchanted. They clustered around her, secretly feeling and fingering, and repeating in awed tones, "Paris—— Italy——" Annabelle brought out their presents and the room was strewn with wrappings and ribbons in an early unseasonable Christmas whirl.

At last there was a lull in the excitement, a breathing-space when one of the girls asked, "Tell us about it, Miss Annabelle. Where-all did you go, and what-all did you see?"

And Annabelle, sitting bolt upright in her corset on the sofa, began:

"We landed at Southampton, and took the train to London. . . ."

16. *Old—and Alone*

UTAH, 1951

DIGGING the root cellar by herself was sheer durn foolishness. Polly admitted it aloud as she lay on the cellar floor with the beam that should have shored up one side wall lying across her middle. Sometimes Curt was right; he had a wide streak of his father in him and he was frequently wrong, but every once in a while he took after her folks.

She pulled herself together and inched her right arm free of the weight of the beam. It moved easily; couldn't be broken, then—and the shoulder blade and collar bone must be all right, too. That was a relief. She could manage to set an ankle or a leg if she had to, but she'd never been able to figure out any way a body could set her own arm or shóulder or collar bone.

With the free right arm she shifted the beam, and felt a stabbing pain in her left side as the weight was moved aside. Ribs, then. Well, Lord knew, broken ribs were nothing to worry about. Painful for a while, maybe, but they didn't lay you up any. They were just hampering.

Bit by bit, never admitting how keen the pain was, Polly worked free of the beam and collected herself from the floor. Now that the anesthetic of shock had worn off, each movement was a separate throb. However, if you hadn't anybody to do it for you, you did it for yourself. She scrambled up the ladder and out of the hole she had dug for the cellar, to lie flat and panting on the ground at its edge. After what seemed like quite a long while, she pulled herself upright and worked her way back to the house.

In the bedroom she stripped and took stock. She was sure of three ribs; two others might also be broken, but she couldn't be positive. Anyway, three were enough. They would do to go on with. She found an old sheet and tore it in strips. Then she tied an end of the first strip to the foot of her old iron bed, held the other tightly against her waist, and solemnly revolved bedwards. The strip held, and she wound herself into a cummerbund, almost tight enough to stop her breathing and certainly as good, she informed herself, as any hospital cast.

Hospitals, anyway! Hospitals always seemed to make an awful fuss about mighty small things. Curt's wife, now. Running to the hospital every time she had a baby, and taking ether and things as if having a baby weren't as natural for a woman as breathing. It might be she had more babies this way than if she had to do it without help. She certainly did manage to get to the hospital every whipstitch. Maybe all she wanted was to lie down and rest!

The bed tempted Polly as she untied the end of the bandage from its foot, but she resisted. After all, lying down might be inviting trouble. She'd all her life had a fear of lying down and not being able to get up. Better to stay on her feet and keep moving as long as she could and then do her resting sitting up in a chair.

She went along out to the kitchen to look at the alarm clock she had carried there when she rose at four, ignoring the mantle clock in the dining room. Ten-thirty. If only keeping track of the days were as easy as keeping track of the hours! The first year or so she'd been alone up here on the edge of the Forest Reserve she'd marked the days off on a calendar. But that had been a mighty long time ago; she'd taken out the claim in 1918, end of the First War, and this was 1951—thirty-three years. And Ben pulled out the end of the first winter, leaving her alone with Curt. Yes, that was right. Curt was three when she started to build the cabin, and he was thirty-five now. And he'd made her a grandmother five times over. He was doing all right—he managed to support his family with his job down in town.

Well, she'd built the first one-room cabin by herself; she'd added the other rooms and converted the first one to a kitchen singlehanded; she'd done about everything on the place alone. That made it hers, closely hers, and precious. Curt always let on he was mad when he came home from school in the summers and found new rooms or other improvements. About the only thing he'd ever helped with, though, was the roofing job four years ago. He'd come driving along the trail in the pick-up, with the back end loaded with tar and tar-paper and stuff, and announced he was going to reroof the place for her. It was sweet of him—he was a sweet boy and thoughtful—but, Laws! He was a clumsy workman. She'd finally had to show him how to go about roofing, and at the end of the job she'd done more of the work than he had.

She eased off the stove lid and poked in a piece of wood. Bending was hard; she'd have to figure out some way to keep the wood higher off the floor until she felt a little better. The coffeepot held the remains of her breakfast coffee, carefully saved for lunch. She set it on to heat, and deposited herself carefully in the old rocker, within reach of the tin cup and the pot. Nothing like a good hot cup of coffee to perk you up when you felt a little under the weather. A good thing she'd never developed a taste for spirits. A winter's supply of coffee was hard enough to pack up the trail a-horseback without having the extra weight of bottles.

And that reminded her. The root cellar. Oh, she was an old simpleton! She could have waited until Breck Jones, the Ranger, came along. Breck was due any day now on his monthly tour around the Forest. He'd have stopped off for a couple of days to help her, if she'd asked him to. Then she'd have had her cellar, instead of a mess of broken ribs to think about. No more cellar for her—not until spring. And the hole lying there open to the daylight, so all the cows on this side of the mountain could fall into it if they took a notion to. Soon as Breck showed up, he'd have to run a strand of wire around that hole. She wouldn't even try to do it now. She was a smart woman—she knew when she was licked!

She poured herself a cup of coffee and considered the more serious aspects of the situation. She had plenty to eat in the house—more than enough to run her till spring. The wood was ricked up on the back porch within easy reach—that was one thing she always made sure of every summer. The stock was out on the Reserve, and they'd have to stay there; if they got off her leased land on to the government area—and they most likely would—it would be just too bad. She grinned slightly to herself. Nobody could expect a poor old gray-haired lady, all alone in the world and with Goodness knew how many stove-in ribs, to get on a horse and round up cattle in the snow. Twenty-five head of stock wouldn't do any permanent damage to the government land. It wouldn't be the first time they'd been on it, come right down to it. How was a poor cow to read boundary signs? Cattle were good for land, anyway. Aside from enriching it by returning its own products to it, they kept the trails open and reduced the danger of fires. She'd always been glad and thankful this Reserve had been spared a fire.

She looked through the kitchen window, across the swale to the wall of pines that marked the edge of the Reserve. Horses; two men on horseback, coming along the trail under the overhang of the Indian picture rocks. The curved bluff face was a gateway, the pecked warriors its guardians, at the entrance to her land. She'd chosen this spot for the house with that in mind. If the ancient figures twining spookily along the rocks didn't scare people away, they were good people and had a reason to be here.

The Ranger's flat-brimmed four-dented Stetson was unmistakable. So was his slouch in the saddle. The man with him rode at ease, like a Westerner, but he was less used to riding, lately, than Breck. She watched them cross the swale and tie their horses at the gate. Planning a short visit, then. They came along the path. The delphiniums and geraniums that bordered it were dried and withered by frost now, shaking their last seeds on the men's boots. Breck would never step on a person's porch, never knock on a person's door, without giving notice. Nor did he now. He paused with his feet still planted on the path and called,

"Hello, Polly. You home?"

She opened the door. "Come right in, Breck. Glad to see you. Bring your friend."

A grin split the Ranger's face. "That's no friend, that's my brother. Meet Mrs. Mathews, Don."

"Howdy, Mrs. Mathews. Pleased to meet you." Well, if he was a brother of Breck's, he'd be bound to have good manners.

"Come on in, boys."

"Juuuuuuust a minute, Polly. What's that hole in the ground doing over there?"

"Oh, that! Tell you about that later. Come on in and have a cup coffee. The pot's hot this minute."

But Breck left the steps for a minute to cross between the rose bed and the mulched-down iris rows and inspect the hole. When he returned, his face was concerned. "When did that shoring timber pull loose, Polly?"

"I already told you I'd tell you all about it. For the Land's sake, do you have to stand out there and chatter? Firing questions at a person? I've got a good fire and a hot pot of coffee in the kitchen. Come in and set. Didn't your mother teach you manners, or have you forgot them all?"

She could feel his eyes on her back as she turned and led the way indoors. It must be the feeling of close inspection that made her clumsy. She clanged the two clean tin cups together and spilled the first spoon of sugar on the floor. Butterfingers! She hated messy housekeeping.

With their hats off the two men looked alike—enough alike to be brothers—all right. Breck was leaner and harder and red-browner; Don had the look of a man who spent most of his time indoors at a desk. She'd like to hear what he did; Breck had never mentioned he had a brother before. Well, likely, if he wanted her to know, he'd tell her. She'd been too well brought up ever to ask personal questions herself.

"Stay to dinner, Breck?"

"Might's well, Polly. Thanks." He turned to his brother. "This is the lady I was telling you about, Don. Best cook this side of the mountain. Best blacksmith. Best gardener. Cans the most stuff every summer. Built the house here all by herself . . ."

"Curt helped me put the roof on," Polly loyally interrupted.

". . . and now, by all the signs, she's digging herself a root cellar. And speaking of that, what happened to the shoring timber, Polly?"

"It slipped."

"I can see that for myself. Mind telling me the rest of the story?"

"That's all. It slipped. If I'd-a had the right kind of jack to hold it, it wouldn't have. I should have ordered one, but the calf crop was a little short this year and I hated to spend the money. After the timber slipped, I sort of gave up the notion of building for this year. It's late in the season to start a root cellar, and I don't really need it. I was just putting in the time between the last of the garden and canning and the first snow . . ."

"Polly, did you get in the way of that timber when it fell?"

"Breck, you ask too many questions. I've told you that before. Yes, I got in the way of the timber, but you can see for yourself that I'm all right. I'd be obliged if you'd string a wire around that hole before you leave, to keep the cows out, that's all."

"Will do, Polly. How near's dinner ready?"

" 'Bout an hour."

"Plenty of time. Come on, Don, make a hand. We'll fence in the lady's root cellar, since she's going to feed us."

Watching them go along the path, Polly reflected that she knew what Breck was saying as well as if she'd heard it: "Wonderful woman in her own way. Seventy-six years old, and look at her, straight as a young girl. Straighter than most of them. Married once before she came here, and the children from that marriage, and their children, are grown; she's a great-grandmother. Only one lives near her's Curt—son of her second husband and a lot younger than the others. Better put two strands around here. Take the wire pullers and the hammer; I'll carry the post-hole digger.

"She stays up here by herself and runs cattle on the Reserve. Always friendly, always hospitable, but she keeps to herself. Never had too many head of stock, but always managed to get along. Any one of the children would be glad to have her with them, but she likes it up here. Says she likes the quiet and wants to be independent as long as she holds out."

That might be a glorified version of the conversation, Polly reflected. Perhaps its trend was less cheerful, went more like this: "Poor old soul. Five children, and one of them just eighty miles away, but she lives up here all alone. Doesn't want help; says she doesn't need it. I've worked with her on jobs before, but I never knew her to ask me or anyone to do one for her. Nobody knows just how she gets by; she can't qualify for a state pension because she's got her own place and her own stock, but that doesn't mean she's always got money to buy her food—"

Lands, but the imagined conversation was getting sad! She'd start believing it herself, any minute. Those boys were working like beavers out there; first thing she knew, they'd be finished and coming in hungry. And she hadn't even started to get their dinner. Of course, coming in on her unexpected that way all they'd expect to get was canned food, that was a comfort.

She paused for a minute before the shelves, considering. Might's well give them canned venison—it was tasty and a treat if you weren't used to it. Breck would never ask her where she got it. He'd eaten moonlight beef too often and on too many tables not to keep his mouth shut. Why should she bother with permits and limits, anyway? She'd been here before the Reserve was, and the deer were pests—always eating the young shoots in her garden in the spring. She had to protect herself, didn't she?

There were potatoes and onions in the bins under the shelves. She set the can of meat on the kitchen table and returned to scoop out the vegetables. She sure was stiffening up—had to carry them almost one at a time. Now, if the deer'd had their way, they'd all be eating their venison plain, without any potatoes or onions.

She selected a jar of wild plums for dessert and a glass of wild blackberry jelly to go with the meat. Too bad she couldn't

205

give the boys fresh fruit, and they'd have to eat their sourdough biscuits without butter, but likely they wouldn't mind. She glanced towards the window again. They were locking the tool shed, and there were two wires strung, tight and smooth, about the hole behind them. That was all right, then. She went to the door and called:

"Chuck! Come and get it!"

The men washed up at the bench by the kitchen door and came to the table. They seated themselves and paused, waiting. Breck sure knew her ways, and he always remembered his manners. She bowed her head above her own plate and repeated the blessing, "Bless this food to our use, Oh Lord, and our bodies to Your service. Amen."

They ate almost in silence. Eating was serious business. Breck poised his fork above the meat platter, once, while he asked, "Mutton, Polly?" with a grin.

She grinned, too, and gave him the standard answer, "A smart man knows what he's eating and shuts his mouth on it."

When they reached the end of the meat-potatoes-sourdough biscuits part of the meal and she had refilled the coffee cups, Breck rose. "Wait a minute, folks. I've got something for dessert." He left the room. A good boy. He never forgot her sweet tooth.

She opened the box of cookies and set it out on the table. The second box—the one with the chocolates—Breck stashed behind the mantle clock. She was supposed to find it there when she dusted, after the boys had left. Anyway, chocolates would keep and cookies wouldn't. They'd dry out and get stale.

Each man took a cookie, but that was only for manners, to keep her company. They'd rather smoke and she knew it; knew, too, that they were waiting for permission. She gave it.

"Go on, boys. Light up."

Now was the time for conversation, for catching up. She'd just have to ask questions. She was dying to know.

"What business is Don in, Breck?"

"No business, Polly. He's with the State Welfare Board."

"What!" her hands clutched the tablecloth before her as the pain in her ribs clutched at her breath. It was coming; she'd always known it would come. Someday some snooper would get around to meddling in her business; tell her she was too old to manage her own affairs; send her to town to live with Curt and his family—all that noise, and all crowded together in a six-room house! And no two women could get along under the same roof, especially if one of them was married to the other's son!—or, worse, they would send her to an old ladies' home. This was it. Breck was doing this to her—she had trusted him like her own boy. She felt sick all over.

Her exclamation must have sounded less sharp in the men's ears than it had in her own, because Breck was answering her calmly. "He works with Child Welfare; delinquent boys."

"Shucks!" She was so relieved at the sound of his words that she could laugh. "There aren't any delinquent boys. All there are's delinquent parents."

Don leaned towards her, his eyes bright and warm with interest and response. "That's what I say, Polly. (May I say Polly? Breck always does.) Boys are good, if they grow up right and in good surroundings. It's the parents who don't give them love and understanding who are at fault."

"Poor little fellers! Mothers running around to picture shows and worse, and smoking cigarets. And fathers God knows where. I brought my boy up by myself after the old man left us, and he's a good boy—a good father and a good citizen. A mother's more important to a boy than a man, some ways."

"Both parents are important. But you're right; when the mother isn't on her job, things go really wrong. Let me tell you about one boy we have—fine kid, about twelve. Family are oil-field followers; never have had a settled home. This kid hasn't known when he came home at night whether they'd be living in the house he left them in, or whether they'd have moved on. Eight children in the family, he's the next oldest, and mother says herself she doesn't know for sure who the fathers of the last four are."

"The poor kid! A woman like that doesn't deserve to have children. The oldest a boy, too?"

"A girl. We're already taking care of her—she got into trouble with a married man last year. But this boy. Never sure where he lived, never sure where his next meal was coming from. He got to picking up odd pieces of pipe around the yards and selling them. Said he wanted to buy something to eat."

Polly's dinner was a lump in her throat, choking her. She shifted in her chair, trying to ease the pain and pressure against her bandage. "What that boy needs is a real home."

"You're right," Don said. "I wish we could find one for him. But the police picked him up last week for trying to sell stolen goods, and no one around town where he lives will take him on probation from the juvenile officers. Looks like it's reform school for him."

"That's as bad as jail. He'll never live it down."

"Yes. That's the worst part of the whole business."

In her mind, Polly ran over the list of supplies in the storeroom. Plenty enough for two. She straightened in her chair, caught her breath at the pain, and forced a smile. "Nobody will take him?"

"We can't find a soul who wants to bother with a twelve-year-old boy with a police record."

"I'll take him," she said. "You send him on up to me. Put him on the bus, and Curt can bring him up from town in the pick-up. Stop off when you go down and tell him so. The kid can stay here this winter; I've got enough on hand for him to eat, and he can work out his board and room helping me. One thing, though. You'll have to hurry, before the snow comes and Curt can't get the truck through."

Don looked a little dazed, and considerably relieved.

"I believe you've got something there. We can do it. You don't have to worry about running short of anything you need; we pay the expenses of the boys we place in foster homes, and you'll have a check coming along every month, regularly, to cover his food and clothes and a little over. I'll send the papers up with the boy for you to sign—no, I'll mail them to you. He might lose them."

"Curt brings the mail up when he comes on an errand; the letters won't get here any sooner if you do mail them. No. You send them by him. Give him a sense of responsibility. If he loses them, I'll show him what a bother it makes for everybody. He's old enough to take care of an envelope with some papers in it. As for the check, you can send it if you've a mind to and I'll not say it won't come in handy, but I'd take the boy anyway, if you didn't pay a cent."

"What have you got on the place here for him to do?"

Polly glanced sidewise at Breck, and Breck grinned back at her.

"Oh, odd jobs. He can help me keep the cattle off the government land, if he can ride. If he can't, I'll teach him. And he can hustle wood and dig paths and feed the horses. If he runs out of everything else to do, he can learn kitchen work—never hurts a man to know how to rustle his own chuck. In between times I'll teach him to handle a rifle—he can shoot at tin cans, Breck, so don't look so curious—and cut quilt pieces. Oh, I'll keep him busy. Come spring, we'll finish the root cellar. What's his name?"

"Bob. Bob Daniels."

"Good name. There used to be some Danielses down the river. They went broke in the drought in thirty-six, but they were mighty nice people. This boy might be kin to them."

"Could be; I don't know. Well, that's settled."

Breck rose and gathered his hat from the deer prongs by the door. "Come on, Don. Time we were telling the lady good-bye and getting back to work. Can't sit here loafing all day."

"Right. Let's go. Good-bye, Polly. It's mighty kind of you to take the kid. You're doing a good piece of work, for him and for the state." He was gentleman enough not to add, "For yourself, too." Instead, he held out his hand, and said, "I'll be up when the snow's off, to see how you're both making out."

She leaned a little against the door jamb, to watch them unhitch, mount, and ride off, before she turned back to the table to gather up the dishes and start towards the kitchen with them. Mighty nice boys, both of them. She snitched a cookie and ate it slowly, thoughtfully. The load off her shoulders was bigger than she liked to face up to. Now it was gone, she knew what it had been: unconfessed fear of being alone with her broken ribs all winter. She knew, too, that she was sickeningly tired, and that she hurt all over. But then, she thought as she slowly, carefully straightened her shoulders, having company when you weren't used to it always was wearing. It did leave you tired.

It was fortunate she did not frame to herself the words the men exchanged on the Trail into the Reserve:

"Mighty good piece of work, Don."

"That boy'll be all right, now. He's in good hands."

"Sure. He may learn to shoot at a deer before he pots at a tin can—but why not give him a good big mark that'll be easy to hit? But what I mean is, I've worried a lot about Polly. I sure have hated to think of her going through another winter alone at her age. I hated it worse when she wouldn't tell me what happened when that timber slipped. I could tell by the way she was sitting something gave, and if she'd been a man, I'd have taken a look to see what was wrong, but, hell! you can't go to work and undress a nice old lady."

"I wouldn't worry about Polly," Don remarked thoughtfully. "You'll only have to worry about her if she ever leaves her home. Then she'll wither and die like the annuals in her garden when the frost hits them. As long as she's on her mountain and taking care of herself and somebody else, Polly'll be all right."

PART SIX

What Do They Do With Their Spare Time?

MOST RANCH WOMEN *will tell you two things, without any hesitation whatever. One is that they wouldn't know how to recognize a dull moment if they met it on the street. The other is that on isolated ranches a little entertainment goes a long way. Any event that is out of the ordinary, however simple it may seem to the jaded city eye, is something for the ranch woman and her children to treasure in memory for the rest of their lives.*

It is because entertainments, in the usual sense of the word, come so seldom to the ranch family that they are so important. Each family relies on its own resources to make the most of what happens from day to day. Jokes are hoarded and grow time-worn in the telling, until they lose meaning for all save the teller and his special, trained audience. Television is still to be installed on most ranches—the radio batteries often must be saved so Father can hear the news broadcast.

So much of the fun to be had on ranches comes, like the rodeo (however you pronounce THAT word), from the skills of daily life. And the things that come from completely outside (and that again includes professional rodeos) are Great Events. But all the same, or perhaps for that very reason, one of the most frequently used farewells of the cow country is: "So long! Have fun!"

17. *This Is the Way We Go to Church*

NEBRASKA, 1952

EDITH slept in on Sunday morning, so it was almost daylight when she opened her eyes. That meant seven o'clock in September, and to be in bed at seven was almost unheard-of luxury on any working ranch. Fred and the children must be starved! What did they mean, treating her as if she were sick? She blinked and tried to remember what had finally awakened her. The sound was repeated from the direction of the kitchen; it was a kind of muffled clang, followed by a suppressed shriek. Such a noise could portend anything, from a new calf born out of its season to a fallen windmill blade. Edith rose from her bed in haste and entered the kitchen with one arm still groping behind her for the sleeve of her dressing gown.

The scene that met her eyes was relatively peaceful. Small Dave was under the table, peacefully occupied with four spools, a grimy length of string, and a Sunday School picture card. Randy was setting the table, with the knives and forks reversed because he was left-handed, and Fred stood at the stove, following the directions which Sharon relayed to him a sentence at a time. She read them aloud, in her turn, from Mrs. Irma Rombauer's *The Joy of Cooking*. Their faces were not joyful, neither were they sad, only unbelievably concentrated.

"Stir slowly and drop by spoonfuls on a hot, lightly-greased griddle," Sharon instructed her father, and raised her eyes momentarily from the book. "Oh, MOther!" she wailed. "We were going to surprise you! We wanted to bring you Breakfast in Bed!"

"I am surprised," Edith said. "Very much surprised. But can't I stay up and be surprised?" Her eye caught Fred's. Very slowly he shook his head, one eyelid drooping imperceptibly downward. "All right," Edith agreed. "I'll go back to bed and be properly surprised." Sharon beamed delightedly, and Edith resigned herself to a succession of surprises.

She prepared for them by encasing herself in her trousseau negligee and putting clean slips on the pillows before she got back into bed and lazily reposed. She reached for *The Cardinal*, reflecting that this was a good chance to get beyond page 120, where two weeks' reading had landed her last week end. Reflecting also that there was good reason why maribou had gone out of style, she pushed back her sleeves and settled down. She had reached page 130 when the door opened and the procession entered.

First Dave, bearing the last chrysanthemums from the garden, their stems thrust chokily into a Mason jar. Then Randy with a napkin over his arm and the last bunch of newspapers, from Thursday's mail, under the other. Then Fred, carrying the laden bed tray. Last of all a somewhat twittering presiding goddess, Sharon, her cheeks flushed proudly, her small front encased in Edith's last clean white apron.

"Goodness!" Edith exclaimed. "It isn't my birthday and I never felt better in my life. Why do I get all this attention?"

"It's Sunday, Mother," Sharon explained, "and that means a day of rest. And we thought you probably needed one worse than anybody except Daddy—but he had to help get yours ready."

"Thank you, all," said Edith, feeling her throat close almost painfully. She accepted the tray when Fred placed it across her and, closely watched by her audience of four, she took her first bite.

214

"Is it good, Mother?" Sharon demanded. "We followed just what it said in the book. Is it all right?"

"It's wonderful," Edith assured her. "I never ate better hot cakes and bacon in all my life. Now hadn't all of you better go along and get your own breakfasts before they're cold?"

Reluctantly, they departed. Edith enjoyed the hot cakes and coffee, and recalled that after all Fred was a pretty good camp cook. This meal was certainly well within his limitations, even if it were a little ambitious for Sharon.

She heard the tinkle of the telephone as she finished the last of her coffee, and a minute later Randy's voice reached her, raised to a fine carrying pitch. "Moooother! It's Aunt Laverne on the phone and she wants to talk to you."

"Well," Laverne said after the first "hello's" had been exchanged and they were sure the wire was clear, "you sound very fresh and chipper."

"I slept till seven and had Breakfast in Bed," Edith informed her. All her family were in the room, listening intently to be sure that she forgot nothing. "My family decided to make Sunday a day of rest for me." She felt something push her from behind and sat down abruptly on the chair Randy shoved under her. Sharon materialized at her elbow with another cup of coffee, and Fred, evidently remembering certain honeymoon episodes which she had almost forgotten, came around the table to pull her sleeves up above her elbows so the feathers wouldn't drip into the cup. Edith giggled into the phone. "They're still doing it," she told her aunt.

"That's nice," Laverne said. "You'll have to tell me how it turned out—sometime when we have plenty of time to talk." There was a sudden, intense buzzing on the line. "Drat these fence-line phones!" Laverne ejaculated. "There's a cow rubbing against the wire somewhere."

"Fred's going to ride fence tomorrow," Edith said. "He'll take care of any loose staples between here and there."

"Good," Laverne said. "What was I saying? Oh, yes. I wanted to tell you there's a missionary at the Fowler's. We'll have preaching at the schoolhouse this afternoon."

"What kind of missionary?" Edith inquired. Fred and the children looked up, interested and delighted.

"I don't know exactly," Laverne replied. "The Fowlers are Episcopalians, aren't they? Well, Church of England—it's the same thing. Maybe an Episcopalian minister."

"Doesn't have to be," said Edith. "He could be a Presbyterian or a Methodist." The telephone buzzed again, persistently. "What time, Laverne?" she asked urgently.

"Oh, whenever you can get there," Laverne said, her voice dimming as the noise on the line increased. "Better come right after ———" The buzzing swallowed her words.

"Fred," Edith said, hanging up the phone, "you'll have to fix that fence. The cow's got the staple clear out, and I'll bet she's got the wire down on the ground by now. There won't be a phone working anywhere along the creek till you get it attended to."

"Somewhere between here and there?" Fred inquired. "Won't take long to fix, if I can find it." His brows drew together slightly. "I wanted to mend the harness for the hay frame," he said reluctantly. "Sunday's about the only chance I get for jobs like that."

"Remember what you promised," Edith said. It was the one thing she insisted on and had ever since they were married. She would not be without a means of calling for help if there were a fire or if one of the children were taken sick. The fence-line telephone, powered with batteries that ran from the Winchargers, linked the six families along the forty miles of the creek. True, none of them could communicate with the telephone lines thirty miles away along the highway, but you could get a car out from Laverne's place in any weather, so there was always a link with town and the doctor for all of them.

"Go and see what you can do, Fred," Edith instructed, "and try to get back for lunch. I feel rested and wonderful, thanks to all of you, and guilty about sending you out this way, but it'll have to be done."

"Sure," said Fred. "Come on, son. You ride with me. We

216

can start in the middle of the fence and work out. With two of us it shouldn't take very long."

Edith watched the two men of the family ride away, with their tools at their belts, a little uneasily. Eight years old, she thought, was *young* to be fooling with electricity. Although, working with his father, Randy learned skills without the profanity he might hear from professionals. Boys had to learn, and the sooner the better. It wasn't any more dangerous than handling cattle, she supposed, and he'd been riding on local round-ups since before he was seven. Still, cattle were something *natural,* and storage batteries had an artificial quality. She distrusted them.

"Sharon," she said, clearing her mind of gloomy thoughts, "you wanted to wash your hair. If you'll go and do it, I'll get these dishes out of the way and be ready to pin up the curls. That will give you a share of the Sunday rest, too. It wouldn't be fair for you to have to cook *and* wash the dishes."

Sharon beamed and vanished. Edith returned to her own room and exchanged the satin negligee for blue jeans and a clean shirt. She rammed her feet into sneakers, tied on the apron Sharon had discarded on the back of a chair, and surveyed the kitchen. It dimly crossed her mind that it might have been more restful to have had only her own, accustomed dishes to wash. Fred and Sharon between them seemed to have used everything. She throttled the thought as unworthy and ungrateful, and cleaned and straightened out the kitchen as quickly as she could. By the time Sharon stood moistly before her, a bottle of wave lotion and a box of bobby pins in one hand, a rat-tail comb and the hand dryer in the other, the kitchen was at least presentable.

"Aunt Laverne must have meant for us to come to the schoolhouse right after lunch," Edith reflected aloud as she pinned up her daughter's hair. She looked quickly at the clock. "My Goodness, it's after nine already. Where does Sunday go to? It never lasts as long as other days. Of course, I started this one late."

"Can I help you with lunch, Mother?"

"Yes, if you want to," Edith said. "I thought perhaps you'd had enough cooking for one day."

"Oh, well, Mother," Sharon replied, "that wasn't really fun-cooking; Dad was helping, and I had to let him stick to things he knew how to cook." She fixed on her mother a penetrating and entirely female look. "You know how men are, Mother," Sharon said from the profound wisdom of twelve years. "You have to let them have their way so you can get yours."

Heavens! Edith reflected. Where do they get it from so soon? This is starting a little young. But she agreed with Sharon, and gave her consent to a fun-cooking lunch. That meant food rather out of the ordinary, and sometimes things they discovered that none of them liked, but it also meant that they learned a lot of new words. If they ever did get into a French restaurant, they would certainly know how and what to order.

While Sharon sat down with the cookbook to work out her fun-cooking menu, Edith made her bed and changed the sheets to match the pillows. The linen closet had been neglected for weeks, and since this was Sunday and she had no regular chores breathing down the back of her neck, she took time to straighten things out and to put piles of towels and wash cloths within the children's reach on the lower shelves. A hasty survey of her own closet, which followed, was alarming. That would have to go till another Sunday, two closets in one day was too much. She would need nylons to wear to church this afternoon, and she gathered up her two remaining pairs of sheer stockings and took them to the bathroom to wash.

"Mother," Sharon reported as Edith hung the stockings on the towel rack to dry, "here's a recipe for curry."

And Fred could not endure any hot, highly seasoned food, even if it had been really safe for the children to eat! Edith examined the recipe. "I'm afraid not, darling," she said finally. "It says here, 'Simmer for four hours.' There isn't time, it's ten-fifteen now. Let's try to find something that's quicker to do."

The back door banged. "Mooother!" Randy called. "I found it! A great big staple out, just about half a mile past the middle of the fence towards Aunt Laverne's. Moother! Is there anything to eat? I'm hungry!"

That was the way it went on a ranch, Edith thought. The menfolks expected to eat when they came in, and the act of entering the house brought on their appetites, no matter how short a time they had been gone. "Just a peanut butter sandwich," she directed her son, and turned her attention to Sharon and the cookbook again. The telephone tinkled.

This time it was Mrs. Fowler. "Laverne said she told you about the services this afternoon," she began. She lowered her voice a notch. "Of course, he's a Non-Conformist, as we say at home in England—Methodists, you call them here, I believe." Forty years and an act of Congress were not sufficient to naturalize Mrs. Fowler. "But actually a very nice little man, and it's been some time since we had any services. I wonder if you'd mind playing a few hymns, Edith."

"Of course not," Edith said warmly. "I'd love to. What did you have in mind, Mrs. Fowler?" She might as well inquire. Mrs. Fowler would tell her anyway.

"Oh," Mrs. Fowler said, "some of the simple, familiar ones. Perhaps 'Onward, Christian Soldiers'—the children love that. And 'Holy, Holy, Holy,' because it *is* the Trinity season. And then we ought to have one for the Offertory—"

"The Doxology," Edith put in. The children loved that, too, and she loved to hear them sing it.

"The Doxology," Mrs. Fowler agreed. "And then—well, I don't know. What do you think? We ought to have one more."

"Why not, 'My Country 'Tis of Thee?'" Edith suggested. That was a tune they all knew and could sing. Probably "Onward Christian Soldiers" was too. She had her doubts about "Holy, Holy, Holy."

"Very well," said Mrs. Fowler. "That ought to be enough, don't you think? We'll see you at two, then."

She hung up. Edith glanced at the clock and went directly to the piano. She was rusty; she'd have to have at least half an hour's practice before the service. But as soon as she opened the piano and began to play, the children came clustering around her with requests. Fred came quietly into the room, in his hands the harness and the tools for mending it. Edith surrendered to her family. "Old Black Joe" for Randy, and "London Bridge Is Falling Down" for Dave, and "Why Do I Love You" for Sharon. Then, without Fred's asking for it, "Believe Me If All Those Endearing Young Charms." It wasn't the practicing she had set out to do, but it did limber up her fingers.

"Goodness!" she said suddenly, as her eyes fell on the clock, "it's a quarter of twelve. We'll have to let the fun-cooking go for this time, Sharon, and just scramble together a pick-up lunch. And we'll have to hurry at that, to get over to the schoolhouse by two. We shouldn't have got started on the music!"

"I'd just as soon have the singing," Sharon observed, and her father, with the memory of some fun-cooking episodes in mind said, "I'd rather."

However, there was still time to work out a compromise. Sharon was allowed to grill the cheese sandwiches in the skillet, the way they were done in the drugstore in Scottsbluff. And, as a treat, Edith opened a jug of cider she had brought out from town with the last grocery order. She stood firm on one point during the meal. Cider was not a substitute for milk and was to be drunk only after the milk had been disposed of.

Also, they used paper plates and napkins and did not set the table. This made the meal officially a kitchen picnic, and the children loved it. The whole business was over, and the dishes were out of the way, by twelve-thirty.

There followed a period of intense, hushed, rustling activity, while they all dressed for church. This time of concentration was broken only by an occasional anguished cry of "Moooother! My hair isn't quite dry!" or, "Moooother! Randy's pounding my head with the hair brush!" or, "Edith! Haven't I got *any* clean socks?"

By one o'clock not only were they all clothed, but Edith felt that she retained an unusually large proportion of her right mind. Perhaps because of the extra rest that morning, she felt almost serene as she took Dave back to the house to the bathroom while Fred and the older children waited for them in the car.

There was a Sunday stillness over the landscape, a peace that went beyond the gold of the cottonwoods—like the color of sultana raisins, Edith always thought—and the high, unyielding blue of the sky. Just a few puffy white clouds—cushions for the angels to sit on, Sharon had said once when she was small—drifted across it. Even the spurts of dust that rose when the cottonwoods dropped leaves on the road ahead of the car seemed relaxed and peaceful and less hurried than on weekdays. Setting aside a day for rest was a wonderful, quieting idea, even if all it did was give you time to notice and enjoy the natural things you took for granted most of the time.

Mrs. Fowler met them outside the schoolhouse, a broad smile of welcome on her face. "We have thirty people here, and some more still coming," she announced. "Mr. Elgin stopped as he came along the highway, and invited everybody he saw to come here for services today. I think it was so thoughtful of him—and he's new to this part of the country, too. *Such* a nice little man."

Some of the thirty people were already inside the building. Laverne was there, with her husband, Uncle Ed. He had built a fire in the wood furnace, to take the week-end chill off the building. The teacher's desk had been moved to the center of the space at the front of the building, facing the row of seats and the tables for the children. Someone—probably Laverne—had covered the desk with a clean white cloth. Mrs. Fowler must have brought the claret-colored chrysanthemums. No one else raised flowers quite like hers. The little missionary—a compact, energetic young man, considerably taller than Mrs. Fowler's diminutive implied—was talking with a group of men near the door.

There was a moment's pause, not a time of silence, but of hush. The last-comers entered the door a few moments before the hands of Edith's watch reached two. The children, seated at their own desks, stopped shuffling their feet; the adults, on folding chairs they had brought with them or on cushions carried in from their cars, were motionless. Mr. Elgin turned from the door and came to the front of the room. He nodded to Edith, already seated at the upright piano.

"Let us all sing together, 'Onward Christian Soldiers,'" he said.

None of them there in the schoolhouse sang very well, but they were used to singing together. The children knew the hymn and loved it, and their voices led the others, loud and strong:

> *Like* a mighty army,
> Moves the Church of God—
> Brothers, we are treading,
> *Where* the saints have trod—

Saints could be anybody; Mrs. Fowler, singing as if she saw fields that were green, instead of the dust-colored prairies beyond the window; Laverne, her face white and tired because she wasn't well and probably hadn't slept—she'd never tell any one about that—Sharon, even, with a small, unmentioned blister on her thumb from getting Breakfast in Bed for her mother. Saints were all around you . . .

> *On*ward, then, ye people,
> *Join* the happy throng,
> Blend with ours your voices
> *In* the triumph song.
> *Glory*, laud, and honor—
> Unto Christ the King—

Randy loved that majestic, rolling string of words and the manful chords that accompanied them. That was his voice now, soaring a little off-pitch above the others. She could not see him, but she knew how he looked, the shut-eyed, open-mouthed ecstacy of his freckles as he ended the stanza:

> *This* through countless ages
> MEN and angels sing!
> *On*ward Christian soldiers—

It was a good hymn; it was one of the best. Edith closed the hymn book on the music rack and rejoined her family for the Lord's Prayer and the reading from the Psalms.

"The Heavens declare the glory of God, and the firmament sheweth his handy-work; One day telleth another, and one night certifieth another; There is neither speech nor language but . . . Their sound is gone out into all lands; and their words to the ends of the world."

It was good, it was all good, and the idea of such a day was best of all. A day when you met the neighbors and gathered with them. A day when you forgot—really—about work and the problems work created. A day for sitting and thinking, for not even planning meals, for letting things happen happily. They all needed it sometimes. Sitting there, listening to the reading of the Scripture lesson, Edith tried to remember when they had last had services on Platte River. Not since the roads opened last April, and even then everybody couldn't get there because so many of the men had been busy with the early calf crop.

The one thing that would take her to town to live even for a little while would be the chance it afforded to take the children to Sunday School every week, instead of three or four times a year. They did love it so. Even when it meant settling back at the end of a relatively unfamiliar hymn, "Holy, Holy, Holy," to listen to a sermon intended for adults, they loved it.

Mr. Elgin was a gentle, kindly man. His message was essentially: Peace on earth to men of good will; Love of God and love of neighbors. He conveyed it by means of the parable of the Good Shepherd.

They took up the collection and sang the Doxology at the end of the sermon. The neighborhood had long ago agreed on the division of funds from these interdenominational services: one-third to the upkeep of the schoolhouse; one-third to the missionary to pay his traveling expenses; one third to the American Board of Missions so that missionaries might be supplied to them and to other communities like theirs.

Then the last hymn, everybody standing together and singing, "My Country, 'Tis of Thee." Edith could hear Mrs. Fowler doggedly following the tune with the words of "God Save the

King." Mrs. Fowler said she did so out of habit. Fred said on the way home that in the present state of British politics it was a habit some of the king's subjects should cultivate.

They all relaxed and laughed a little and took off their mental and spiritual tight shoes once they were in the car and headed for home. Formality in religion was fine, but it didn't go far unless you lived what you believed. Edith was proud to think that her family lived their religion. That was a satisfying thought. As long as they could believe and live their religion, church in the schoolhouse four times a year and Bible readings and family prayers at home would give them all the guidance they needed.

18. *This Is the Way the Ladies Ride*

SOUTH DAKOTA, 1951

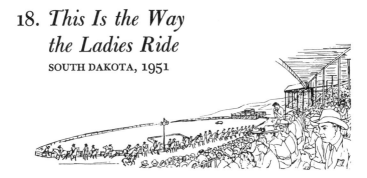

WINONA must have been influenced by the photographs in *Vogue* without knowing it. All the lovely, long-necked, long-waisted ladies swishing through its pages trailed stoles across their drooping shoulders that season. If Winona had not subconsciously noticed that stoles and other wrapping wraps were being worn, she might have rejected her grandmother's shawl and worn a lumber-jacket instead.

But the morning was damp and chilly and she was in a hurry. Grandmother came hurrying from the old log house with the shawl when she saw Winona come out to start the car. And there *had* been those illustrations in *Vogue*. Winona accepted the square of Roman-striped sheer woolen and wrapped it around her, grateful for its warmth and only casually aware of its beauty.

She covered the twenty miles into town in twenty-five minutes, the delay being the result of getting in and out of the car to open and close gates. And she had to slow down when she reached the edge of town and drive more deliberately along the streets. But she got to the station in plenty of time. There wasn't even a smudge of smoke down the tracks to show that the train was coming.

The platform was crowded with people. There were men in high-topped, high-heeled boots and steeple-crowned felt hats. There were some women in blue jeans, with hats and jackets like those of the men, and other women who wore their church-going dresses and gloves and flowered hats. There was also a group of Indians, the men easily distinguished from the whites by their swinging braids; the other women wrapped in shawls as Winona was. White or Indian, most of the women held boxes or bundles.

She went to join her own people and stood with them, shivering a little from cold and excitement and lack of breakfast, listening to the squeals and squeaks and rattles and bangs of the local band, holding her package tightly.

The noise of the band was caught up and drowned in the sudden wonking of the Diesel. With only that noise for warning, the big engine slid to a stop beside the platform. The racket of young, healthy, wildly human voices made itself heard vociferously. The 891st Division was a former National Guard unit. Passing through its home town was a major event for the families as well as for the service personnel.

MP's stood, forcing impassivity, on the steps of the coaches. They chanted monotonously: "Nobody on or off. Nobody on or off." Families ran along the platform, gazing upward, stumbling on the rough concrete underfoot. Individuals walked more slowly, up one side of the train and down the other until they found the faces they sought, or others almost equally familiar, and with them, guidance. Winona saw both her brothers as soon as the train stopped. They stood side by side on the steps of the last coach, white-lettered brassards proclaiming their importance to the world. Old Singing Weasel, beside her, nudged her with his elbow. "Young men's soldier society," he said in Indian, and chuckled.

Perhaps it was just as well she was an Indian. She, at least, had been taught by her elders to keep her feelings and face under control. She could not speak to her brothers when they were on duty; they would never have forgiven her. She could only, for the moment, look at them and let them look at her.

She looked and wondered how in the world she was going to give them the sack of fruit, cakes, candy, and cigarettes hugged against her inside the folds of the shawl. These lordly creatures, even if they were allowed to relax from their military duties, could never accept a brown paper bag from the Safeway.

The problem was solved even as she became aware that it existed. Out of the washroom window beside Bill's head another Indian face projected itself, grinning broadly.

"Hiya, Winnie," Jack Longtassel shouted. "What you got there—dried beef?"

She ran across to the train and stood beside her brothers, passing the sack up under their eyes to their friend. "I brought this for all of you, Jack," she said loudly and firmly. "You be sure you divide with them."

"Swell, Winnie," Jack grinned again. "They already said they'd divide with me if I did the talking for them. Mom wrote me she couldn't make it down to the train. They're haying in the north meadow, she said."

"They got it all in last night," Winona told him rapidly, "and started on the patch in Bitter Creek Bottoms this morning—or they were going to. Your mother's bucking the rake. She sure makes a good hand. I think she and your Dad will get the whole cutting in—just the two of them."

"Thanks, Winnie." His face sobered. "What about your folks?"

"Mom's all right. She can get up for an hour in the afternoon, now, and they may let her walk next month. She's got to stay on at the San, though. The doctor won't even guess when she can come home. George and Grandma and I are holding the place down. We can't get help and we've given up trying. George and I got our hay in last week—as much of it as we're going to cut. Most of it we'll let the cattle harvest for themselves. We've got three hundred yearlings and they look fine. George cut out three of them to sell to the Chamber of Commerce for the rodeo, and got slaughterhouse prices for them."

"Say, that's all right! George's quite a hand for fifteen. How do you manage, Winnie?"

"Oh, I ride and work with George, and we let Grandma handle the books and the stock records. She's slow, but she's sure. Carlisle sure taught Indians two things: how to read and write and how to keep house. We couldn't get along without Grandma."

"Cowgirl Winnie! You better run for rodeo queen next month, Win. Be the first time they ever had a real cowhand run."

"Dope! Indians don't run for rodeo queens!" Her eyes went beyond him to her brothers, where they stood on the steps, trying to hear everything that was said, trying to look as if they heard nothing. "Tell them good-bye for me," she called as the Diesel wailed again. "Tell them the old people are waiting to kill beef. Tell them that Grandma sent them many lucks!"

Jack waved, but whatever he said was lost in a final screech and a shout from the head of the train. The wheels turned slowly, then more rapidly, as they took up a steady clicking across the ties. The MP's saluted the band and its flag as they soared past, then turned and swung and were lost inside the coaches. The train was gone, and Winona, standing on the platform, shivered all over once as she saw the dust devil twist along the tracks and mark the end of the last visit home.

What she needed was breakfast, she told herself firmly as she walked back to the car. Breakfast, and especially a hot cup of coffee. She had been too rushed and excited to swallow anything before she left home.

Now she drove directly into town and stopped on the main street. She parked the car and dropped a precautionary nickle into the meter; then, with the shawl still hugged about her for warmth, she walked quickly into a small café.

At first she was simply grateful to be warm and to sit down; then she began again to think about a cup of coffee. After a time her thoughts became urgent. The clock over the counter showed that she had been there fifteen minutes. There were people at the counter and in the other booths, and only one waitress. Winona could see for herself that the girl was busy. But when half an hour passed and most of the crowd had thinned out, Winona decided to take action. She was less chilled than she had been, but she was decidedly hungry. Perhaps the girl had not noticed her, sitting alone in the back of a booth. She rose, and went to balance on one of the counter stools. The waitress paused before her briefly, and Winona gave the girl her order, a little surprised to see that it was not written down on the waitress' pad.

Another interminable wait followed. People about her were served; indeed, newcomers entered and were attended to and left the restaurant. The waitress passed before Winona again.

"Please," Winona said, "could you bring me a cup of coffee?"

The girl looked at her and went away without speaking. A moment later, a man came from the kitchen and stood as the waitress had before Winona.

"Look," he said in a low tone. "We don't serve Indians here. We don't serve anybody but whites," he reiterated as Winona looked at him blankly.

She got up quietly, the shawl still folded around her, as softly draped as any stole in *Vogue*. Without a word she left the place. Once on the street she turned towards her car. Something blurred her vision; she was not sure where she had parked. She smacked into something solid, and her tears took form and ran down her cheeks, clearing her eyes so she could see who obstructed her way. It was Harry Ferguson, the rancher from up the river.

"What's the matter with you?" he demanded, clutching her elbow.

Chokily, Winona tried to tell him, and something of what she got out must have made some sense. Ferguson piloted her by the elbow he still gripped and settled her in his car at the curb. Then he left her, and when he returned she had dried her eyes. He was carefully carrying a tray when she saw him emerge from the door of the restaurant. On the tray were doughnuts and a sweet roll and two mugs of coffee.

"Ada would say this wasn't a balanced breakfast," Harry remarked, "but I always say that anything on a tray on your knees is a balanced meal as far as I'm concerned. Drink your coffee, Winnie. There's plenty more where that came from. And have a doughnut."

Winona obeyed him, and while she ate and drank, the rancher beside her consumed his own cup of coffee, half a doughnut, and two homemade cigarettes. He went back to the café once for seconds of coffee. When Winona had finished the other doughnut and a half, the sweet roll, and her coffee, she felt like a new woman.

"Thank you," she said finally, crumpling her paper napkin on the tray. Then she really looked for the first time at the man's face. "Don't feel so bad," she consoled him. "It's happened before and it will again. It's nothing to get upset about."

Ferguson shook his head. "It's something to get very much upset about," he corrected her. "Look at the line-up. You went down to the train this morning to see your brothers off for Korea. How are they, by the way?"

"I didn't get to talk to them," Winona replied. "They're both MP's and they were on duty. But they looked fine."

"That makes it worse. You didn't even get to talk to them. Your brother Bates died on the Bataan death march and your father worked himself to death in forty-five as a C.B. Your mother's in the T. B. sanatorium, and there you are, with only your grandmother and one fifteen-year-old brother left, running that ranch. More than running it, doing a good job of it. It's a damned outrage when a girl like you can't get a meal in a cheap dirty-spoon café."

"It's the first time," Winona remarked thoughtfully. "I've eaten there before when I was in a hurry. I guess it's the shawl. I've never worn a shawl to town before. But I was in a rush...."

Ferguson lighted another cigarette. "Shawl or no shawl," he insisted, "it makes no difference. Indians are doing as much as anybody, and more than a lot of people, to hold this country together. It's a damned outrage when they don't get decent treatment."

"Oh, don't worry about it; it isn't worth while. I should have been at the ranch two hours ago anyhow. I'll stay put out there, and forget all about it."

"You can't. I won't let you." Ferguson suddenly grinned. "I'm going to write a letter to the paper. That's the first thing.

And then I'm going to keep on reminding the people in this community what kind of neighbors the Indians around here are." He reached over and patted her lightly on the shoulder. "Cheer up, Winnie. I'll let them know you can do something besides supply them with rodeo stock."

Winona slid out of his car and turned towards her own. She giggled, but when she spoke her voice was still bitter. "Jack Longtassel said I ought to run for rodeo queen. He said it would be the first time a real cowhand ever got elected to that job."

"Did he now?" Ferguson inquired. "Did he?"

The letter came out in the paper that same evening, and it was published on the back page, in the "Paid Advertising" section. It was quite a long letter, a full column, and Ferguson must have paid a good bit of money to have it printed. The letter recited the incident of the morning as briefly and objectively as anyone in a hot anger could have reported it. Then the letter continued with a review of Winona's family history and a mention of her present occupation: cattle raiser. It cited the contribution made by Indians to the nation's food supply, both in terms of the historic past and in those of contemporary production. And it ended by nominating Winona as a candidate for rodeo queen. "It is high time," the letter ended, "that our Indian friends and neighbors received the respect and honor that are due them."

Winona laughed when she read the letter; then she clipped it to send to Jack as soon as she got his APO number. After that she spent a restful evening checking the breeding records with her grandmother and went to bed. In the morning she left early with George to mend fence, and forgot about everything but the high price of barbed wire.

In fact she did not think of the incident again for a week; not until she drove to the sanatorium to visit her mother. They sat out on a long screened porch, overlooking the hills and the green of the meadows, while they talked.

"Don't run for queen," Winona's mother said. "We don't do those things, you know. It isn't modest to go around *asking* people for an honor."

"Don't worry, darling," Winona replied. "I haven't time to

run for anything but fence-busting yearlings. If they want me for queen, they'll have to find somebody to take care of the place for me while I'm in town being crowned. Either that or come out to the ranch for the coronation. I'm busy."

Her mother lay quietly looking out at the hills. "You know," she said presently, "it's a funny thing. I always wanted you to be a missionary, but I was willing to compromise and let you take a teacher's training course. Anything to get you away from the reservation and out into the world to do good. Now you have to come back to the reservation and do a man's work to live. And you end up by going back to the blanket," she smiled dimly, to show that was meant for a joke, "and being insulted by white people in the nearest town because you're an Indian. The world hasn't changed at all in some ways since I was a girl."

Winona stroked her mother's hand lightly, and they sat wordlessly until the bell in the corridor rang and drove visitors home with its clangor. It was a funny thing, Winona thought, driving home. Grandma had been born in a tipi and was sent to Carlisle with other children of tribal chiefs. That amounted to being a prisoner of war. Grandma had learned English and housekeeping and all that such knowledge implied in her day, and she had married another Carlisle graduate and had sent her daughter east to be educated, first at a girls' boarding school and then at a music conservatory.

Mother had toured the country, singing in concerts. She had refused to wear a buckskin dress on the concert platform and insisted on being judged as an artist and not as an Indian. She had married the first man in her tribe to take a college degree— Father had been trained at an eastern engineering college. In a way they had both been worldly and successful people before they came back to the reservation and began ranching, extending their allotment holdings with leased land. The ranching idea had been mother's. She wanted her children to live in the country while they were growing up.

Bates went to the state agricultural college and played football. Winona dodged the car around a rabbit and remembered the wild year when Bates was a senior and saved the conference championship for the school. She was a freshman and was wondering why in the world there was a state law that compelled her to take courses in agriculture before she could secure a teacher's certificate. Now she wished she had taken nothing but agriculture, as the younger boys did when they came along after the war. Certainly she never had a chance to use any of the other subjects. French and history—who wanted to study them in the ranch country? Anyway, she never got to teach. As soon as she graduated, she went to work as a hand on the family ranch.

Well, it was still the family ranch, and now it was up to her to keep it that. And if she sat around wondering what would have happened if she had taught school or why Harry Ferguson thought it did any good to write letters to newspapers, she would never get the hay crop in. What she had to think about right now was running the stock through the chutes tomorrow and getting the fly spray on as much of each of them as possible. Lucky George had seen that ad for the underline spray. Getting the stuff along the lower parts of the creatures was a major job without it.

Again Winona forgot about the rodeo. There was a post card in the box when she stopped; a card signed by Jack as well as her brothers, giving their APO. "Thanks for the grub," was scrawled across one end, and "Yeah! Cowgirl! Ride 'em!" on the other. That must be Jack and his idea of a joke. She handed the card over to her grandmother to be answered with the rest of the ranch correspondence. After all, when you set out to spray three hundred yearlings, each with violent objections to being sprayed, you get up before daylight if possible. Correspondence is a luxury to save for winter.

The delegation arrived when Winona was balanced on top of the chute, with the long-armed spray clutched firmly under her arm. George, in the corral, was shouting and waving his arms, driving the last steers into the chute. Winona hauled back on the spray trigger and a fine mist enveloped the leading steer.

Someone gave her a swat on the bottom and she swung

around, still with the spray trigger depressed, and drenched her tormentor, too surprised to stop at once even when she recognized Singing Weasel. Then her hand relaxed. Singing Weasel was shouting with glee.

"See!" he yelled at the other tribal councilmen, who were still clustered around the Indian Service station wagon, well beyond Winona's aim with the spray. "She knows she's got the right to play jokes on her uncle! A fine girl!"

Winona wondered what made Singing Weasel her uncle all of a sudden; then remembered that he was one of Grandma's multitude of cousins. All right, so he probably was her uncle, Indian fashion. She still clutched the spray. "Get back, all my uncles, until I finish this," she ordered. George hupped and waved his arms again, and she drenched the last three steers with fly spray. Then she climbed down, pulled off her gloves and hat, and shook hands. "What's on your mind?" she asked Singing Weasel.

The old man was not to be hurried. He squatted deliberately on the ground by the corral and waited till the other councilmen joined him. Only after all the men had lighted cigarettes did he speak.

"We have come to invite you to run for rodeo queen," he said when they had disposed of the weather, their own health, that of Winona's mother and grandmother, and his wife's.

"I haven't got time," Winona said, and added, "Thank you just the same."

But Singing Weasel had made up his mind. "See," he said to the other older men. "She knows what is right and how to behave. She does not accept immediately. She is waiting to be urged. Niece, these are all good men, your friends. They want you to run for rodeo queen. It is their idea, not mine. They just brought me along because they know you haven't the right to refuse your uncle anything."

"I've got to refuse," Winona protested. "I've got the government veterinarian coming to shoot the stock for anthrax next week."

"She wants to be urged again," crowed Singing Weasel. "Oh,

234

what a pleasure it is, in these modern days, to find a young woman who is properly brought up and has good manners."

An approving murmur of response ran through the group of councilmen. The old man smiled benignly on Winona. "You must run for queen," he said. "After all, it is only because of that letter in the paper about you that we have decided to have a candidate for queen. You have already been nominated."

That time Winona paused before she answered, when she did speak, she was less curt. "My uncle," she said, "you know and I know that such things happen; hadn't we all better forget about it? Won't we be happier if we do? Those were very ignorant and careless people. Why should we worry about what they think or say or do?"

Singing Weasel stood quite still as he faced her. "My niece, for the fourth time I am asking you to be our tribal candidate for queen. Because the fourth time must be the last, I make the one request you cannot refuse. Because of your brothers and our other fine young men, in order to show respect for them, I tell you that you must be our candidate for queen."

He was a smart old man, anyway you looked at it. That *was* the one request Winona could never refuse. She knew it and he knew it. She hesitated only a moment longer; then she nodded.

"Very well, my uncle. I'll have to accept. I will be the tribal candidate for queen. And now, for Goodness' sake, go on back to the council house and let me get these steers out in the pasture before my brothers and our other fine young men have to starve to death for lack of meat."

Each councilman came up and gravely shook hands with Winona, putting into her calloused palms their own brown, soft, small ones. Cowboys and Indians, she thought, smiling to herself. Always vain of their hands, always wearing gloves and rubbing on tallow to keep the skin soft. The delegation teetered away on their high heels, and Winona got back to work.

Grandmother kept track of the rodeo plans for her. On the morning the show was scheduled to open she came into Winona's bedroom before daylight, and shook her granddaughter's foot through the bed clothes. "Come on and get up," the old

235

woman ordered. "You've got to get busy. Some of the yearlings got through the south pasture fence in the night. I've already sent George out to run them back."

Winona came out of bed in one movement and reached for her clothes in a second. "Where are they?" she asked, without bothering to find out where her grandmother got the information. Grandma was like a lot of other old timers. When it came to things like that, she just *knew*.

"Down at the haystacks in the creek meadow," Grandma said. "I'll have breakfast and some water hot for your bath when you get back."

By the time the yearlings had been returned to their legal pasture it was seven o'clock, and the parade was scheduled for ten. In the interval, Winona would have to do her regular chores, bathe, dress, and get into town. The time gap was alarmingly short. "I just can't go," she said to George on the way back to the house. "I know I'll never make it. You can take the car and go in and tell them there isn't going to be any Indian entry."

Grandma, however, had everything under control. The chickens were fed and the board floor under the roosts raked clean. The bum lambs in the fenced yard beside the milking corral had been cared for. Breakfast was on the table, and Grandma, already bathed and fresh in a clean cotton print dress, was pouring coffee when they entered the kitchen.

"George," she directed, "you go and have your bath while Winona eats. Then you can have breakfast while she's dressing."

Winona stowed away eggs and hot cakes and bacon briskly. When she got up for her second cup of coffee, Grandma spoke again. "I laid your clothes out on the bed, all ready for you," she observed. "I knew you hadn't got around to thinking about what you'd wear, so I took care of it for you."

"Oh, Lord! The buckskin dress!" Winona exclaimed. If there was anything she did not want to wear on this particular occasion, it was the buckskin dress. The garment was old and fragile, and the big blue and white pony beads that decorated its neck and sleeves were likely to loosen and scatter with the slightest movement of the wearer. Besides, the dress was an heirloom; it had belonged to Grandma's grandmother and its associations were precious. In addition to her consideration for this particular dress, Winona didn't want to wear buckskin in the parade.

But Grandma shook her head. "You see," she remarked.

George appeared from the bathroom. "O.K., Winnie," he said to his sister. "Say, what about the horses? You want me to slick 'em down and load them in the trailer?"

Again Grandma took charge. "I fixed about horses," she said. "Go on and get ready, Winona, and George, you eat your breakfast. Horses are in town for you to ride."

Maybe it was Quaker raising and maybe it was mother-wit, born of the centuries and generations when Indian women had to be prepared for anything before it happened. Whatever it was, Grandma was firmly in charge of the situation and of her grandchildren. She was boss of the ranch, and she might well wind up running the whole rodeo at the rate she was going.

Winona scrubbed briefly, then took a minute or two to soak before she got out of the tub and went down the hall to her bedroom. Inside the door she paused and stared at the clothes that were spread out on the bed. Grandma had indeed gone to town: frontier pants and shirt of aqua gabardine, with yoke inserts of golden tan. Embroidery in rose and gold and deepest green; roses and foliage looping and twining across the front yoke and shoulders of the shirt and down the side seams of the trousers. A flat-crowned Stetson of the same golden tan as the inserts. Boots, their tops stitched tan leather, inlaid with butterflies and wild roses of turquoise blue. A new and perfectly useless lariat, braided of gold and turquoise silk rope. And the crowning glory of a new belt, carved and stamped and silverfitted, with watch-band to match. It was the perfect outfit for a rodeo queen, but how in the world had Grandma managed it? How had she even known what to manage for?

Grandma was waiting in the car when Winona came out. Grandma, wrapped in the striped woolen shawl, was enthroned in the center of the back seat. The front was covered with a spotless sheet. "You let George drive," Grandma instructed Winona. "You're too nervous. Turn around and let me see how you look."

"It's beautiful, Grandma," Winona said, obediently turning. "I never saw a nicer outfit. How did you ever get it without my finding out?"

"Well, it's good material, and you don't look any worse than most of them with your bottom poking out," said Grandma. "As for how I got it, what are all the Sears catalogs around the house for, now we have a bathroom? I wrote to Denver and told them to send me one rodeo queen's outfit. Complete. I had some money put away, and I used that."

Grandma's money-put-away. The little buckskin bags that smelled of herbs hung in her closet and were folded among the clothes in her dresser drawers. Theoretically and officially those bags held Indian perfume for sachet and to keep the moths out; actually there was none of them that would not yield up a wad of tightly folded bills if it were opened. Grandma's money-put-away had pulled the family through tight times and had given the children small luxuries in good ones. Where would they all have been, all these years, without Grandma's money-put-away?

They were approaching the edge of town. Suddenly Winona was aware of flags and bunting draped across the streets, of other cars decorated with ribbons of colored crepe paper for the parade, of horns banging aimlessly and uselessly and merrily. People and movement and noise, and it all added up to fun. Winona felt herself relax on the car seat. Maybe she had been taking things too seriously lately. Everybody was entitled to a day off once in a while.

"Where do you want to go, Grandma?" George asked.

"You go to the line-up," Grandma directed him. "I'll get along. Somebody will take me into town from there. Go on."

The line-up was in the park on the edge of town, and about all that could be said at the moment was that there was nothing resembling a straight line anywhere in sight. Four high school bands, in as many different uniforms, were wiggling protoplasmic masses at the four corners of the park. The parade marshals, on horses chosen for their stolidity, plopped through the dust, trying to capture the attention of the clowns, of the queen-candidates, of the escorts, and of the local politicians and state dignitaries who had abandoned their convertibles to mingle with the mob, to have some fun, and to raise a few votes. Behind the tossing movement were the more solid forms of the floats, and beyond them again the indifferent forms of the hills and the indelible blue of the sky.

George parked on the edge of the skirmish, and Grandma rolled down her window, peered out, and beckoned. Harry Ferguson appeared at the side of the car. He was afoot and he led two horses. "These suit you, Winona?" he inquired.

Winona knew that perfectly matched pair of palominos—who in that part of the world did not? Their golden-tan bodies were curried to satiny perfection; the spun-glass whiteness of their manes and tails had been sleeked and waved until it rippled like timothy ready for cutting, touched by a light wind. Those Arabians were perfect parade horses, spirited and high-stepping without being spooky; velvet-mouthed but so intelligent and used to crowds that a rider could hold the lines with fingertips and without worry; so vain of themselves that they liked to be paraded. Range horses hated it all, but these might have been bred and trained for a circus. They were terrific showoffs.

"Come on, kid," Ferguson said. "I'll drive Grandma into town. I've worked these and walked them, so they won't be too fresh for you to handle." He grinned. "Remember, they'll be all right as long as you leave them alone. If they want to stand up, let them; they're trained to do it, it's part of their act. Don't try to pull them down and they won't spill you. I wouldn't get up till you're ready to start; just line up wherever the marshals tell you and wait till they give you the word to go."

Grandma's brown face, at the rear window, cracked into a reluctant smile as the white man took George's place at the wheel of the car. "Pretty horse, pretty girl. You have many lucks. We look for you in town."

Surprisingly, the parade was only twenty minutes late in starting. It curved informally around the square park, rounding the corners in a series of swerves. A flag, a band, and a convertible full of important men to be looked at. A float, a group of marchers, a queen-candidate and her escort and attendants, and a float and a convertible and another band. Then the succession repeated again and again, with clowns on bicycles and donkeys and old Model T's fringing the edges of the more orderly ribbon of paraders. Dogs barked, a few horses fretted their bits or reared, the drums ruffled softly to set the pace, and then were as still as the trumpets until the straightaway of Broadway was reached and the parade really strung out and started moving.

There was a little wind to push the dust along the pavement ahead of them. George and Winona rode behind the Indian School band and the group of old-time Indians who always rode and never walked, although they were down in the parade program as "marchers." Behind the two palominos rode the queen-candidate's attendants; two girls in white buckskin and elks' teeth, with striped shawls across their laps and over the horns of their high-pommeled, old-time women's saddles. Just for a moment, when she saw her attendants, Winona wondered if she should have worn buckskin, too. Then her palomino stood up on his hind legs and walked forward four paces, and she devoted her entire attention to the horse.

The matched pair, now pacing sedately side by side, had been trained to take their cues in a way that Winona did not at first understand. Then she realized that the horses reared every hundred steps. The action had nothing to do with anything but distance covered. Composedly, every hundred steps, the pair stood up and walked four steps forward, then dropped down and took the next hundred steps. If their rearing happened to coincide with something else that was going on, it was fortunate but it was also fortuitous.

So it was that Winona and George had nothing to do with the horses' rising to their hind feet at the first notes of "The Star-spangled Banner," nor again when they passed the flag-draped reviewing stand. It was not in obedience to their riders, but to long and thorough training, that the palominos rose to salute

Grandma, when they passed her seated in the car before the small café that Winona had hoped she had forgotten. And it was entirely involuntary on Winona's part that she appeared as a superb, rather than an everyday, capable rider, all the length of the town and out to the fairgrounds and the corral behind the grandstand.

"Looked pretty good," observed Grandma, materializing by the gate as Winona dismounted. "You leave George to hitch them. Don't off-saddle, boy, or they'll roll and you'll have to groom them again. It isn't too hot for them to stand a couple of hours until it's time for the grandstand parade."

They drove back to the picnic area in the park, and Grandma produced a basket from the back seat of the car. Inside were fried chicken, bread and butter, potato salad, ripe tomatoes from the garden, and two thermos jars of coffee. "No cake," said Grandma. "Sweet stuff makes you sweat. Salt is better. Put lots of salt on your tomato, Winnie, and tie this dish towel around your neck before you eat it."

"Where's Harry Ferguson?" George asked around a mouthful of potato salad.

"Gone to have lunch with the Chamber of Commerce," Grandma informed them. "He drove me out to the fairgrounds to meet you and went on back to town with some other men."

It was dreamy quiet and peaceful, sitting there in the park under the trees. It was like sitting with her mother on the porch of the San, Winona reflected. Next week visiting day came around again, and she could see her mother and tell her all about the rodeo. She'd have to be careful to remember everything that happened. And she'd also have to remember so she could write to Jack and her brothers.

Now Grandma was organizing again. She supervised the gathering together and repacking of the lunch and the reloading of the car. She inspected Winona and brushed an almost imaginary twig from her shoulder. She directed their progress through thickening traffic as they returned to the fairgrounds, and selected the one parking spot that was equi-distant from the grandstand and the horse corral. With everything under control, she left her grandchildren to get their horses and make ready for the second parade of the day.

This was a repetition, on a slightly smaller and much more crowded scale, of the proceedings of the morning. There were no floats. On the other hand, the band members seemed more lively than before, and their numbers appeared to have increased. And the state dignitaries and the local politicians, all slightly flushed with lunch and the highballs that had preceded it, were inclined to talk more loudly and impressively than they had previously.

But the little cool breeze was there to freshen the horses and their riders, and the sun shone on the hills and the flats where the fairgrounds were set. The sky stretched its blueness above the corrals and the pens and the bawling calves waiting for the roping. It was the best kind of summer afternoon.

Now that she knew what the horses could be expected to do, Winona planned a little ahead, as Grandma would have. She figured as closely as she could the distance between the corral and the judges' stand. If she and George mounted at the gate the horses would salute three times in the course of the parade; once as they came before the grandstand; once in its center as they faced the judges, and again at the far end. Possibly Harry Ferguson had trained them with the length of the grandstand in mind; he often rode in parades.

It worked out perfectly. The horses saluted exactly as Winona had planned. Then they were at the end of the stand and they turned—again the horses seemed to know exactly what to do— and rode back to the center. Here the queen-candidates formed a mounted line, with their escorts behind them. Some of the horses were restless, and some of the girls had a hard time holding their mounts. One, evidently a town girl, dropped her lines and unashamedly clutched her saddle horn. The pick-up men backed their way into the line on either side of her, and her horse quieted down. But the palomino, once he had again saluted the judges, stood as still as a rock. Winona eased herself in the saddle and looked out over the crowd.

242

She did not expect to recognize anybody, just to see spots of color here and there. But she did, after a moment, easily identify three of the occupants of the judges' box. Ferguson she might have expected; after all, he was a well-known cattleman. The restaurant man—yes, as a local merchant, he had a right to be there. But the third—what was Grandma doing, wrapped in her shawl, in the box behind the restaurant man? And why was she bending forward and whispering to him with such intensity?

The mounted judges rode down the line of girls, and beckoned each in turn to ride forward and salute the crowd. As each separated herself from the bunch, a judge raised his hand and applause rolled up. The other judge held a stop watch to time the cheers. Winona and the palomino did, she thought, very well. Ferguson was applauding even before the air was split with a throat-trembling, spine-tingling yell—Grandma was making herself heard with a good old traditional war whoop. And when Grandma yelled like that, right in his ear, the restaurant man stood up and yelled, too. Moreover, he threw his hat in the air and he gave three rousing cheers.

The mounted judges continued the length of the line and came back. Winona and two other girls were beckoned forward. The palomino knew what to do better than she did. Free of the line of other horses, he cantered in a tight circle, its circumference little more than his own turning length. Then he again saluted the crowd. Again applause rolled, and again Grandma's war cry swelled out. There could be little doubt, even before the formal announcement of the judges' decision, who had won, who was the rodeo queen.

Winona and the palomino led the group back to the corral. Ferguson was waiting to help her dismount. "Go on," he said, "I'll see to the horse. You go on up to the box and sit with your Grandma."

"What did you do?" Winona whispered fiercely. She seized his arm and shook it. "What did Grandma do?" she demanded.

Ferguson was busy off-saddling and he kept his face turned away from her. "She went and sat in the box," he said. "The

243

poor old lady can't speak much English, and she couldn't understand when people told her she was supposed to sit somewhere else." His shoulders jerked slightly.

"Did she draw a knife on him?" Winona insisted.

"Why, how you talk, Winnie." Ferguson faced her, all bland innocence. "Would a sweet little gray-haired old lady like your Grandma—brought up by the Quakers, too—draw a knife on anybody?"

"You bet she would if she happened to feel like it," Winona said. "Tell me. *What* did she do?"

"Why, she just sat there, wrapped up in her shawl, and when anybody asked her to move, she said, 'My grandsons big army chiefs. Kill lots Reds. I teach 'em.' That's all she did, Winnie. As far as I know she didn't even have a knife with her—just that old tin billy-club your dad used to carry for a joke the year he was Indian policeman on the reservation."

The all enveloping shawl! It could hide a college degree and the quality of your table manners. It could also hide a policeman's night stick or a small, gray-haired atom bomb, if necessary.

19. *They Could All Get Killed*

OKLAHOMA, 1951

THE concrete of the grandstand made hard sitting. Catherine Caine wondered if it would seem softer if she relaxed. Certainly she had enough padding of her own—she ought not to notice whether or not the concrete were comfortable. She consoled herself with the thought that even the old sofa on the back porch of the ranch house felt pretty firm when she sat down on it with her girdle on.

Before and below her the earth of the race track showed the striations of the rake that had gone over it earlier in the day. The pens in the center field had been newly whitewashed and gleamed boldly. They were the focus of a constant, purposeful activity of men and boys; a buzzing haze of blue jeans and Stetsons and colored shirts surrounded them. This accustomed movement was enough to distract everyone's attention from the school band and the parade of the Shrine Drill Corps and the rodeo queen and her court on their horses. The parade and all those who composed it were simply incidentals; the real business of the day and the real attention of the audience centered on the whitewashed pens.

The queen-candidates were lined up on the track facing the grandstand. Time for the contestants and the officials to appear.

Catherine wondered how stiff the competition would be. These little small-town, small-time rodeos with purses to match rarely drew the big-time professional contestants. The local boys had at least a fifty-fifty chance here.

Here they came: A convertible with its top down first. It carried the mayor, the county representative to the state legislature, and the three other judges who would do the work of determining points and awarding purses. Now there followed four men, all big, heavy men, on big, heavy horses, men and mounts alike sober and businesslike. These were the pick-ups, the men and horses who did the most dangerous work of the rodeo without applause. Then came the younger, lighter men on the tough little quarter horses—pintos, buckskins, a bayo coyote, an almost-palomino, several workaday bays and sorrels, and a little blue mare. *That* was Bud on Denim, her color matching his shirt and only a shade or two lighter than that of his worn-and-washed levis. Catherine had spent the last week running those pants through the washer with chlorine bleach, to get them the precise shade Bud wanted. "I don't want them to look new, Mother."

The men on the bayo coyote and the near-palomino didn't mind having their clothes look new and fancy; they must be professionals. They wore silk shirts with appliqued flowers in contrasting colors and frontier pants instead of jeans. The handkerchiefs at their throats were thin silk, and the ends of the scarves lifted and waved a little as a breeze wandered down the track and gathered up loose handfuls of dust to play with. No ordinary cotton bandannas would do for these boys.

Catherine had heard Bud and Pop talk about rodeo professionals; male talk, dropped to discreet whispers when they remembered that she was in the next room and might be listening. Professionals rode dirty—they rode to win, by any means that came handy. That wasn't the worst thing about them. Professionals gambled; in a way, you might say, gambling was their business. They bet their lives against a few hundred dollars every time they went into a bucking chute. Of course, if they won, they made a lot of money in a hurry—ten seconds was a mighty little sliver of time. But if they lost, they lost bad. When a professional won, he didn't use his money sensibly. Instead of investing in a few hundred acres or some good breeding stock or even in a new roping pony, most of them seemed to blow the take on fancy clothes and new cars, on craps and poker and liquor and girls.

Well, the real ranch kids weren't so silly, she thought as the men rode off the race track and clustered back at the horse corral behind the stock pens. A ranch boy like Bud took rodeos differently. He'd spend all year practicing his roping throws, but he needed to use a rope in his business sometimes. Practicing roping was really practicing his trade. Those kids rode all the time, wherever they went and whatever they did. Catherine had heard of men who rode fence in jeeps. They ought to try that in the north pasture at the ranch! You certainly couldn't get around there on anything but a horse.

Pop had been a little upset about Bud's bulldogging. It did take weight off the calves and toughen them some, to use too good stock to practice on. Even roping practice would wear a calf down. But Bud had had his own calves from the time he started. She had known, if his father didn't, that the reason Bud had accepted a scrub calf instead of a purebred for his first 4-H project, and the reason he wasn't disappointed when it weighed the lightest in the school at the end of the year, was that Bud didn't want a blocky calf, he wanted a calf he could rope. The boy had been building up his own herd ever since he was ten, and the money for the first stock he ever bought had come by way of that tough, scrawny calf. He'd won the junior stock roping at the fair when he was eleven. Two-thirds of the money he had spent for good, square, solid beef stock, but the rest had gone into his hobby and he'd bought scrubs.

Well, he'd paid for it himself, and it wasn't as expensive as stamp collecting, from what Catherine had read. Here she sat, for the fourteenth time, and felt just as sick and sinking inside as she had at Bud's first rodeo, when he was eleven. She never would get over it; every rodeo meant that she went to bed with a sick headache for the next three days. Bud had never put two and two together, and she didn't intend to help him do it. She was not going to ask him to stop.

It had got so now that she lived all the year round planning for the next rodeo, as Bud himself did. She listened mechanically to the voice that emerged from the loud-speaker, calling the names and numbers of the contestants. As always, she heard only one. "Number twenty-two, Bud Caine, on Denim. Entered for bucking horse, calf-roping, and steer-riding."

"Move over, Mother." Pop deposited himself beside her and grinned cheerfully. As always, she wondered how he could be so relaxed. "Pays to get here early," he continued. "Was there anybody else in the place when you picked these seats?"

"They were starting to come in. Pop, who are the pick-up men?"

"Didn't you hear the announcer? Slim James, Jack Elliott, Toothpick Barnes, and Injun Arrington. Now, don't worry, Mother. They're the best pick-up team we've ever had."

"I'm not worried."

"Not much." He slid his arm around her and hugged her shamelessly, right there in the grandstand, where anybody who looked away from the infield for a second could see them. "Your shoulders feel like a washboard, that's all. Relax. Enjoy yourself. Listen to the band."

The band ended the discussion before it could fairly get started by slamming into "The Star-spangled Banner." The audience rose to attention amid a rain of spilled cokes, dropped programs, and precariously clutched babies. The riders out on the field grabbed off their hats and tried to hold their horses to attention. The two professional riders were conspicuously unsuccessful at this maneuver. Their horses, supposedly trained to instant obedience, revolved like two highly independent merry-go-rounds. Denim stood rigid, one pointed forefoot barely tipped to the ground, her ears pricked stiffly. This was one of Denim's best tricks, rehearsed nightly to the phonograph. It got her what she wanted now. There was a ripple of amused attention from the audience, and Bud slid forward along her neck as the

248

last note ceased with pain and slipped Denim her sugar lump. She nodded and ducked her head in response. The band sat down and stowed instruments under chairs. The rodeo was really starting now.

Something was wrong with the light, Catherine noticed. It was yellower than it should be at two o'clock of an August afternoon. She nudged her husband.

"Think it'll rain, Pop?"

"Hope so, Mother, we need it. Hey! Not until this is over!"

He was as bad as any of the rest of them. So set on seeing men and horses strain themselves out, maybe get hurt or killed, that he didn't care whether it rained or not. That *was* a black cloud gathering in the north. There was a coolish edge to the strengthening wind. Well ——— The first rider was out of the chute.

It was one of the professionals, and he had drawn a big black horse. It was the meanest of all rides, a sunfisher. The horse went straight up and came down spraddled. It looked less sensational than some other forms of bucking, but it was extremely dangerous. Professional or not, Catherine was relieved that the man stuck on. Ten seconds passed. The referee raised his hat. The pick-up men and their wise, solid horses drew alongside the rider. One of the pick-ups slid his arm around the professional, and the younger man transferred his weight to the other's stirrup, letting the outlaw slide from beneath him to be drawn away by the second pick-up.

"Nice ride," said Pop, severely nonpartisan.

"Where did they get the stock, Pop?"

"Slim James's horses; that's why he's riding pick-up now. He knows pretty well ahead of time what they'll do."

"What about the roping stock?"

"Some ranch down in Texas shipped it up. I don't know the man's name; heard it but I forget it. Brahmas, though, and they traveled all right. Look full of fight."

She wanted to scream, to pound him with her fists, to shriek aloud and stop his talk of steers full of fight. Instead she sat calmly, watching the pick-ups intervene to lift one man from his saddle at the end of ten seconds, draw off the horse from a rider who had sprawled on the ground immediately in front of the chute, catching another almost before he could hit the ground and snatch him out of the way of his horse's twisting hooves. The only friend Catherine had in the world was the wind that was, coquettishly and with little flippant puffs, leading a big black cloud nearer and nearer to the grandstand.

Then the chute opened again and she saw the Number Twenty-two arm band she had been waiting for. He had drawn a buckskin, a rocking-chair horse. Bud was ready for him. The horse rolled forward and back, first his hind legs and then his forelegs in the air, and Bud rolled with him, his upraised arm and raking heels beating out a precise, rollicking rhythm against the horse's ribs. At the end of ten seconds, he waved the pick-ups away and rode the buckskin over to the closed corral, slid from the horse's back to the rails, and dropped to the ground.

"Bud Caine, and a beautiful ride," the loud-speaker droned. "A nice ride for Number Twenty-two. Let's give Bud a hand, folks."

Catherine relaxed her clenched fists and pounded her numb palms against one another, the indecent exhibition lost in the enthusiasm of the crowd. She slowly sat down, wondering when she had risen to her feet. She breathed deeply and half-perceived that the air was chilly. That was over, and it *was* a beautiful ride.

The bucking-horse contest was over. The calf-roping and steer-riding remained to be endured. Those three were the events that every contestant had to enter if he wanted to score for the rodeo as a whole. Wild-cow milking and relay races and some other events were thrown in to amuse the crowd and to keep people from getting restless from suspense. But riding and roping and horse-breaking were part of real ranch work, and the rodeos still centered around them, as the old, original roundups had.

The band lifted instruments and began to play. The loud-speaker blared. "The original mounted square dance troupe, from Burkburnett, Texas. Riding an old-fashioned Virginia reel at a full gallop, ladies and gentlemen. Just watch this, now. You don't see anything like it very often."

Pretty. The band played, more carefully and precisely than they usually played, the slightly jerky old "Arkansas Traveler." Eight mounted riders, on four matched pairs of ponies: two black, two white, two sorrel, and two gray, cantered out on the track. The riders' shirts were matched, too, and each rider carried a long staff with a guidon fluttering from it. They formed their square, with the horses dancing in anticipation, and then, as the band repeated the first bars of the old tune, horses lay belly-flat to the ground and riders stretched above their saddlehorns. Timing and precision were perfect. It was beautiful and skillful riding, and Catherine's heart rose again to her mouth. There was no sense to this kind of business, and half the riders in the square were girls. Suppose two of those flying horses collided, down there? The dancers would surely be killed.

But the square was danced almost before she had time to comprehend its danger. The horses were pulled up on their hind legs to salute the grandstand, the bandmaster waved to the caller out there on one of the pens with a microphone in his hand and his legs twined around the top rail. The team cantered off the field again, and the audience settled back for more serious business.

"Want me to get you a coat, Mother?"

Catherine shook her head. She was shivering all over, but it was as likely to be excitement as cold. All trace of sunlight was gone from the infield now, and it looked as drably gray as the skies that lowered over it.

"Calf-roping," droned the announcer.

Catherine wondered if it were worse to have Bud ride early in the contest and see him killed immediately, or if she didn't suffer more when she watched the other contestants get through and out of the way before he appeared. This time it was a compromise. He had drawn a middle number.

"Well!" Catherine exclaimed as the chute gate opened and the first calf appeared. "I don't see why they call this calf-roping! Those are yearlings, I'll just bet, and heavy, too."

Pop grinned sidelong at her. "You don't mind this so much, Mother, do you?"

"He's got Denim to help him. He doesn't have to ride it alone," Catherine answered and wondered why her husband guffawed.

But Denim was a help. Her tough little belly stretched out as straight and flat as her back-pointed ears, when the time came. She was as easy to ride as a sofa and as steady as a bale of hay, but she was fast. Skillfully, Denim kept even with the wildly galloping, twisting calf until Bud had thrown his rope. He rode her always with an open bridle. As the rope soared past her eye, Denim stopped, putting on her own brakes without a touch on the lines. Bud dropped from the saddle in a quick, swarming motion, the pigging string between his teeth. Denim stood like an intelligent rock, giving him enough play on the lariat to catch and turn the calf and then holding the rope taut while he tied. Bud sprang up, his arms at full stretch above his head, Denim continued to stand with her head turned approvingly towards him, the lines still tight on the calf until after the judges had checked the tie.

"Thirteen seconds for Number Twenty-two. Thirteen seconds for Bud Caine. The boy's making a nice ride this afternoon. Let's all give him a hand, folks, him and his pretty little Denim."

Catherine watched Bud swing back into his saddle and Denim proudly pace him out of the ring. The little mare knew when things went right; you couldn't fool her. If Bud had missed his throw and lost his loop that afternoon, she would have been as disgusted as his father—or, Catherine thought with a rush of private honesty—as his mother. They all three had their hearts in there for Bud to win: Pop and Denim and she herself. Catherine wiped a spatter of rain from her face. Water dripped from the front eaves of the grandstand.

The calf-roping continued after the rain started, but Catherine found it dull. The horses slipped and slid and moved at a walk instead of a canter, to keep their footing at all. The men were soaked, their shirts were plastered against their bodies. Only the judges brought out slickers; the contestants and the pick-ups needed their arms free. A horse skidded and went down, his rider under him. It was a big buckskin, the almost-palomino. The professional, then. Not one of the local boys.

One of the pick-ups caught the bridle and swung the horse away from the prostrate man. He bent over the casualty, then straightened and raised one arm. An ambulance swung out of its hiding-place behind the stock pens—bad luck to let the contestants see the ambulance before it was needed—and stormed across the field, water spraying away from it on either side as if it were a speedboat. Its gong bonged, its siren wailed, its red headlight flashed on and off madly.

"A short ride but a merry one," Pop said beside her. "Those boys sure put on an act when they get their chance." He was referring to the ambulance crew, who were making a great business of getting the stretcher out and loading the injured man on it. "He's not bad hurt," Pop said reassuringly. "I saw him lift his head and look around to count the crowd. Wanted to make sure they were all there watching him get kilt."

"Ladies and gentlemen," the loud-speaker yammered, "that was Bucky Pendleton got throwed. He isn't hurt bad, but the Doc says he better not ride any more this afternoon. He done his best while he was still up and around. Let's all give Bucky Pendleton a hand, folks."

The applause rolled around Catherine, and another voice rolled, too. This was no ordinary summer storm. Water no longer dripped from the front of the stand; it was a solid curtain between her and the pens. She could not see the field, could not even dimly make out what went on there. And she *had* to see. The steer-riding came next. That was what she had been dreading all afternoon. Steer-riding was a terrible thing. Men got killed, not only hurt, but really killed, in steer-riding contests. She *had* to see Bud ride; if anything happened to him, she wanted to know about it right away. She *had* to be able to rise and to run down the stair beside her. She would go out of the grandstand and be at the track gate when the ambulance came through and slowed on the cattle guard. She could open its door and get in and . . .

The loud-speaker was croaking again. "Ladies and gentlemen, we regret to announce that this is the end of the afternoon's entertainment because of rain. Those of you haven't got your hay in will feel as bad about this as the rest of us. We sure hate to disappoint you, folks, but the boys say it's no use trying to ride when the judges can't see them. This ends this afternoon's entertainment, ladies and gentlemen, but we hope to see you all back here again in front of the grandstand tomorrow, when we promise the sun will be shining." The droning clacked off abruptly.

"Oh, shoot!" said Catherine. "I wanted to see Bud ride his steer."

20. *Merry Christmas*

MONTANA, 1952

IN the Larsen household on Powder River there were certain special, privately observed holidays as there are in all good homes. Generally such intimate celebrations have only rather casual associations with the calendar. They are not as rigid as birthdays, Fourth of July, or Christmas. Rather they are sliding dates, with a blessed informality of occurrence, like Easter or Thanksgiving. Specifically, the Larsens celebrated among themselves the three-day rodeo in early summer and the arrival of the Montgomery Ward catalog just before fall.

After the JL Ranch ceased to be known as Larsens' and became known as Brookses', the pleasant customs were continued. Sometime in June or July, even Jack left the cattle to themselves for twenty-four hours and went with the rest of the family through the smoking dust and blazing heat of the flats to the blacktop highway and so to town. This was a wonderful day, to be remembered and talked about at least until the next rodeo came around, and, comparatively, for months after that.

Margie could remember the catalog's appearance in the mail, from her own, earliest childhood, as well as she remembered the thrill that was an integral part of it. Deliberately she recreated for her own children the tension of the days before the catalog arrived. It became a ritual for all of them, a ritual that never diminished in importance or lost in meaning.

255

"I wonder where it is," Margie would murmur as she sorted and laid out in piles the semiweekly mail. The newspapers in one stack, opened and laid flat, so Jack could get first crack at them before the children looked at the funnies. After that she kept the stack in the kitchen where she could look quickly at the society page, run her eye down the column of Powder River notes, and glance surreptitiously, because grown-ups weren't supposed to be interested in such things, at L'il Abner and Pogo.

"I don't see it here at all," she would mutter, laying out the letters; three stacks for the bunkhouse, one for each of the hands; a purple-edged pink envelope scrawled and doodled with pencil for Dorothy, from one of the other pre-teen-agers in the Valley; seven long, crisp, white envelopes, with printed returns in the upper left-hand corners for Jack—the crackle of the paper alone was enough to tell her they had originated with commission houses in Omaha and Kansas City and with the bank —and two small, neat, plain white envelopes for herself, from her mother and her sister in Seattle. They never forgot. She made a separate stack of the announcements of bargain magazine subscriptions, hardware-store sales, and warnings of the dire things that happened to chickens deprived of Blank-Blank's feeds. The boys would feel dreadful if they didn't get any mail, so these fourth-class temptations were always reserved for them.

Now was the time for Dorothy to ask, as if she didn't know the answer, "What are you looking for, Mother?"

And for Margie to reply, "The catalog. Here it is almost September and time for the new Monkey Ward catalog to be out. It'll have to get here pretty soon, or there won't be time to get an order in and back by Christmas."

That was always a terrifying thought, no matter how familiar. Suppose the catalog didn't get there in time. Suppose the order didn't get mailed in time. Suppose the Christmas presents didn't arrive—it was as hard to suppose that the twenty-fifth of December wouldn't roll around. Still, there was one time when it almost happened.

The catalog got there all right, and right on time, on the fourteenth of August, which was its scheduled publication date.

But the rodeo was late that year and it started on the very next day, the fifteenth. They had been waiting for the rodeo to start since its earliest possible opening date in mid-June, and had built up to a state of almost unbearable suspense in the interval. Since the delay had been caused by waiting for the arrival of the Greatest of Movie Cowboys and His Trick Horse, it was not to be supposed that any other excitement could supplant the rodeo breathlessness until that was over. So the big, square, brown-cardboard-and-paper parcel containing the catalog was put aside on top of the piano until it could receive proper care and attention, and was forgotten for almost two weeks, impossible as that later seemed.

Afterwards Margie said it must have been because she was used to a certain interval of time between the rodeo and the catalog, and when the rodeo was over, she didn't expect the catalog to show up right away. That may have been the reason, or it may have been because they were all busy shifting the cattle down from the mountains to the lower winter pastures along the river and near the house. The JL was short-handed that year, and Margie had to ride all day and every day with Jack until the job was finished. Fortunately Dorothy was ten years old and perfectly able to take care of the boys, the cooking, and most of the housework. Jack brought the Christmas tree down from the upper slopes on one of his trips, and stored it in the root cellar for future use.

It wasn't until the cattle had been moved and Margie began to think about fall and school opening that she remembered the catalog. The mail had come and she automatically began the ritual as she sorted. "I wonder where it is," she said almost under her breath. The ritual fell apart then, for the children burst into howls of laughter.

"There it is, Mother," Dorothy panted, when she could speak. "Right on the piano behind you."

Margie broke down and shouted, too, then she suddenly sobered. "It's been here two weeks already," she exclaimed. "I wonder if it's going to be too late to get the order off . . ." She stopped, for the children stood about her white-faced and stricken.

257

"Can't we get it off before Christmas?" Jack, Junior, wailed, and little Fred clutched at her hand, and gasped, "Won't Santa Claus get here this year, Mother? Not at all?"

"Oh, I think we can manage," Margie soothed them. "We'll all have to get busy right away and think hard, though. We can get the Christmas order off now, and maybe order the other things for the house a little later." It meant extra shipping charges, she thought anxiously, but the money would have to be spent. You couldn't—you simply couldn't—have a Christmas without presents, with children in the house.

She looked quickly over the mail on the table and was relieved to see that there was nothing to claim the attention of any child. The folder on power mowers and the tempting booklet on egg-mash she slipped to the bottom of Jack's pile. He could be trusted to dispose of them in the coal stove as soon as he found them. And Dorothy's girl friends, for once, had neglected the perpetual letter writing that furnished all the girls with involuntary exercises in penmanship and composition.

"I tell you what," Margie said to her brood. "We'll start in right now, as if the catalog had just come. You can all sit down and look at it right after lunch and make your lists and write your letters to Santa Claus this evening. Then Dad and I will take it after dinner and start making out our orders."

Lunch received only cursory attention at the JL Ranch that noon. Margie hard-boiled eggs and sliced bread and laid out a plate of butter, a jar of peanut butter, one of wild plum jam, and a pitcher of molasses that Jack's mother had sent from Missouri. She scouted up some apples to be eaten with the catalog for extra flavor, and she served the whole meal on paper plates so Dorothy and Little Jack wouldn't feel that they had dishes to do. As soon as the scraps had been gathered together—she remembered as she looked at the egg shells that her mother often said egg shells would convince anybody of the truth of the Biblical story of the twelve baskets of fragments—she removed the tablecloth and laid the solidly tempting brown package out on the table.

Scissors in the hand poised above the outermost string, she paused. "Have you all got pencils and paper?"

"Yes, Mother." A treble, tremolo trio. The scissors swooped down, and the stiff string parted and snapped back and away from the brown paper. A knife, then, to slit the butcher's tape that sealed the ends of the parcel. Then the real struggle: pulling with one hand at the catalog and pushing the wrappings back and away from its vividly printed cover with the other. And as the butterfly printing emerged from its cocoon, the hands of the children, obedient to the commands of the eyes fixed upon her, followed and imitated each motion as she made it. As the final tug and shove succeeded and she held the catalog for a moment before she dropped it on the table top, they all four breathed together, deeply and gaspingly, for the first time, it seemed, in minutes and minutes. This was the first great emotional peak of the catalog season, when the volume rested on the table before them, unsullied, shining, and waiting to yield its secrets to each of them in turn.

The moment held them, taut and silken, while they breathed twice, and then it was gone. Little Fred, in his highchair between the older two, leaned forward and demanded, "Which page is wagons?" Time moved and breaths came normally again. Margie seated herself across the table, with her own paper and pencil within reach. It was understood and established that she would not look at the catalog now, however great its temptations. Now she was Fred's stenographer, as before she had served each older child.

Little Fred found the page of wagons, because the youngest child had the right to look first. And while Jack and Dorothy had outgrown playing with wagons, they had not got beyond looking at pictures of them.

Each child made two lists, one of the things he wanted to buy to give as presents; the other, in the form of a letter to Santa Claus, of the things he hoped to receive. Each list was supposed to be an absolute secret and it was a respected tradition that neither of the older ones should hear the lists Fred dictated to his mother. The purchase lists were, in some ways, more intricate to make up. Each child had his own Christmas money, saved from the allowance he earned for doing chores. Purchases had to be figured within the amounts on hand, with no speculation as to whether additional sums could be earned between ordering and delivery. Money for Christmas presents had to be given to their father when he wrote the check and sealed the envelope for the family's whole order. There was much arithmetic and more wiggling before the exact amounts were calculated. Dorothy did it by laying the coins aside in separate piles as she listed the articles. Jack insisted on doing it in his head, although the process was slow and agonizing. Once in a while Margie and Big Jack discussed the desirability of asking the children to pay pro-rata shares of the shipping costs. So far nothing had been done about that. Faced with the calculations that might result from establishing that rule, Margie turned away. She would pay the children's shipping charges herself if need be, for the time being.

The real struggle did not come, as far as she was concerned, until after dinner when the children were in bed. Then she and Jack sat down with the catalog on the table before them, to correlate the lists. This meant much checking and cross-checking. If one child had asked for a present another planned to give, that could be checked off his letter. If there were requests that were immediately impossible, like Dorothy's listing of a diamond lavalier—genuine 18 K gold-washed—or Jack's wish for a .30-calibre rifle, guaranteed to knock over elk at any conceivable distance if the rifle-man were big enough to hold the gun, they were checked off.

It was the intermediates that were difficult. Did Dorothy *really* want a Bonnie Braids Baby Doll, that opened and shut its eyes, had real, curly, Orlon hair, and said "Wah?" Or was she simply seduced by the photograph and the reproduced strip from Dick Tracy below it? Was Young Jack old enough for a .22? He would discard a B-B gun as sissy and unsuitable, they knew. Would he accept a small-calibre rifle as a more manly weapon? What would Fred do with a red wagon if he had it? Would a wagon be any fun at all for a boy who had never lived, and never would live, on sidewalks?

Their own choices for the children were usually utilitarian first: sweaters, leather belts to wear with jeans; socks (with one neon pair for each child and the rest plain cotton); and dressing gowns. Underwear, pajamas, shirts, and blouses were so obviously functional that no amount of wrapping could make them acceptable as gifts. Besides, those things had to be ordered regularly, at set intervals throughout the year. There was no sense in cluttering the Christmas order with them.

This time, with the delay between receiving the catalog and getting the order ready, Jack agreed to send two orders. Usually he was adamant on combining the Christmas order with the one for winter supplies. Not to do so meant extra shipping costs and an extra trip to the railroad. Margie clinched her side of the discussion by pointing out that perhaps the company would send two medium-sized orders by express, while they were almost sure to send one big order by freight. Delivery would be more prompt, and perhaps, if the first order came *very* promptly, Jack could wait until the second one arrived and pick them both up on a single trip to town.

Jack gloomily replied to that suggestion that he'd better get into town the first time the roads were clear, if there were any sign of either order. Otherwise they might have to revise the calendar and hold Christmas sometime in the spring.

On the following evening they completed their lists and filled out the order form. They added a barrel—ten pounds—of hard candy, for the school Christmas tree, if the roads were open enough to have one. They included a string of tree lights and a dozen extra bulbs, and Margie ordered ten yards of old-fashioned tinsel because it meant Christmas to her in a way that tin-foil icicles never could. They included two and a half pounds of maple sugar for the grown-ups along the Valley, ten candy canes for emergencies, and a Luxury Box of chocolates for themselves. Last of all, friends and relatives having been remembered, each included a gift for the other, and folded the paper so that particular item would not show. They had to tell each other the cost so the check could be written. That is, Margie had to tell Jack, and he always insisted that it was only fair for him to tell her.

Followed the time of waiting. This was an indeterminate period, midway between the ritual of the catalog and the far less set ritual of Christmas. Christmas plans were always subject to change without notice; the catalog ordering had never been altered before—certainly not since Margie could remember. They took their time, and the making out of the regular winter order, which included emergency-shelf groceries, household and barn supplies, and restocking of the first aid kits and the family medicine chest, filled a part of the interval. Once or twice someone thought of something that could have gone on the Christmas order and included that item in the second list, always with the proviso, "It'll do for birthdays if it gets here after Christmas."

Snow came early that year, as if to threaten them still more. It fell and packed, light and dry and powdery to begin with, dense and solid as ice-blocks after it had lain for a time. They fed the cattle on snow shoes or skis, and moved large quantities of feed at a time whenever they had their turn at the community caterpillar. The creek froze over, and every once in so often a steer went through the skim of ice and had to be fished out by a wet, muttering Jack, frequently with Margie's help. They both skirted the edge of pneumonia rather closely that winter.

Nobody stirred off the place unnecessarily. When a thing was within walking distance, they walked on snowshoes or skied; otherwise they rode and let the horses flounder. The car was up on blocks with the battery in the tank house where it could be connected to the Wincharger and recharged at regular intervals. Jack had put on mud tires in the fall before he jacked the car up, so it would take only a few minutes to get started if they had to take it out to go somewhere. He frequently expressed a hope that they wouldn't have to go.

In their preoccupation with the weather and with the problems of staying alive and healthy, both parents forgot about the Christmas order from time to time. Never for long, however.

One or another of the children was there to remind them; speculating, wondering, wishing, hoping that the order would get there and get there on time.

The notice came on the twenty-third of December, just after another fall of snow. Jack rode Jingo down to the mail box, and came back with the post card in his hand, separated from the other mail. He handed it all to Margie at the back door and turned Jingo around, headed for the garage. As soon as he had unsaddled and fed, he went to the tank house for the battery. By the time Margie had her jacket on and was out of the house, he was getting the blocks out from under the axles.

It never entered their heads that he should not go. The only problem that occurred to them was: When would he get back? The condition of the fifty miles of dirt road between the ranch and the highway could not possibly be anything but bad. Beyond that, the blacktop crossed a high ridge through the banks of a deep cut. It was not a pass, but it was uncomfortably like one. That trough, a half-mile long, was sometimes closed to traffic for a month at a time in winter. Still, the Highway Department might have been able to keep it open.

Right at the last moment, Margie had an idea. "Wait a minute," she said, turning to go into the house and speaking over her shoulder, "I'll get some clothes together and we'll all go with you. We can stay at mother's or get a hotel room if she has a house full, and we'll all have Christmas in town this year."

Jack shook his head. "Wouldn't be the same as Christmas at the ranch," he said. He slung out of the yard, with the mud tires gripping feebly at the icy surface of the snow. Not until he was out of sight did it dawn on Margie that he was probably thinking of the certain discomfort and possible danger for her and for the children if they all went with him.

As she started lunch, she found herself hoping that by some miracle the second order might have arrived also. That was almost too much to expect, but she could dream. She *needed* that new spatula or she wouldn't have ordered it. The handle of the old one had got charred when she took it out to cook for the roundup, and it was almost worn through now. And they were running low on other things: baking-powder and the special vanilla extract that she ordered from the catalog and hand lotion. In this weather they all used hand lotion constantly and gallons of it were expended.

She kept the children busy, and they all got through that day without too much trouble or too many trips to the window. If they saw Jack coming now, it would mean that the roads were impassable and he had had to turn back. As long as they did not see him, she insisted firmly to herself, it meant that he was on his way.

The next day, Christmas Eve, was more difficult. Suddenly that what-shall-we-have-for-Christmas-if-there-isn't-any-delivery crisis was upon them. The need for improvisation, fortunately, kept them all too busy to spend much time at the window. And the invention of popcorn strings, and loops of paper chains made from the colored advertising sections of magazines, occupied the children. From the back of her dresser drawer Margie excavated a little bottle of silver radiator paint, left from the days when she resilvered evening slippers for college dances. She thinned it with nail-polish remover and supplied each child with a small water-color brush from their old school paint-boxes. The radiator paint, generously supplemented with nail polish, added color and variety to the pop-corn strings.

Pancakes and maple sugar were their traditional Christmas Eve supper. The maple sugar was, Margie hoped, on the way. Luckily the children liked sorghum syrup almost as well. They got through supper very well and, as soon as the dishes were washed, gathered expectantly around the piano.

With the lights out—all except the big light over the gate— Margie and the children sang their Christmas carols. They saved "We Three Kings of Orient Are" for the last. That one was special. Each child, with a little help from Margie, sang one of the verses that described the gifts of the three kings. As they sang, they went to pin their stockings to the family bulletin board behind the coal stove. The bulletin board was bare except for the string of brightly colored letters that said MERRY CHRIST-MAS across its top. And as each child finished singing and hanging his stocking, there was a scuttle through the hall and the sound of a plunge and a bounce into bed. Margie sang the last verse alone:

Glorious, now, behold him arise,
King, and God, and sacrifice,
Heaven sings Alleluia—
Alleluia, the earth replies . . .

There were rustles and giggles down the hall as she closed the piano and then profound silence that signaled a determined imitative effort at sleep. Then, finally, stilled, regular breathing.

They were so good, she thought—and wondered what on earth she had to put in their stockings. They knew as well as she did that there would probably be nothing but token presents for them in the morning. Yet not one of them had complained—or even seemed concerned—about the turn their luck had taken. None of them—she heard a rustle behind her and turned to see Dorothy.

"Mother," Dorothy asked, "do you expect Dad any time soon?"

"I expect him when he gets here," Margie said steadily.

"Well," Dorothy began, and hesitated. She started over. "You see, Mother, I'm the oldest." There was another pause. "Mother, I know who fills the stockings. I have for a long time, but I wouldn't let on to the boys. And I thought, maybe, if you were alone . . ."

"Yes," Margie said. "That's a wonderful idea. I can use some help."

She knew that Dorothy was almost as worried about Jack as she was herself, too worried to sleep, apparently. If she sent her daughter back to bed, she would only add hurt feelings to Dorothy's other distress. "I can use some help," she repeated. "Let's go out in the kitchen and close the door, so we won't wake the boys."

She had sugar and butter, but no cocoa or vanilla, so fudge was out of the question. There was sorghum, and she hit on the happy idea of taffy. Jack's family had sent a sack of peanuts

265

in the fall, and she spread some on a cookie sheet and put them in the oven to roast. There were always apples in the cellar, and she brought up a basket and set Dorothy to work picking out and polishing the best of them. At least they would have something to put in the stockings.

They were engulfed in the warm smells of cooking sugar and roasting peanuts and the cool smell of the apples when Margie heard the noise in the yard. Only the car could make that sound. Before she did anything else, before she even went to open the door and tug on her jacket on her way to help Jack unload, she pulled the coffeepot forward to the front of the stove. When Jack came in, with the first bundle in his arms, the coffee smell was overriding all other odors.

"Made it," Jack said briefly, setting down his load. "It's snowing again, but they had the blacktop scraped clear over the rise." He kissed Dorothy on the top of her head and held Margie off at arm's length to kiss her gingerly on the forehead. "I'm too cold to get near either of you. What are you doing out of bed, Snooks?"

"Helping Mother," Dorothy said briskly. "I'll go to bed as soon as we pull the candy."

It was a wildly hilarious taffy-pull in the kitchen that Christmas Eve, the more exciting because it had to be accompanied by whispering instead of speech. The candy couldn't wait for the packages to be opened, and they pulled it immediately, Dorothy and Margie working with it while Jack took off his icy clothes in the basement, and put on his dressing gown. By the time he came upstairs the candy was cut and cold, and they could each try a piece with their coffee. Even Dorothy had a cup of coffee—enough coffee to color and warm a cup of milk.

"Let's all go to bed," Jack said, licking the last taffy off the inside of his mouth, but still speaking blurrily. "The packages will still be here in the morning. The stockings can be filled because we have plenty to put in them without unpacking. Then we can all have a big Christmas together, from start to finish. Everybody can help open things."

"We still have to fill the stockings," Dorothy reminded him, and he agreed; the stockings really ought to be filled on Christmas Eve.

"We'll have to hurry then," Margie said, "It's eleven now. It won't be Christmas Eve much longer. Each of us can fill one, and then we'll go to bed."

She noticed, as they all went sleepily to work, that Dorothy was filling Fred's stocking, with her back turned to the place where her own hung and where her father was busy.

21. *Merrily*
We Dance and Sing
WYOMING, 1951

T
HE Old-Timers' picnic was always set for late
in summer, as near the end of haying as possible.
Long ago a movable rather than a set date had
proved the only feasible way to time the celebration. There
were always some people away up in the mountains who hadn't
got all their hay in even in late August. Goodness knew, Rebecca
reflected, this wasn't the first year the Higgenses themselves
were behind with their baling.

She intended to enjoy herself this time. The boys and their
wives would carry all the load; she and Bill could kind of coast
along and have a good time visiting. What with only six people
staying in the house for the week end, and three of them women
who were able and willing to do their full share of cooking and
housework, she hardly had enough to do to make planning
worth while. She stretched luxuriously in bed, thinking of the
automatic dishwasher Bill had installed in the kitchen for her
last birthday and of all the worlds of leisure it had bestowed
upon her.

She peered across the room at the clock on the dressing table.
Heavens! It was six-thirty! Way up in the day! It was a shameful
hour to be lying in bed, with guests in the house, on the day
of the Old-Timers' picnic. And then she relaxed again. The girls

were preparing the lunch and bringing enough to the picnic grounds to feed everyone. The Association always provided the beef and coffee from the dues. She hadn't a thing to think about. Really, it was wonderful, like being company herself.

However, time was a-wasting, and no matter who brought lunch she would have to do something about breakfast. She took time for a bath—now she really felt lazy, taking her bath before breakfast and sitting down in the tub instead of splashing through it before she dropped into bed at night. She dressed fresh and clean from the skin out, adding dabs of talcum and cologne as she went along. Bill would say she smelled real hussy; and it was silly, fussing with things like that in the morning. She giggled like a bride, and smelling bridal she approached the kitchen.

She was as near as she had ever come to being bridal, she recalled as she measured the coffee. The first meal she and Bill ate in their own house—and that was the first meal after their wedding breakfast at noon—his old uncle was there with them. Natural enough that Bill's mother, who had taken care of the old man for years, should be glad to get him relocated while she went off on a trip. But still! A lot of the neighbors had talked, and some had even spoken of it to Rebecca. They thought it was kind of odd that the bridegroom's mother went off on the wedding journey and the young couple stayed at home.

Oh, well, Rebecca reflected philosophically, breaking eggs in a bowl and beating them—scrambled would be a nice change, and kind of partified—you could get used to anything, even being hung, if you had to. And the winter she and Bill had spent alone two years ago, after all the children were married, had been the lonesomest time she remembered in her whole life. It certainly seemed more natural having people in the house.

Zoe Emsdorff was the first guest in the kitchen. You could count on Zoe. She and Rebecca had known each other so long and had spent so much time together in their early days that they knew each other's ways as well as they knew their own. Just as well, too, now that Zoe had got so hard of hearing. She had her hearing aid and she did her best to lip-read, but conversation with her was a kind of groping in the dark now. You couldn't embarrass her by writing notes to her—not before strangers, certainly.

The automatic dishwasher practically did the cleaning up by itself. While it splashed away and her guests made their personal preparations for the picnic, Rebecca got down the old family picnic basket. The girls never took enough paper plates, and somebody was almost sure to forget napkins. Besides, there would be coffee mugs to take for themselves and their guests. The big old basket looked lonesome and empty standing there on the kitchen table. She added a jar of bread-and-butter pickles and a loaf of homemade bread to keep the coffee cups company. Extra cream never did anybody any harm, and they could almost certainly use another pound of butter. And the graham crackers for the babies—the girls would be sure to remember, but in case they didn't . . .

The basket looked more comfortable now; not exactly full, but certainly not rumbling with emptiness. She left it where it was and started for the bedroom. A car whished by the window. Bill and Herman Emsdorff were headed for the picnic grounds. She'd have to take the pickup or hitch a ride with somebody. Well, Bill would never trust anybody else to carve a whole beef, and he and Herman had been trotting in couples as long as she and Zoe had. *That* was all right.

She opened her closet and considered the question of dresses. She didn't want to be too dressed up, but still she didn't want to look tacky. She had that new blue linen sun-backed outfit. Muriel had helped her choose it when they were in Sheridan last fall and found it on sale at the Specialty Shop. Muriel insisted it was becoming, and Delft blue had always been one of her best colors, but she hesitated. Sun-backed. It would be kind of—well—naked. Then she smiled to herself and leveled off her chin. She'd just wear it, though Zoe was going in a tailored suit. If she smelled like a bride, she might's well dress like one, and there weren't too many women her age had kept their figures even as well as she had.

It did look pretty, the blue sun-backed dress. With the little bolero jacket over her shoulders, it wasn't naked at all. She added the somewhat battered coconut straw hat that had sheltered her gardening for the last ten years. She was ready for the day, and as soon as she got her slicker from the back porch, the weather could do whatever it pleased. She wouldn't care.

Zoe was waiting for her in the kitchen. "I put in some canned ham and that foreign patty dee foy grass Bill likes so much," she said. "Herman had me bring them along for a surprise." The flat tonelessness of her voice rippled with happiness. She held out her hand and showed Rebecca a bunch of keys. "Herman left us our car; he said you'd drive. I gave it up when I got so unsteady."

Rebecca hugged her. "Thanks, darling," she shrieked into the microphone on her friend's chest. "Where are the others? Everybody ready?"

"All waiting for you," Zoe answered.

Rebecca inspected the basket one last time and added salt and pepper, just in case. There were a number of strange objects in the basket besides the canned ham and the paté. Evidently her other guests had been adding their contributions to the day. It was sweet and thoughtful of them, but Rebecca wished they hadn't bothered. They might have trusted her. Nobody had ever gone hungry at the Higgenses, even when they all had to eat double portions of boiled potatoes to fill up.

There was the usual business of sorting people out and deciding to take two cars after all. She and Zoe and the picnic basket rattled across the cattle guard and down the road. Downhill all the way, past the sheep barn and the shipping corrals and the hay meadows, with her own boys and the Indian hands sweating themselves bone-dry to get the last cutting baled.

The smell of coffee met her like a welcoming hand as the car turned into the grove. Somone—oh, yes, it was the youngest Barker girl—reached into the car and pinned red ribbons on Zoe and Rebecca. "Old-Timers' Picnic. 1900– ?" was lettered on them in gold. That meant that she and Zoe had been part of the community since before statehood. She herded the car, leaping with it as it sprang from chuckhole to snag, across the open center of the grove to the gap in the trees on the east side. The Higgenses had parked their car and eaten dinner in that space so long that now it was left open for them by community consent. You might say they had reserved seats.

She stood on the rear bumper and peered across the crowd. Bill raised one enormous arm where he stood at the long trestle table beside the barbecue pit, slicing the beef. She felt herself blushing all the way up from the bottom of the sun-back. She might be an old silly, but it was nice to have your husband stop whatever he was doing and notice when you came into a crowd. She climbed hastily down and set about organizing things for dinner. She dispatched one guest with a covered tin bucket to bring coffee from the great tin trough that steamed gently above a banked fire. Two others carried the bread board between them, to bring meat from the serving table. Putting the bread board in the car had been so automatic that she couldn't for the life of her remember doing it.

The day was windless and golden with sun. The Bighorns, white-crested, were so much a part of Rebecca's world that she seldom consciously saw them, but at times like this she was acutely aware that she would miss them if they were gone. The smell of crushed mint underfoot, of broken pine branches overhead, and of dust from the road mingled with the comfortable fragrance of the coffee and the smell of roasting meat that always carried with it a suggestion of wildness, of pirates and mountain men and Indians around their respective campfires. Rebecca breathed deeply. A little of her own perfume mixed in her nostrils with the pot pourri and sweetened it.

Bill came over and welcomed them all as if he had had breakfast somewhere else with other people. "Where are the boys?" he asked when the greetings were done.

"They'll be along," Rebecca said easily, and turned to see the first of the family cars drive up. Just in time, right when Bill got interested and before he got impatient. Two of the boys set up the card tables to serve on. The girls brought out and opened their baskets. Somebody laid a rug on the ground and turned the babies loose on it to be watched by whatever uncles or guests were not otherwise occupied. All around them other families were laying out their picnic dinners and getting down to the serious business of the day.

One of the perennial puzzles of the Old-Timers' picnic was how people who ordinarily finished their meals in fifteen minutes could manage to spend as much as two hours eating this one. Maybe they ate slowly because the food tasted good; maybe the food tasted good because they ate slowly. It didn't matter a whole lot anyway. Eating together outdoors in the sun was a happy, blessed sort of thing, best of all because they were all together. She felt Bill's eyes on her and glanced sidewise at him from under the brim of the old coconut straw hat.

"You're looking mighty fussed up and pretty, Mother," he observed.

She felt herself blushing all over again and turned her head aside. "Oh, this old thing," she said. "Something I got on sale last fall in Sheridan."

"Don't remember I ever saw it," Bill commented. "But whether it's new or old it suits you. I like to see a woman wear that color of blue."

The old silly! Silly as she was! Married forty years and a grandfather six times over, and still flirting with her. And she was flirting right back. If they didn't look out, they'd likely fall in love all over again. Couple of plain old fools.

Later she and Zoe joined the crowd that drifted over to the west side of the grove for the program. The first time in a long time a Higgens hadn't been on it, Rebecca thought. But they were all the wrong ages now; the boys and their wives too old and the children still too young. Bill, of course—but Bill would drum for the dance that night. He couldn't very well take part in the afternoon program too.

She looked about her, relaxing as well as she could on the backless bench. The reunion and picnic certainly brought them all out of their holes. There was Babe, as straight and slim as when she was riding in rodeos sidesaddle and stopping shows all across the country as the first girl roper. Babe was boss of her own ranch now, boss of it as much as Bill Higgens was boss of his, and Babe had grown sons helping her, too. She was still built like a split willow, even if her hair was white.

Robert Meeker had maybe aged the most of any Old-Timer, but then he was—good gracious, he couldn't be!—but he was eighty-seven. You'd expect a man to show at least some of his years when they'd run up like that. It was a little surprising that he should look so much like that Egyptian mummy Bill had taken her to see in the museum when they were in New York that time. Maybe his years showed on Bob more than they needed to because his wife was as plumply red-headed as she'd been at thirty. Come to think of it, she was at least twenty years younger than Robert—maybe more. The real Old-Timers had always waited quite a while to marry.

Good lands! That was Old Grandma Ezekiel White, in the old-fashioned slat sun-bonnet. She must be a hundred if she was a day. Grandma was sitting upright in her wheel chair with her hands folded on her cane and her blind eyes fixed before her in the direction of the platform. Her printed calico dress was as fresh and her sun-bonnet ruffle as crisp as if she had done them up herself instead of leaving everything to her grandson's wife. Grandma had always been dressy. It would be a comfort to her to be told how nice she looked, and Rebecca made a mental note to do so at the end of the program.

There was a piano in the rear of the truck backing into place beside the platform. Helen Daniels got up and tried it with her finger. Now that was sweet of Helen, to have her piano brought all the way out from town, when jolting it around that way would mean an extra tuning job when she got it home. The piano sounded all right; so far, it hadn't been hurt by traveling. A real nice thing to have a piano; they had never had one for the program before. Yet come to think of it, pianos had been part of home out here from the beginning, when they had to be hauled out across the plains by ox-team. It was fitting and proper, as Bill would say, to have a piano here today and to have it in a truck.

Who was that getting up on the platform in white shirt sleeves? Old Reverend Boys, bless his heart. The red ribbon looked out of place on him; he never wore any colors but black and white, but it was cute of him to wear it. The old preacher raised his hand and they all rose in a rustle of skirts and dropped programs. The invocation droned along. Where was the old Reverend's wife, who had come out from Pennsylvania with him when he took the pastorate? They had to put her away after her second baby died. Was she still living, poor soul, shut away in the State Hospital? It was an awful thing to happen to a woman —and to the man, for that matter.

Now the program proper began. "The Star-spangled Banner," with everybody standing and singing. A little girl from way back over the mountain, who Gave A Reading. Two little boys—their parents lived down Hay Creek Way—solemnly tap-dancing. Two older girls, one pounding "The Stars and Stripes Forever" out of Helen's piano, the other smiling all over her pretty face as she twirled and twisted her heavy, shiny baton. One of the girls whispered to Rebecca that those two went to school in town, and the one with the baton was the state champion. They came from the little Swedish community across the rim of the Basin. Ranch kids learned to entertain themselves early in life. They had to if they wanted to be entertained.

The State Senator rose. Rebecca saw Bill and Herman drift away from the corner of the platform, where they had been leaning and off through the shade under the trees in the direction of the baseball diamond. The game wouldn't start until the program was over. She thought it was kind of rude of them to walk out on the Senator like that, even if they couldn't stand his politics and had voted against him. It was only right and fair to hear what the man had to say whether you agreed with him or not. This year she wasn't going to let them get away with that lame excuse about umpiring the ball game! Wait till she got those two home!

End of the Senator's speech. Applause. Helen sitting down at the piano. The sun had shifted considerably across the clearing. Helen played two of her "Show pieces," one of them the one where she crossed her wrists in three places, and then started on the old songs. "Down by the Old Mill Stream." "When You and I Were Young, Maggie." "Should Old Acquaintance Be Forgot." They were all standing and singing together. Bill and Herman had come back from the diamond and were joining in.

Rebecca and Zoe gathered themselves together at the end of the program. Slowly they made their way across the clearing, stopping for chats that prolonged to visits as they went. The daughters-in-law had picked everything up and taken it all home in their own cars. Time for the older people to drive home for a nap before the dance.

Rebecca considered changing for the evening, then decided against it. She couldn't dance with Bill on the platform drumming for the orchestra; she hadn't anybody to dance with. Oh, maybe she and Herman would step a turn. Zoe wouldn't mind. She was definitely out of the dancing, she said. But the blue linen was comfortable to get around in. It still looked surprisingly fresh; there must be something in this crease-resistant chemical business. The first linen dress Rebecca remembered owning, in the year after she was married, had creased something awful. Fifteen minutes after she put it on it looked as if she had worn it all day. And now she'd worn a linen dress all day and it looked as if she'd put it on fifteen minutes ago. Modern science certainly was wonderful. And Bill liked the color of this dress.

It was clouding up a little outside the window as she brushed her hair. Oh, dear, it would be a shame if it rained now, after being so beautiful all day. Or would it? The picnic was what counted to the real Old-Timers like Bob and Grandma Ezekiel White and the Reverend Boys. Their strength wouldn't hold out for the dance, even to watch it. And the young folks didn't care. The first spatter of rain on the windshield startled her only a little.

The orchestra sat on a raised and covered platform, and the dancers trod a concrete slab below. There was a five-strand barbed-wire fence with a gate in it around the dance floor, to keep out anybody who hadn't paid his fifty cents for the evening's dancing. As their escorts paid the fifty cents, the ladies held out their left palms, and the gatekeeper stamped each with indelible ink. Then the lady and whatever gent was with her could come and go as she pleased.

Somebody was calling a square as Rebecca parked the car, and the sets on the floor were galloping through what they called a Virginia reel. If you'd ever danced a real Virginia reel, with all the couples in long facing lines, forming lanes and arches for the leading couples, you knew this business of splitting up in eights like double quadrilles wasn't even a good imitation. But bless their hearts, the children enjoyed thinking they were real square dancers, and why spoil their fun for them? It was the best kind of exercise. Let them enjoy it. And the caller was good, with the rain sluicing off the end of his nose, even if he went so fast and loud nobody could follow him and some of the squares got snarled. Rebecca giggled to herself. The poor babies! Getting tangled in a Virginia reel! As if anybody could!

The square was over. The orchestra tuned a little, and swept into "Just a Love Nest." Funny how a lot of old tunes were coming back. Herman came over and bowed to Zoe. Sweet of him; lots of men wouldn't remember that the first duty dance belonged to the wife. Zoe shook her head, and Herman bowed and offered his arm to Rebecca. They stepped through the gate on to the floor.

The rain had let up a little, but the waxed concrete was sticky underfoot. You couldn't glide; waltz or no waltz, you had to hop. But it was fun in a way, and it was fun to look up and try to catch Bill's solemn eye, as he sat on the platform above her and single-mindedly, relentlessly drummed. His lips moved wordlessly as he counted. Nobody could ever tell that Bill loved what he was doing to look at him. He glanced down at a break, and saw them. He shook his drumstick threateningly at Herman and then grinned at them both to show he didn't mean it. In proof he had the orchestra play "The Blue Danube" for the next dance. That was a real old-fashioned waltz! Most of the younger couples left the floor and gave the Old-Timers room to spread themselves.

Only once a year they all got together like that. The thought crossed Rebecca's mind as she dropped asleep at dawn. Only once a year, and they never let themselves think or speak of the ones who had dropped off since last year. Only once a year, and they'd all be tired for a week to come. But it was worth it. She and Bill only had to drive in from the ranch—barely ten miles—but Herman and Zoe had come 150 miles for the reunion, and other people had come from farther away than that—some from clear across the country. Ranch people always traveled big distances to their get-togethers; it was right and proper—as Bill would say—for them to do it this way every summer. It had been a good day from start to finish. She slept, smiling with remembered pleasure.

"Well, here they are, my fifty men and women," Robert Browning began the epilogue to a volume of his poetry. And here, gentlemen of the cattle country, are my portraits of your wives, your children, and yourselves. Let's not have any shooting —the days of range wars are long over.

I have tried to be honest. I have received complaints that I have painted too rosy a picture of the ranch woman's life. But remember what I said in the beginning: I have yet to hear a ranch woman admit that her life is hell, and most of them tend to identify it with Heaven. If it reads romantically, blame the women who described it, not me. But if there are errors in fact, as distinguished from errors in interpretation, in this book, mine be the blame.

Eighteen months, six thousand miles, fifty-two close personal interviews. And yet the book is incomplete, as it is faulty. So, take it as it is, Gentlemen and Ladies who made it possible. It's been swell knowing you! So long, and I'll be seeing you.

Bibliography

Way back yonder, in my first chapter, I said that no industry in America is so fully documented as the cattle business. Each year sees the list of titles on the business as a whole, and on various parts thereof, swelling and expanding.

Curiously enough, except for technical publications, the greatest number of books about the cattle business is concerned with a single phase of it: the pioneer period. Those twenty years have been so thoroughly covered that it seems that now might be the time for a bright, budding young Ph.D. in history, agriculture, or library science to compile a bibliography on the subject for a dissertation.

I have not compiled a bibliography on the subject. I have not even listed all the pertinent titles in my own library. I have ignored fiction entirely. I have skipped privately printed volumes of personal reminiscence. I have disregarded all but one of the innumerable periodicals concerned with the subject and region—and have included that one because it goes beyond regionalism.

What I here submit for your inspection is a list of books that I think are worth reading in themselves, that are available in most public libraries, and that will give some idea of the ranch life of today and of the factors that have contributed to it. All these titles, and many more, have gone into the making of this book.

Abbott, E. C. and Smith, Helena Huntington. *We Pointed Them North*. New York, Farrar and Rinehart, 1939.
Adams, Ramon F. *Come an' Get It: The Story of the Old Cowboy Cook*. Norman, University of Oklahoma Press, 1952.
———. *Western Words: A Dictionary of the Range, Cow Camp, and Trail*. Norman, University of Oklahoma Press, 1946.
Anderson, Edgar. *Plants, Man, and Life*. Boston, Little, Brown, 1952.
Boatright, Mody C. and Day, Donald. *From Hell to Breakfast*. Austin, Texas Folklore Society, 1944.
Cleaveland, Agnes Morley. *No Life for a Lady*. Boston, Houghton Mifflin, 1941.
Debo, Angie. *Oklahoma: Foot-loose and Fancy Free*. Norman, University of Oklahoma Press, 1949.
Denhardt, Robert. *The Horse of the Americas*. Norman, University of Oklahoma Press, 1947.
Dobie, J. Frank. *The Longhorns*. Boston, Little, Brown, 1941.
———. *Vaquero of the Brush Country*. Dallas, Southwest Press, 1929.
Gard, Wayne. *Frontier Justice*. Norman, University of Oklahoma Press, 1949.
Haley, J. Evetts. *Charles Goodnight: Cowman and Plainsman*. Norman, University of Oklahoma Press, 1949.
Jackson, Clarence S. *Picture Maker of the Old West: William H. Jackson*. New York, Scribner's, 1947.
James, Will. *Sand*. New York, Scribner's, 1929.
Landscape: A Magazine of Human Geography. Santa Fé, Landscape, 1951–.
Peplow, Bonnie, and Peplow, Ed. *Roundup Recipes, with the Help of the Arizona Cowbelles*. Cleveland, World Publishing Company, 1951.
Rhodes, May. *Hired Man on Horseback: The Life of Eugene Manlove Rhodes*. Boston, Houghton, Mifflin, 1938.
Russell, Charles M. *Good Medicine*. Garden City, Doubleday, 1930.
———. *Trails Plowed Under*. Garden City, Doubleday, 1935.
Sandoz, Mari. *Old Jules*. Boston, Little, Brown, 1935.

Saunderson, Mont H. *Western Land and Water Use.* Norman, University of Oklahoma Press, 1950.

Sonnichsen, C. L. *Cowboys and Cattle Kings: Life on the Range Today.* Norman, University of Oklahoma Press, 1950.

United States Congress. *Final Report of the United States De Soto Expedition Commission.* 76 Cong., 1 sess. *House Doc.* 71. Washington, 1939.

Vestal, Stanley. *Short Grass Country.* New York, Duell, 1941.

Ward, Elizabeth. *No Dudes, Few Women; Life with a Navaho Range Rider.* Albuquerque, University of New Mexico Press, 1950.

Woolley, Leonard. *Ur of the Chaldees.* Harmondsworth, Middlesex, England, Penguin Books, 1929.

Woolley, Leonard. *Ur: The First Phases.* London, King Penguin Books, 1946.

Acknowledgments

No one writes a book single-handedly, and that statement is more true of this book than of most others. In a sense, this is a compilation, made up from many sources.

There may be, in the list that follows, the names of persons who do not even remember the help they gave me. There is not one that I do not remember warmly, for assistance in interviews, in letters, in brief meetings at conferences. My fear is that names I should remember have been omitted, rather than that too many have been included.

This list is made by states, and by the towns in the states. It is alphabetical; there is no intention to give anyone more or less credit than is his due. I cannot assess the good feeling and the willingness to supply information of these people. To all of them I give my most humble and hearty thanks.

ALICE MARRIOTT

Nambe, New Mexico
January 15, 1953

ALABAMA
Darlington: J. Ernest Lambert

ARIZONA
Flagstaff: John G. Babbitt
Globe: Louie P. Horrell

Joseph City: Mrs. Wallace W. Crawford
Phoenix: Charles E. Blaine, Mrs. Elliott S. Hunphrey, Mrs. Keith
Rimrock: Mr. and Mrs. Bruce Brockett
Sonoita: Frank S. Boice
Tucson: Henry G. Boice
Wilcox: Mrs. Joe Lane

CALIFORNIA
Caliente, Kern County: Mrs. Walter Rankin
Hollister: John Baumgartner, Jr.
Ione: Loren C. Bamert
Long Beach: Fred H. Bixby
Madrone: Mrs. Eva N. Kirby, Mr. and Mrs. Jere Sheldon
Maricopa: Hubbard Russell
Red Bluff: Drs. Bob and Jeanette Von Tour
Willows: Mrs. H. C. Compton

COLORADO
Denver: Mr. and Mrs. Radford Hall, Mr. and Mrs. F. E. Mollin,
    Lyle Liggett, Fred Rosenstock
Loveland: Mr. and Mrs. Lyman Linger
Nathrop: Frank Fehling
Red Feather Lakes: Mrs. A. J. Beckstead
Roggen: Stafford Painter
Sterling: Arthur A. Smith

FLORIDA
Fort Meade: Mrs. Katie L. Durrance
Kissimmee: Irlo Bronson
Miami Beach: Mr. and Mrs. A. Frankel
Orlando: Cushman S. Radebaugh

GEORGIA
Waycross: E. C. Hall

IDAHO
Challis: Mrs. Frank Burstedt

Acknowledgments

Idaho Falls: Mr. and Mrs. John Smith, Mrs. Thomas Yearian
Malad: Dave Jones
Twin Falls: Mrs. Adelaide Hawes

KANSAS
Burdett: Mr. and Mrs. O. W. Lynam
Garnett: Bob White
Leoti: Mr. and Mrs. Herb Barr
Sitka, Clark County: Mr. and Mrs. Jesse Clair Harper, Mrs. Mel
  Harper

LOUISIANA
Luling: Mr. and Mrs. Harry Post
Gurley: George Gayden, Jr.
Natchez: Sylvan Friedman
Welsh: Mrs. A. L. McBurney

MISSISSIPPI
Walls: A. B. Freeman

MISSOURI
Kansas City: Mr. and Mrs. Ray Cuff

MONTANA
Ashland: Father Marion Roessler
Deer Lodge: C. K. Warren
Forsyth: Mrs. Freeman Philbrick
Lame Deer: Carl Larsen, Rufus Wallowing
Miles City: Mrs. Milton Simpson
Powderville: Mr. and Mrs. Pete Hill and Family

NEBRASKA
Alliance: Robert Howard, W. A. Johnson
Bassett: Mrs. Julia Bradock
Bridgeport: Bernard Coulter
Burwell: Mrs. George Dewey
Cody: Mrs. Ada Adamson

Gordon: J. H. Vinton
Hyannis: Miss Floy Buchanan, Mrs. Steen Castle, Mrs. Essie
    Davis, Mrs. Helen Hager, Tom Quinn
Kennedy: Mrs. Cyrus Wolfenden
Keystone: Mrs. Joe Lee
Newport: Mrs. Vic Thompson
Sutherland: Mrs. May Trego
Valentine: Mrs. P. C. Shockley

NEVADA
Arthur: Mrs. Robert Duval
Deeth: William B. Wright
Elko: Mrs. Isabel Griswald
Gardnerville: Mr. and Mrs. Fred H. Dressler

NEW MEXICO
Albert: Mrs. T. E. Mitchell, Albert K. Mitchell
Carlsbad: Mr. and Mrs. Roy Forehand
Deming: A. D. Brownfield
Lordsburg: Mrs. Victor Culberson
Nambe: Jose de la Cruz Romero, Mr. and Mrs. Pablo Roybal,
    Mrs. Margaret Schoonover, Mrs. Adele M. Stevenson,
    Wynderllyn Folsom
Rutherton: Mrs. Carl E. Johnson

NORTH DAKOTA
Bismarck: Thore Naaden
Bowman: John H. Hanson
Medora: Mr. and Mrs. Don L. Short

OKLAHOMA
Lawton: Wayne Rowe
Norman: Graham Johnson
Oklahoma City: Mr. and Mrs. Carl Neumann
Saddle Mountain: Mr. and Mrs. R. L. McElhaney

OREGON
Burns: Mrs. Clara Hanley

Acknowledgments

Paulina: Robert Lister
Prineville: Harry Stearns
Seneca: Mrs. Bob Lemcke

SOUTH DAKOTA
Agar: John E. Sutton
Ludlow: Claude Olson
Midland: Mrs. Ralph Jones
Rapid City: Mrs. Bernadine Benedict, Mrs. Mamie Owens Du-
    hamel, Mrs. Adelaide Fallon, Mrs. Orpha Haxby, Emmett
    Horgan, W. M. Rasmussen, Dr. Warren E. Wilson

TEXAS
Canyon: J. Evetts Haley
El Paso: C. L. Sonnichsen, Mrs. W. W. Turney
Fort Worth: J. M. Reynolds
Kent: Mrs. W. D. Reynolds
Marfa: Mrs. L. C. Brite
Ozona: Monroe Baggett
Pampa: Mr. and Mrs. W. W. Heskew
Rocksprings: Miss Lena Strackbein
San Angelo: Ray W. Willoughby

UTAH
Ferron: Mrs. Jesse M. Conover
Green River: Mrs. Hazel Ekker
Heber: L. C. Montgomery
Jensen: Kirk Dudley, Clyde Haslem, Mrs. Josie B. Morris
Sterling: Mrs. Arta Ottasen
Vernal: Hugh Colton

WASHINGTON
Ellensburg: Mrs. Rufus Schnebly, R. L. Rutter, Jr.

WYOMING
Bighorn: Mr. and Mrs. Carlo Beuf
Buffalo: Mrs. Fred Hesse

Caspar: Mrs. George Snodgrass
Cody: Lloyd Taggart
Cheyenne: Russell Thorpe
Dayton: Mr. and Mrs. Ray Bryan
Hyattville: Mr. and Mrs. Sam C. Hyatt and Family
Kaycee: Mr. and Mrs. William Bailey, Mr. and Mrs. J. Elmer Brock, Mr. and Mrs. Walter Elm, Mrs. Floyd Reno, Mrs. Luther Todd
Laramie: Mrs. G. E. Sundby
Moorcroft: Mrs. Joe Watt
Sheridan: Mr. and Mrs. James Crew Reynolds, Earl Newell, Mr. and Mrs. F. H. Sinclair, Mrs. Lillian Smith, Ray Tarbell, Miss Jennie Williams
Wolf: Mr. and Mrs. Charles Kane